Praise fo:

MW01094229

"Nancy King's appreciation ...
ling is matched only by the breadth of her experience in
teaching through story. Across many years and wide travels
she has evolved a highly original and eminently effective
method of using stories and the storyteller's craft to build
community and guide fellow travelers on the path of personal knowledge—which, after all, is the most mythic journey of all. Now, in the true spirit of storytelling, she generously offers her discoveries to all who are wise enough to accept them. In addition, enfolded within and appended at the
end of this masterful manual for teaching through story is a
delightfully varied selection of folktales from many world
cultures. Everyone who uses or hopes to use stories to facilitate personal growth, promote empowerment and strengthen
community will thank Nancy for writing *Dancing with Wonder*. It is a handbook that should never be far from their
reach." **Joe Hayes**

"The wizardry of this book lies in its brilliant stories and its
fascinating narrative about how these stories have healed listeners. Nancy King is a master story teller. In this book she
has revealed not only the sources and power of stories, but
also the key to using them to unlock strength, wisdom, and
creativity." **Jeanne Murray Walker, Professor of English,
University of Delaware and author of *A Deed To the Light***

"I have read a lot of text books in my time, but never before
have I read one that I couldn't put down—one that brought
me to tears with it's wonderful folk tales and personal examples from Nancy's vast experience helping people write
their stories and share their lives." **Donna Robbins, Ph.D.,**

Business Coach, Organization Development Consultant and former adjunct professor, Pepperdine University, School of Education & Psychology Placitas, New Mexico

"Dancing with Wonder is a beautiful revelation of the healing stories that wait to be told within each one of us. I know of no one else who has worked with stories in this way—as a spontaneous gift emerging from the individual soul, bringing healing and renewal to the teller and the listeners." **David L. Hart, Ph.D., Jungian Analyst and author of *The Water of Life: Spiritual Renewal in the Fairy Tale***

"Nancy King plunges her readers into the heart and soul of stories and into the healing potential of storytelling itself. Wondrous, world-wide examples of stories, as well as the effects of painting them, singing them, drawing them, are sprinkled throughout her text. She enchants as she educates. This book is inspiring!" **Demaris Wehr, Ph.D., Jungian psychotherapist and peacebuilder; author of *Jung and Feminism***

"As an artist, I have experienced first hand Nancy King using the techniques she writes about in Dancing With Wonder: Self-Discovery Through Stories. I have seen how imagemaking and storymaking improved and enhanced the imagination and creativity of people with whom she worked. She created a caring community in which people felt comfortable sharing their images and stories. I highly recommend this thoughtful and finely written book for readers who love stories and for all those who want to discover and explore their creative potential, by themselves or with others." **Susan Duhan Felix, Internationally Exhibited Artist**

Dancing
with
Wonder

Dancing with Wonder

✳

Self-Discovery through Stories

Nancy King, Ph.D.

CHAMPION PRESS, LTD.
BELGIUM, WISCONSIN
Copyright © 2005 Nancy King

ISBN: 1932783504
LCCN: 2005922973

Manufactured in the United States of America

10 9 8 7 6 5 4 3 2 1

For

Claudia Reder

ACKNOWLEDGEMENTS

If ever a midwife birthed a baby, Claudia Reder birthed this book. Her faith, questions, suggestions, and encouragement kept me going throughout significant and difficult changes in my life. I am blessed to call her friend.

I thank David Hart and Seth Rubin who helped me to discover and honor my stories. Anita Grunbaum, Karin Gustafsson, Fidele Persson, Marianne Nikolov, Alida Gersie, and the late Stig Starrsjo, as well as students, workshop participants, and various university faculty who made it possible for me to learn and teach in the United States, England, Sweden, Denmark, Norway, Canada, Hungary, and Mexico.

I am grateful to have had the opportunity to work with participants in the University of Delaware's International Institute who came from Russia, Kyrgyzstan, Kazakhstan, Uzbekistan, the Ukraine, and Germany. Their willingness to explore, share experience, and confront personal and national prejudice made it possible for us to create a community where it was safe to ask for help, and to examine and express our ideas, attitudes, thoughts and feelings.

I am thankful for the help of Demaris Wehr, David Hart, Louise Rubin, Christine King, Donna Robbins, Sage Magdelene, Richard Carlson, and Jesse Hoover, who read, asked questions and commented on various versions and drafts.

Nancy Rosenfeld, my agent, and Brook Noel, along with the staff, at Champion Press made the publishing of this book possible and brought joy to the process.

Contents

Introduction   17

25/ Imagemaking
The Power of Imagemaking   26
Imagemaking as a Way of Knowing   33
Tension and Trickster   38
  "Caterpillar and the Wild Animals" (Africa)   44
Releasing Memory   47
Recovering Memory   48
  "Li Chi the Serpent Slayer" (China)   49

56 / Storymaking
The Power of Speaking in Role   58
One Story, Many Meanings   52
  "How Light Came to the People" (Native American)   62
Archeology of the Self   69
  "Ulu and the Breadfruit Tree" (Polynesia)   70
The Healing Power of a Story   72
  "The Healing Water" (Native American)   73

81 / Experiencing the Storymaking Process
The Power of Sharing   82
Group Contribution   83
  "The Light Keeper's Box" (Venezuela)   83
  "Ant and Elephant" (India)   90
Finding Stories   96
  "Hummingbird and Panther" (Brazil)   97
Revealing the Concealed   105

108 / Story Journeys

Hidden in Plain Sight   110

Read but Not Written   112

    "The Fern Girl" (Eastern Europe)   112

Popping-out Stories   122

    "The Black Patch" (Author)   123

    "The Black Patch Revisited" (Author)   132

    "Digging Out from Under" (Author)   134

Variations on a Theme   136

    "Dynamite Pretty" (Workshop Student)   144

Moving through Nothingness   149

Character Autobiography   155

    "Macha the Red" (Ireland)   156

    "The People Could Fly" (African American)   162

Helping a Friend   165

    "The Basket" (San People)   165

Changes in Meaning over Time   173

    "How People Came to the Land

    that was Home" (Native American)   173

184 / Creating A Story Journey

Creating a Storymaking Community   185

Beginning   186

Creating a Structure   187

Starting with a Story   189

Starting with an Image, Feeling, or Intuition   191

Structuring a Session   193

Framing the Session   193

Designing Imagemaking-paints   194

Designing Imagemaking-clay   196

Designing Activities   199

Sharing the Work   201
Reflection   203

205 / Sample Structures

"The Poor Tailor" (Eastern Europe)   205
"Coyote Gets His Name" (Native American)   207
"The Magic Brush" (China)   214
"The Coming of Fog" (Canadian Indian)   220
"Anniko" (Africa)   228
"The Tug of War" (Africa)   235
"Catherine's Fate" (Sicily)   243
"Stan and the Dragon" (Rumania)   257

264 / Problematical and
Unresolved Stories for Experienced Storymakers

"The Journeys of Little Duck" (Australia)   265
"The Old Man and the Villagers (Africa)   271
"The Whippoorwill's Story" (Native American)   278
"The Golden Fish" (Burma)   284

292 / Suggestions for Storymaking Activities:
Prompts, Props, and Ideas for Creating Structures

Trickster Masks   291
Making a Character Mask   291
Making a Life Mask   292
Trickster Chants   293
Group Poem   293
Group Story   294
Group Painting   295
Need/Want/Wish   295
Journey to Get/Receive/Find/What You Want   295

Sending/Receiving a Letter: As One Character
  and Answering as Another 298
Creating a Story from a Person's Question 298
One-Minute Monologue 299
Alter-Ego Dialogue 300

301 / Stories to Stimulate Storymaking Sessions
 "Suho and the White Horse" (Mongolia) 301
 "The Vases of Harmony" (Gypsy) 304
 "The Little Parrot" (Tibet) 304
 "The Location of Wisdom" (Laos) 306
 "Why the Akha Wear Black Dresses" (Laos) 306
 "Speaking Truth" (Thailand) 307
 "The Night of the Wolves" (Poland) 308
 "Why People are Different" (Brazil) 310
 "Getting a Ride" (West Sahara) 311
 "How Some Wild Animals Became Tame" (India) 312
 "The Gift of the Pointing Stick"(Inuit) 313
 "Who Gave You Permission?" (Maori) 317
 "Sweet Music" (Brazil) 318
 "The Education of Finn McCoul" (Ireland) 319
 "Coyote and The Mouse Maids" (Native American) 323
 "The Past is Prologue" (Hindu) 325
 "The Power of Song" (Russia) 326
 "The Gift of Fire" (Mexico) 328
 "The Necklace (South Africa) 329
 "Truth is Truth" (Iran) 330
 "The Way of Things" (Canadian Indian) 331
 "The Story Bag" (Korea) 335

About the Author   339
Selected Bibliography   341

INTRODUCTION

Stories move in circles, they don't move in straight lines. So it helps if you listen in circles because there are stories inside stories and stories between stories, and finding your way through them is as easy and as hard as finding your way home. And part of the finding is the getting lost, because when you're lost, you have to look around and listen. *Because God Loves Stories,* by Steve Zeitlin, Editor.

THE NINE WOMEN from Kazakhstan were sitting in a three quarter circle. At each end sat two interpreters, prepared to simultaneously translate the women's words from Russian into English. Ranging in age from early twenties to mid-sixties, the women had come to the United States to attend workshops and give presentations on mediation and non-violent conflict resolution. Each defied cultural norms by refusing to remain silent in the face of brutal border disputes, bloody school battles, and continuing domestic violence. Separately, they had organized their various communities to support dialog, negotiation and other peaceful means as alternatives to habitual and traditional violent resolutions. "There has been too much killing, too much bloodshed," said one of the women.

I am a storyteller and a storymaker. I facilitate workshops, helping participants to make a community where they can safely create and share their own stories.

The women from Kazakhstan were interested in how they might use stories as an aid in their quest to teach people to share ideas and experiences, to negotiate rather than fight.

After hearing an Indian story, "Ant and Elephant," (p. 90) the women finger-painted an image from the story and then wrote some words evoked by the story and the image. Eventually these words grew into stories. After the third woman shared the story she had created, Eleni, a woman who looked to be in her sixties challenged me, "What good are stories when my husband is beating me?" The other women nodded their heads—they had seen and suffered what I could barely imagine. The young Russian interpreter practically choked as he translated her words. The tension was palpable; all eyes were focused on me.

I gasped and then managed to say, "No good at all. First the beatings have to stop. Absolutely!" The women nodded in agreement, continuing to stare intently at me. "But then, when the violence stops, what do you do with your pain? How do you heal from the damage done to your soul and spirit?" Eleni stared at me, challenging me to look away.

I knew that how I answered would determine the way our work together would continue. "In my experience, one way to heal is to tell your story to people who are ready to listen."

"Okay," she said, spitting out her words, "I tell you my story." She was married at thirteen and had borne eight children, four of whom survived to adulthood. Her husband beats her regularly. After thirty-two years of marriage she has long since given up trying to figure out how to avoid his wrath and rage or what she might have done to cause his anger. There was no way. There was no cause. There was no provocation. The beatings came in good times and bad. She didn't have to tell the other women; they knew and waited for my reaction. A bitter smile formed on Eleni's face. The male translator looked helplessly at the other translator, a woman, who refused to step in and take over the translating.

After a very long, deep breath, I handed each woman a four-inch square of paper. "Thank you for telling us your story. Let us paint a blessing for Eleni and then write some words of comfort for her." While Eleni waited, her eyes still focused on me, the women quickly painted their images and after writing, looked up at me expectantly. "We'll give Eleni our images one at a time and if you feel like saying something to her, that's fine."

One by one the women put their small pictures in front of her, some whispering words, others patting her on her shoulder. When I placed my image in front of her, since I didn't speak Kazakh or Russian, I had to speak loud enough for the interpreter to hear and felt very vulnerable. "I appreciate your willingness to share your story. I'm sure it takes a lot of courage to tell us. I will remember your story." Gently touching her shoulder, I walked back to my seat, hoping my words were comforting.

Eleni looked intently at the images before speaking, eying each of us, including the interpreters, remaining silent for an uncomfortable length of time. We waited. Then, with tears in her eyes, she said, "Thank you. Is first time I tell my story. Is first time there is someone listening."

The Kazakh women grew up in a culture where

beating women is acceptable and traditional. They learned to keep their feelings to themselves for the most part. What was the point of complaining about such a common experience? Yet, when given an opportunity to talk, these women spoke with painful eloquence—many speaking their truth in public for the first time.

After our storymaking session, at a dinner at my home, one of the older women, speaking through a female interpreter said, "We were invited to come to the United States because we have started programs that explore alternatives to violence in our schools and community. Now we have to stop the violence in our homes." Even before the interpreter could translate for me, the women cheered and toasted, "To the end of beatings."

The interpreter asked Eleni, "You seemed different after you got the blessings. What happened? After all, they couldn't change your experience or even what might happen when you go home. What difference can a few scraps of paper make?"

Eleni nodded, taking time to formulate her answer. "Is difficult to explain. I was feeling pain. Closed inside myself. When Nancy told people to make blessing to give me I was angry. What did she think little pieces of paper could do? But then, when the women gave them to me and I looked at them, something happened. Like my closedness opened a little. Somehow I felt better."

The interpreter asked, "How long did *feeling better* last?"

Eleni smiled. "Is still feeling good."

Stories are an endless source of vitality, power, healing, and information. When we share our stories, the energy released through the telling helps restore our sense of balance both within ourselves and in relationship to the group. We communicate aspects of our lives through stories, which is why when one person tells what happened, many of those listening respond with stories of their own. Sharing stories creates community by helping us connect to each other in meaningful ways.

THE YEARNING TO be heard without being judged is fundamental to our sense of well-being. Bearing witness to another's experience is a gift and a responsibility. All too often, as we listen to someone, we are thinking about what we want to say or do in response. The Kazakh women listened intently to each other, leaving space to take in what was said before responding. Once again, I experienced the healing power of telling one's story, of paying attention to the speaker and what was being said. The responses of the Kazakh women made an indelible impression on me. Once again the power of stories helped participants to create community, evoke new questions, reflect on past experience, and imagine new possibilities.

Storymaking participants find their way into the story by making images with finger-paints or clay, from an abstract prompt, in one minute or less. An abstract prompt is one for which there is no specific object to reproduce. The task might be to paint or sculpt an image of an abstract idea such as "courage" or "fear" or "open" or "unusual." Obviously, there is no one or right way to make these kinds of images. A concrete prompt such as the task to paint or sculpt a chair or a tree, however, conjures up specific images and participants can easily feel they "can't do it right." All the activities in a storymaking session are designed to help participants discover the power of metaphor and association of new stories evoked by old stories. Creating an image in one minute or less makes it possible to give unplanned shape and form to an idea or feeling without censorship. When words or phrases evoked by the image are immediately written down, participants connect nonverbal images with verbal associations. There is no time to plan, judge or analyze. Sharing the words and images within a small group can stimulate a profound knowing, an insight amplified by the listeners' exploratory responses, especially when someone has no words to explain or describe thoughts and/or feelings.

In a culture that requires explanations, when we can't find the words we need, are we lost in our silence? Does muteness equal ignorance? Does silence equal complicity? There are many reasons for silence: fear, lack of experience in honestly expressing thoughts and feelings, embarrassment, lack of trust... Whatever the cause, in my storymaking experience, participants learn to move through their silence, to trust the power of first thoughts and imagery, and to give voice to what was previously hidden from view—inner stories. These may be memories, created stories colored by experience, variations of stories we've read or been told, or spontaneous stories that seem to come from nowhere.

The issue of fact or fiction is irrelevant in storymaking as Eudora Welty wrote: "I create fiction to tell truth." A story can be accurate as far as facts go but be an emotional lie. Yet filtered through the power of experience and feelings, a created story may feel truthful. Even if we feel a need to hide our truths or fear the consequences of spontaneous storytelling, there is comfort in the wisdom of the psyche. Whatever we say or write without coercion or pressure is appropriate. We work at layers and levels uncontaminated by fear, going deeper only when it feels safe, as our confidence and courage permit. What makes the process of storymaking such a mystery to me is that stories emerge with no prior thinking or planning--a response to the story heard, an issue of concern, or perhaps a feeling that haunts us.

We are storytellers.

Dancing with Wonder is a book of stories about stories and storymaking. What informs my writing is a love of stories—hearing, writing, and telling them. This book offers suggestions to help readers embark on their own adventures in storymaking. Included are a number of journey stories that are meant to stimulate, challenge, support, and help create a vicarious sense of what it is like to participate in a storymaking journey. Most of all, I hope readers experience the joy of hearing, telling, and making stories.

Dancing With Wonder is divided into sections: **Imagemaking** explores the power and purpose of making spontaneous images and suggests a variety of ways in which imagemaking helps us to connect what we feel with what we think. **Storymaking** contains stories that exemplify the process of creating stories. **Experiencing the Storymaking Process** enables readers to begin exploring what it means to be part of a storymaking community. **Story Journeys** describes in detail, sessions of storytelling and storymaking in a variety of settings and groups. Although this section is long, a wide selection of possibilities is included to give readers a sense of what a storymaking session can be like and to provide vicarious experience. I imagine readers making their way through this chapter in a leisurely fashion, according to need and interest. **Sample Structures** suggests a variety of structured activities to help readers begin their story journeys. **Stories for Storymaking** includes stories from around the world that participants have found useful in developing story journeys. *Note* names and situations have been changed to protect the privacy of participants.* **Selected Bibliography** includes collections of stories from countries and cultures around the world.

❄ Try this!

Paint: An image of "Myself as Storyteller in a minute or less.

Write: Some words that come to mind.

Write: A memory or experience that comes to mind. If none does, imagine one.

What role do you play?

How do you feel?

Do you recognize yourself as storyteller?

1
IMAGEMAKING

> Part of our predicament today is due to the
> impoverishment of the natural images in us
> all. This narrow rational awareness that we
> have developed has cut us off from the
> imagemaking thing in us. Meaning comes to
> us in the first place, I believe, straight out of
> life in symbols and images, and this
> meaning is always greater than any concept
> we can consciously make of the image. It is
> greater than any words we can say or
> pictures we can paint. But these images are
> the source of an enormous spiritual and
> psychic energy, if we have access to them.
> When we are cut off from these images we
> lose the transforming energies with which
> we are endowed and we are poor. *Patterns of*
> *Renewal*, Laurens Van der Post

WE LIVE IN a culture where having no words is often
considered the equivalent of not knowing. And yet, we may
sense that even when we remain silent there is something
we would say if we could find the right words. Almost
everyone has experienced a need to speak yet be unable to
find the words that accurately express particular thoughts
and feelings. Why does this happen? Do we really not know
what we want to say? I don't think so. Our inability to find
words can have many causes, one of which is a

disconnection between what we think and how we feel. This may be the result of childhood experiences where adults discounted our ideas and feelings, or of the fear that what we said would be ridiculed. Changing this pattern, particularly if it is well entrenched, is not easy. However, healthy group dynamics can begin to help us trust ourselves as well as other group members. Once we know that what we say will be treated respectfully, we can begin to discover, recover, and uncover our authentic voice.

The activities suggested in this chapter and throughout *Dancing With Wonder* are designed to help readers connect their thoughts and feelings. No prior experience or artistry is required. All that matters is our willingness to begin, without having to know an issue we want to explore or feelings we want to express. We have to recognize and accept that if we try to control and censor our expression, much of what we think and feel will be lost.

The Power of Imagemaking
Breaking lifelong patterns of behavior is difficult. Coping mechanisms develop to protect us from danger or harm, yet they can persist long after their usefulness has become questionable or even unnecessary. Since we seldom wake up one morning and say to ourselves, "Oh, my coping mechanisms are outdated, I need new ones," it usually takes a series of experiences before we begin to recognize the need for change. *Imagemaking can act as a catalyst for both the recognition of outdated habits and behaviors as well as the possibility for developing new ones.*

People attend storymaking workshops for a variety of reasons: to improve and enhance creativity, to deal with life crises, to explore ideas about specific projects, to have fun with stories—sometimes even because a friend is going and wants company. It's rare that two people have the same purpose in mind. This is one of the ways storymaking differs from therapy. In therapy, the "contract" involves a problem and the client comes to the therapist to get help/advice/strategies for dealing with the issue. If the therapy involves a group, usually everyone involved is working on the same problem. In a storymaking workshop, the "contract" is that people will hear a story, paint and/or sculpt, write, share stories, and reflect on what has happened. No one will interpret, define, or tell anyone what anything means. It is always the teller who knows the meaning or asks for help as to what something means.

Donna decided to attend a storymaking workshop titled "Moving On" because she was frustrated at work. Her colleagues continuously teased her about her silence. They accused her of not having anything to say. When participants shared what had brought them to the workshop she told the group, "I have plenty to say; I just can't think of the words fast enough. I'm tired of them making fun of me." People nodded as if they knew all too well what it was like to be ridiculed.

When I told the group members to paint an image of "myself at this moment," Donna painted three red circles. Between the two larger circles was a small circle. Radiating out from the two large circles were thick lines of black that looked as if they were suffocating the small red circle. The black lines encapsulated the small circle, isolating it from the two larger circles. After a minute, I asked the group to stop painting and to write words or phrases that came to mind.

Donna quickly wrote: "You're wrong." "That's not what happened." "Don't be stupid." "How can you think that?" "Are you sure you're our daughter?" "Where on earth did you get that idea?" She was silent for a time, looking at her image and words. Then, very deliberately, she painted a second image. This time she painted a large red circle on top of two smaller red circles. The black lines radiated out from the two small red circles and had no contact with the large red circle that radiated yellow lines in every direction, including the small red circles. She then wrote: "I see." "I feel." "I experience." "I have words." "I can speak."

"Wow," she said, shaking her head, staring at the images she had painted and the words she had written. "Wow," she said again. "This is really something to think about." She looked around the room and then said to me, "When you asked us to paint I wanted to leave. I was always the worst one in art and I didn't believe you when you said that what we were doing was about knowing, not art." She shook her head again. "Just look at what I would have missed if I had left."

"Or if you hadn't written the words that verbalized the problem..." I replied.

"I'm going to frame these paintings, just as a reminder."

"Remember, it's about knowing, not art," I teased, checking her expression to make sure she knew I was supporting rather than criticizing her effort.

Donna disagreed. "To me it is art and I like that it is. Making those paintings reminded me that just because an art teacher told me years ago I had no creativity doesn't mean he was right. I just might buy myself some paints." She paused and then added, "Oh," looking as if she'd been struck by lightning. "Maybe there's a connection... In Psych 101 they say you can't decide to not feel one emotion but feel all the others. Maybe when the teacher said I had no creativity I decided that meant I had nothing to say."

Making images, using the energy of feelings, especially when we don't know why we feel as we do, helps us to learn something about what is going on inside of us. In the workshop with Donna, was Celia, a woman going through a messy divorce who thought she understood why she was upset, but knowing the reason didn't make her feel better. The image she painted reminded her of something that happened years ago on a school playground where she'd been taunted for being different. Writing the words that came to mind enhanced her memory, making it more vivid and detailed. She began to realize that her current situation was affected by painful memories of being yelled at and attacked as a youngster. The old feelings of being alone, unwanted and unprotected were bleeding into her current feelings about being divorced by a husband who had left her for a younger woman. She decided to keep painting, using her feelings of isolation and misery, working mostly with black and brown. She wrote a few words on each picture but had no desire to share either her images or what she wrote.

After painting eight images without stopping, she paused, shook her head, and then reached for the pot of red. Previously, she had begun her images with jagged lines but this time she started with swirls and spirals, painting with red and green. The next one included yellow. In what proved to be the culminating image, she included all the colors and shapes she previously used, and then carefully spread the images around her, gazing at each one, numbering them in the order in which she had made them. Only the words on the last painting were large enough to read from a distance: "I can. I will." Sighing, she turned to the group. "Going through an unwanted divorce is hard enough, but dragging a ton of baggage you don't realize is there makes it a whole lot worse." She shook her head and smiled wryly. "Who could believe something that happened more than thirty years ago would still be so powerful?"

❊ Try this!
Paint: An image of memory.
Sculpt: Some characters evoked by the image and put
         them in relationship to each other.
Write: What comes to mind. If no memory or experi-
         ence is evoked, imagine a situation evoked by
         your image and the sculpted characters.
Reflect: On what you've written.

So many of the people with whom I have worked have stories similar to Celia's. An influential person in their childhood told them they couldn't draw or paint or write or that they had no imagination or creativity. We all have these abilities—they are our birthright. Most of us are not interested in being artists, in seeing our work hanging in galleries or museums, or having our writing published and on the best seller lists. What does matter is the ease with which we are able to express our thoughts and feelings however we wish—authentically and with clarity.

Many, if not most, of us, have at one time or another tried to draw or have had to draw in school, recreational programs, or just because we had a yen to play with color and line. And many, if not most of us, have experienced a sense of failure, an inability to create art, either because we looked at what we drew and threw it away in disgust, or because a teacher or artist told us what we had done was no good. Even the thought of making images may remind us of past failures that left deeply embedded scars. Painting or sculpting might seem too scary to try. What if we're laughed at, denigrated, or judged? Do we even know how to make an image? Not to worry! I have yet to meet a person who couldn't 'smush' paint on paper or squeeze clay into an image.

Imagemaking stimulates a way-of-knowing that bypasses verbalization. It enhances our ability to manifest what we are feeling or intuiting with no intention of creating art or exploring an artistic vision. This is why it is necessary to make images, in less than a minute, whether with clay or paints. By working so quickly, we have no time to plan. We bypass our inner censors, allowing us to concretize first impressions. Using primitive materials like fingerpaint and clay allows our fingers and psyche to create without conscious manipulation. Sticking fingers into pots of paint to smear colors on the paper to express feelings or 'smushing' clay into a form shaped by a wordless vision makes it possible for us to symbolize that which was previously inaccessible. What we make is neither good nor bad, right nor wrong, artistic nor inartistic, it simply *is*. Honoring first thoughts or impressions, and letting the juices flow as they wish, enables us to explore inner thoughts and feelings in unexpectedly complex and marvelous ways.

What we know about our inner life and how we see ourselves not only affects how we understand ourselves in the world, it also impacts the meaning we derive from what we see and hear. Because we take in more information than we consciously process, we know more than we consciously realize. Making images from abstract (nonfigurative) prompts helps connect what we know, but cannot verbalize, to what we know and can express. For example, painting an image of "upset" or "joy" or "promise," followed by words that come to mind, often triggers experiences or feelings we may not have previously remembered.

Creating spontaneous images using primitive materials, working quickly and responsively to a story or an abstract idea, brings to mind words that help us regain access to our knowing. Notions of creativity or artistry prove irrelevant. We need only the motivation to stick fingers into paint or manipulate a piece of clay. The response, which often feels magical, happens without intentionality as long as we actively participate and allow our inner voices to speak without interference or censorship. The poet Rainer Maria Rilke speaks eloquently of this process:

> You must give birth to your images.
> They are the future waiting to be born.
> Fear not the strangeness' you feel.
> The future must enter into you long before it
> happens...
> Just wait for the birth...
> For the hour of new clarity.

✖ Try this!

Paint: An image.

Write: Some words.

Reflect: On what you see and feel.

Imagemaking as a Way of Knowing

The importance of imagemaking struck home for me many years ago when I read a letter Albert Einstein wrote to a fellow mathematician who had asked how he (Einstein) knew what he knew. Einstein responded that initially he didn't know what he knew. In order to discover what he might know, he made images, or "doodles" as he called them, and then wrote equations and words that came to him after the images. He repeated the process until satisfied that he had uncovered whatever it was he knew about what he was doing. Einstein is not the only person who doesn't know what he knows. A participant in a workshop wrote in his journal:

> I had always thought about my inner self as a gloomy, structured figure until I fingerpainted this image. I found myself using bright yellow and drawing unknown shapes. I felt this image was my inner self but I failed to acknowledge its existence. After I painted this image I seemed to hear stories in a new way but I can't explain how.

The magic of imagemaking, working responsively in ways that help us regain access to our knowing, came clear to a group of participants who I asked to make an image of a Story Guide without being told what it was. Immediately all hands went up with one person asking the question for the group, "What's a Story Guide?"

"Just make an image, you'll find out," I responded. Grumbling and muttering to themselves, they dutifully put fingers into pots of paint, shaking their heads, wondering, so they later confessed, if it was too late to drop the course.

Peter's image of his personal Story Guide looked like confetti falling from the sky. He sighed so loudly we all laughed and he joined in, but then, when I asked the group to write the story of the birth of their Story Guide, he protested. "How can I make a story from stuff floating in space? Besides, I don't have a clue what a Story Guide is."

"Look at your image until your fingers start to write," I told him. He shook his head, looking utterly helpless, but everyone else was writing so he picked up his pen. This is what he wrote as he peered at his image titled: Birth of a Story Guide

The clouds in the heavens drifted apart and it was as if the sky itself was splitting. Down to the Earth fell the story. The story fell and fell and when it reached the Earth it shattered into a great many pieces. There were enough pieces of the story for everyone in the land to have. So every person took the story and kept it. Now every piece was different and every person was different as well so the story helped and guided people in different ways. No person was affected in the same way. Each person went on through life, everyone different, but all the same in that they each had a piece of the story.

Shaking his head, he murmured, "All that from an image that made no sense..." He paused, trying to put his bewilderment into words. "Before you asked us to paint an image of a Story Guide I would have said there's no such thing. But then, I painted an image of mine and told how it got born. That's just too weird!"

"What's weird?" someone asked.

"How we can paint an image of something, and tell a story about it, and yet before we were asked to do it, we didn't even know it existed. Now it's gonna be with me for the rest of my life." He hesitated, looking at the group, as if checking out whether he could trust us. "Can I tell you something?" We all nodded. "That's the first story I ever wrote. I can't believe how it poured out of me. And it happened just because I kept looking at my image? This is definitely weird."

ONE OF THE most common questions in response to being asked to paint or sculpt an abstract image is, "Do you mean..." or "Is this what you want?" In fact, what I want is whatever people do. Just as the students experienced disbelief that they could paint or write the story of Story Guide, an entity they knew nothing about, readers need to trust that however they respond, their spontaneous response reflects their unique experience. Trusting and honoring our expression takes time and requires nonjudgmental reaction. This is why my students are not allowed to make comments that reflect judgment but are encouraged to share responses that reflect personal experience, wonder, puzzlement, or an evoked memory.

Try this!

Paint: An image of Story Guide
Write: The story how Story Guide was born.
Share: Your story with someone.
Reflect: On your experience.

I believe we all know more than we are aware of knowing. In the above case, Peter could describe a guide and he knew about stories. His imagination, feelings, and stored knowledge mixed together to produce the image and the story. As part of our reflection at the end of the session, he told the class it was the first time he could remember connecting his thinking and feeling. "It feels safer to keep them separate. Actually, it's not so bad. I'd like to try it again. Maybe separating them isn't such a good idea."

Another student, Joe, painted an image of Story Guide as books on a shelf and then groaned, "Can I have another chance? I need to paint a better image. This one sucks."

I shook my head. "Work with what you painted. Your story is there, waiting for you."

"Look," he pleaded. "I'll do another image real fast–in less than a minute. I'll write so fast you won't even know I did it."

"The image you made is your story. Treasure it." Joe did not look pleased. "Focus your anger on your image. Your story will come, I promise."

Obviously annoyed, he began to write, furious at me and the process, muttering to himself when he finished, "Son of a..." Of course everyone wanted to hear what he wrote. He read almost as if he were reading someone else's writing, practically spitting out his words.

The stories being read and told meant nothing. The more the teacher assigned reading to the student, the more the student hated reading. It just seemed so pointless to him. Why read when there were so many other things he could be doing? Why tell stories? But what confused him more was that he could see that all his friends enjoyed reading and telling stories. What was he missing? Why didn't he like it? Maybe it was the stories his teacher was suggesting. So he went down to the library and looked up stories on different topics. He picked a book, opened it, and sat down. While he was reading he noticed something happening. The blackness he had known as stories his whole life was turning all the colors of the spectrum. And emerging from the story and colors was a man—a shepherd, moreover. From then on, the story shepherd guided the boy on all his treks into books and stories and telling stories.

As soon as he finished reading he looked at the questions on the faces around him and threw up his hands. "I have no idea where my story came from. I was so mad at having to use my image I couldn't think straight. The first thing that came to mind when I looked at my image was a shepherd guiding his followers to the stories that would shape and enrich their lives. And though the birth of my Story Guide might sound like a true story, it's not. Well, it's true until the point where the Story Guide is born, but for some reason, that hasn't happened to me, at least not yet. I try to enjoy reading if it's assigned. I try leisure reading but it's still somewhat of a chore for me. And I know I'm not much of a storyteller. Oh well, maybe some day. Maybe tomorrow..." He grinned.

"Where's your anger?" someone asked.

"I don't know," he said looking puzzled. "It's gone."

How can anger simply disappear? Anger is energy. Joe channeled the energy of his anger into writing his story, thereby transforming and dissipating the angry energy into something useful. If we consider emotion as energy we can explore ways to use this power to our benefit. This may be more difficult when we feel depressed and it seems we have no energy. Yet imagemaking also works in reverse. When we hear a story and then paint or sculpt a reaction or response, we nourish our psyches and very often, as a result, we feel revitalized.

Tension and Trickster

Although I have been writing and telling stories for most of my life, the power, possibility and importance of Trickster stories crystallized after a storymaking session in 1980. I recount what happened in some detail because it was the first time I experienced the transformational power of storymaking. Although the archetype of Trickster is associated with energy, creativity, sexuality, and possibility, it's an archetype that I find troubling because I don't like being tricked. When the colleague with whom I was co-leading a workshop suggested we use it for our next storymaking session, I was less than pleased.

The afternoon before the workshop I taught a drama class on acting and nonverbal communication. The regular teacher, a friend of mine whom I will call Martin, confided he had alienated several of the students and hoped I could help the students regain a sense of community. He participated in one of the groups, acting as director, violating an important precept I had established: No one tells anyone what to say or do. He did both, continually.

During their reflection, the students in his group turned their anger at Martin against me. Thinking I had satisfactorily deflected their rage and had helped them to look at the causes, rather than the symptoms, of their anger, I felt pleased. The group looked more peaceful and relaxed. As I was leaving, Martin yelled at me, accusing me of being dogmatic and unresponsive to "legitimate student complaints." I felt shocked; stunned and sickened that he would talk to me this way, especially in front of the students. These feelings gave way to a sense of shame and self-loathing. The last thing I wanted to do was to meet with another colleague and work with students, but I had previously agreed to meet my workshop co-leader on a street corner and had no way to contact her to cancel my participation in the workshop.

Trying to hide my feelings, we began the workshop as previously designed and planned. Although I usually don't participate in sessions that I lead so I can focus on the responses of group members, my colleague insisted that I do so and rather than make a fuss, I reluctantly agreed.

After painting an image of Trickster (mine was of an abstract elf-like creature painted mostly in yellow but covered with dripping bits of red and black), my co-leader asked participants to jot down answers to seven questions quickly, without censoring. The following questions and my replies will give readers a sense of the storymaking process in concrete terms and of how the scribbled-down answers shaped my written story.

Q1. What is the age of Trickster?
A1. Continually changing, not measurable in human terms
Q2. What is the time of day?
A2. Noon
Q3. Who does Trickster encounter?
A3. A weeping woman
Q4. What do they talk about?
A4. The constant flow of water down to earth
Q5. What is the challenge?
A5. To stop the weeping, the flow of water
Q6. How is the problem overcome?
A6. A time to weep, a time not to weep.
Q7. What is the final result?
A7. Ocean tides...ocean swimming...waves...no drowning

While scribbling my answers I felt a surge of energy that grew stronger after my co-leader asked participants to begin writing their story with the words, "And Lomi was wandering aimlessly..." Although I usually wrote painfully slowly, more rewriting than writing, words now danced onto the page without conscious intention. I wrote with no awareness of time, place, or people. After finishing the story, I sensed workshop participants watching me and felt embarrassed and confused. I didn't know what to do with the feeling inside me that something miraculous had just happened. I desperately wanted time, privacy, and quiet to process my experience. The writing felt like a dream from which I wasn't ready to wake up.

When it was my turn to read I hesitated, afraid my bubble of euphoria would be shattered by participants' reactions. Instead, at the end of the reading, unlike the comments and observations other readers received, no one spoke. Later, several people asked if I had really written the story right then and there. Unnerved, I nodded, still quivering with amazement.

The story's effect surprised me more than writing it. The emotional pain I had been feeling from the drama-workshop-encounter had given way to a sense of inner comfort. Depression, shame, and self-loathing had been replaced by wonder.

Here is the story, written immediately after answering the seven questions.

And Lomi was wandering aimlessly about the earth and heard a great noise and saw great commotion. "What is happening my brothers and sisters?"

In many voices they replied as one, "The earth is being filled with water. We shall soon have no dry land on which to live. We will all drown. You must help us."

So Lomi wandered about looking for the source of the water. Climbing the great current of salty water he found a woman of no great size weeping tears. "Oh help me," she cried. "I angered the gods and they have condemned me to stand here weeping for all eternity."

Lomi answered, "I have no great powers such as those of the gods. I cannot change what they have ordained." The weeping woman wept harder than ever. "But," said Lomi, "it is possible to trick the gods in small ways. You will have to help me." The weeping woman agreed.

"I will change myself into a wind and wind myself around your body to squeeze out all the tears in one great flow. You must not be afraid and fight the wind. It will take time before the new tears come so you will have rest before they start again. But, they will begin once more and you must learn to squeeze them out yourself."

And so it was. Lomi changed into a fierce young wind and wound around the body of the weeping woman, squeezing her tears dry. Peace came over her as the tears stopped. When it was time for them to start again she was rested and the tears flowed more gently. Lomi watched and was pleased. "You have learned quickly and well. I believe the People of Earth will no longer have to worry about their land being flooded."

The weeping woman smiled her thanks and wept a particularly fine stream of water for Lomi's descent. The People of Earth noticed there was a rhythm to the ebb and flow of the water and learned to live with it. They called the changing rhythms of the water, tides, and they gave the name of Ocean to the water filling parts of Earth. They learned to swim and to fish.

Thus did Lomi trick the gods to bring comfort to the People of Earth and peace to the weeping woman.

I identified with the woman weeping endless tears, condemned for all time, with no respite and no appeal. A person I thought was my friend had judged me without consideration for the part he played in his students' anger. To my surprise, help came from the archetype I studiously avoided and consistently dodged. What sensible person trusts a trickster?

This encounter with Trickster made me rethink my previous position. Perhaps not taking the risk to ask for help, refusing to explore my inner trickster, and not wanting to read stories about trickster characters I thought unreliable or untrustworthy was part of the reason for my habitual slow and agonizing way of writing. Maybe I had relied on old patterns. Perhaps the way out was not the way in.

Sharing my story with the workshop participants who generously showed their admiration enhanced my self-esteem. The incident made me wonder if there were other stories inside me waiting to be written. Could anyone experience this process? Even the possibility was exciting and curiously liberating.

Making an image of Trickster not only locates our thoughts and feelings about our inner Trickster, giving clues as to what is happening inside us, it also shows us a way to release energy, even when we are not aware of our tension.

Try this!
Paint: An image of Trickster.
Ask: Trickster a question.
Answer: As if you are your inner trickster.
Reflect: On your experience.

A few months after writing the story, a group of students entered the classroom tense and distracted. We began with everyone painting "an image of myself at this moment," after which, they wrote words that came to mind. Almost everyone's image contained a black cloud, some small, some covering the page. Their words described feelings of fear, anxiety, frustration and shame. When we discussed the images and words, many talked about having to take their first big chemistry test the next period from a teacher well-known for his difficult tests. Although I had planned to work with a creation story I switched gears and told a Trickster tale. When we embrace Trickster energy we nourish our creativity and these students appeared to need all the creative possibility they could muster. We worked with an African story **"Caterpillar and the Wild Animals."**

One day, as Rabbit walked home from the market, he heard a loud voice coming from his house. Rabbit asked, "Who's in my house?"

The creature answered, "I am the most powerful warrior in the world. I crush elephants with my fingers and turn lions into dust. I am invincible."

Terrified, Rabbit ran back to the village. When he saw Leopard, he wailed, "Oh, Leopard, there's a strange creature in my house and he says he's the most powerful warrior in the world. Can you help me?"

"Rabbit, you are such a scaredy-cat. It can't be that bad." But, as soon as Leopard heard the voice boast that it could crush elephants, he said, "I'm very sorry but I just remembered I have to visit my cousin." And off he went.

Rabbit raced around looking for an animal that would help him and saw Jackal. "Oh, Mr. Jackal, please come with me. I can't go home, there's a ferocious creature in my house."

Jackal laughed at Rabbit. "No one is as ferocious as I am. I'll take care of him, don't you worry." But, as soon as Jackal heard that the creature turned lions into dust, he said, "I'm so sorry. I forgot that it's time for me to meet my brother." And off he went.

Rabbit begged many other animals to help him but as soon as they heard the voice, suddenly they all had urgent business requiring their immediate attention. Discouraged, Rabbit walked slowly toward his house, wondering if he would ever be able to go inside again. Frog saw him looking so miserable he asked why. When Rabbit told him, Frog said, "I'll help you."

Rabbit sighed, remembering how all the bigger and more powerful animals had run away but he said politely, "Thank you, Frog."

Frog listened to the mysterious voice yell, "I am the most powerful warrior in the world. I crush elephants with my fingers and turn lions into dust." He took a very deep breath. He took a second deep breath, and then a third.

Frog shouted back, even louder, "I am stronger than the most ferocious warrior. I jump over mountains. I leap across rivers. I fear no one and nothing. Whosoever arouses my wrath is doomed. Forever!"

When the creature inside Rabbit's house heard Frog, it whimpered, "Please don't hurt me, I'm leaving."

The door opened and out crept Caterpillar looking very frightened. When Caterpillar and Frog saw each other, they laughed. Soon all the animals were laughing, even Rabbit.

After hearing the story, the students painted an image of a telling moment, a place in the story that strikes them as powerful, meaningful, interesting, irritating; in other words, any passage that evokes a strong response. After making and sharing their images I asked them to imagine themselves as Rabbit, walking in the woods, meeting a stranger passing by, and telling this creature or person what "really" happened the previous day. People were encouraged to "liberate" their imaginations and to allow Rabbit to tell his story from his point of view. Most people made up versions in which Rabbit acted heroically, not at all bothered by the loud voice, quite ready and willing to act on his own behalf. The stories were very clever, some quite funny and students laughed a lot. Just before the end of the period I asked them to make another "image of myself at this moment." This time there were almost no black clouds and those that remained were considerably smaller than they were originally. The difference shocked the participants. They offered a variety of opinions as to what had happened. Most attributed their more relaxed state to the activities and the laughter, although one student suggested, "Maybe it was because Frog was the smallest animal, yet he was the one who solved the problem. Maybe we're all identifying with Frog..." Everyone laughed as he made frog sounds.

"Just the fact that Frog was the littlest animal and was able to do what the bigger animals were afraid to do gives me hope that even though I'm not a genius, maybe I can pass the test, or better," said Mari.

Joe added, "If we hadn't made the before and after images of 'myself at this moment,' I wouldn't have known how tense I was at the beginning of class and how much better I feel now."

Although they were on their way to deal with a difficult challenge the next period, everyone looked more relaxed and ready to confront the chemistry exam than when they first entered the room. From then on, whenever I worked with highly stressed participants, I asked them to make before and after images of "myself at this moment." Their images often evoked words describing their stress and brought to consciousness feelings previously unknown. Coupling this with a Trickster story enabled us to explore ways to reduce their fear and anxiety. It seems that Trickster has a good track record when it comes to releasing tension, especially when we are unaware of it.

What do you think of when you think of Trickster?

Releasing Memory

Making a spontaneous image may not only unlock memories, it can create a reason to speak. When working with a group of older people at a community center we began with each person painting an image of "beginnings" and then writing words that came to mind. One man who painted a round brown shape with a long yellow blob burst out laughing. Of course everyone wanted to know what was so funny. "I haven't thought about this in seventy years." He started laughing again. "When I was six years old, my dad came downstairs and said, 'Make a cup of tea and a slice of toast and put them and a banana on a tray. Take it upstairs to your mother.' I held it very carefully as I climbed the stairs, wondering what was going on. The door to the bedroom was closed so I had to put the tray down to knock. My dad came up at that moment, took the tray, opened the door, told me to wait, and went inside. A little bit later he came out with a baby. I decided that if you wanted to have a baby all you had to do was take the woman a tray with tea, toast, and a banana." This time everyone joined his laughter.

Suddenly a woman who had never spoken in the two years she had been coming to the center stood up. She had painted a brown rectangle with two tall stick figures, a small stick figure between them, and a small blob of yellow on the brown rectangle. She wrote her words in Yiddish. She seemed to want to talk. People were astonished to see her looking this way and immediately gave her their full attention. She spoke hesitantly, in broken English, but no one misunderstood what she said. She had been born in Russia, and when the authorities told her family to leave, they stipulated her parents could take only one suitcase and one child. But, the family had two children; she was about two, her brother, almost five. Her parents got the biggest suitcase they could find and refitted it, drilling air holes in the cover and lining it with soft cloth. They put her inside and took turns carrying the suitcase all the way to the train station, on to the boat, and across the ocean. She remembered her father as a soft-spoken man, however, when he said in a harsh tone that she must be very quiet, she was. "That was my beginning," she said. "I was born in a suitcase." That was also the beginning of her participation in center activities. No one knew that the woman who painted the suitcase spoke English or why she had remained silent for so long. She never told anyone why she suddenly decided to speak. But, having told her story of her beginning, she found other stories she wanted to tell and soon developed the reputation of being a raconteur.

Recovering Memory
Entering a story through a powerful image can help facilitate the recovery of past experience and feeling. During a workshop titled "Becoming Memory," I structured activities around an old Chinese tale, **"Li Chi the Serpent Slayer."**

In China, a long time ago, a huge serpent was menacing a village--eating animals and crops, and sometimes, even people. The villagers, tired of losing their crops, food and livelihood went to their magistrate and demanded that he protect the community. But no matter what he did, he was unable to stop the rampaging serpent. As a last resort, he sought the advice of a sorcerer who advised the villagers to sacrifice a thirteen year-old maiden in the tenth month of each year to the beast if they wanted him to stop plundering the village. Each year, for nine years, offering the maidens kept the villagers safe from the serpent's devastation.

In the tenth year, Li Chi, a young girl from a poor family, spoke to the magistrate. She volunteered to go up the mountain and sacrifice herself to the serpent if the magistrate would guarantee that her mother and father would be taken care of until they died. She knew that as she and her five sisters married, they would have to leave their home to live with their husband's families and when the last girl was married, their elderly parents would be destitute, alone and without help.

Unlike the maidens who were forced to go with nothing to protect them, Li Chi made a plan. She asked the magistrate to give her a dog, food, flint, and a sword. Although he was reluctant to provide her with what she requested, the magistrate's relief, that this year he would not have to struggle to find a maiden from increasingly unwilling families, overcame his resistance and he satisfied all her requests.

Li Chi went up the mountain with the dog and though she wasn't exactly sure how to find the serpent's cave, the closer they came, the more powerful was the stench. The dog whined in protest. Li Chi, almost overcome by the horrible odor, found it harder and harder to continue yet they kept walking toward the smell. When they reached the cave, she began her preparation, telling the dog what he must do. Using the flint, she made a fire to cook the food she brought. Soon delicious smells wafted back into the cave, enticing the hungry serpent. It slithered out from the cave, rearing its ugly head in search of the food. With a nod from Li Chi, the dog leapt up and clawed the serpent's eyes. Immediately, Li Chi stuck the sword into the neck of the blinded beast, continuing to strike it until the serpent lay dead.

Instead of leaving immediately, Li Chi entered the serpent's cave and collected the bones of all the nine maidens who had been sacrificed to appease the beast's appetite. Reverently, she carried the bones back to the village, not only to show the villagers the serpent was dead, but also to remind the people that the young girls had died for them. Li Chi ensured that they were buried with the proper ceremony and respect.

After hearing the story, each participant painted an image of a telling moment that particularly impressed them. The words evoked by the image of one participant were: "bones, blood, memory, hiding in the bottom of the pile." While writing the words, Jenny said she felt queasy, not sure she could continue participating. Yet, after the first person read what he had written, Jenny volunteered to read her writing.

I faced the monster. I killed the monster. I am free to go, to live my life. Yet I remain in this place of blood and stench and horror. My feet are rooted. They will not move foreword. They will not go down the mountain, to the people who live in fear, who kill young girls to keep themselves safe.

I feel myself moving backward, into the cave. Into the darkness and horror, into the killing ground. I stumble and fall. My fingers touch a bone...and another bone...and another bone. The bones of the maidens sent to their death by their families and teachers and neighbors.

I collect all the bones though there are so many I cannot hold them all. I carry the bones out of the cave, out of their hiding place, into the light, into the sun. I go into and out of the cave until I have brought all of the bones outside.

I make many trips up and down the mountain until all the bones are gathered in a soft bed of green grass in the center of the village. People come to watch in silence...in shame...in resentment. How dare I, a young woman, do what none of them would do. Face the monster. Slay the monster. End its murdering and pillaging.

I will not let the villagers forget the maidens who died to save them. I will mark their graves with words to tell all those who come, who might ask what happened. These young girls were killed because their families and neighbors who were stronger and wiser and older had no courage to do what needed to be done. I will tell the young girls' stories. I will not let them be forgotten. I will tell their stories so that future generations will know what happened here. It can happen again. It must not happen again.

Jenny looked surprised after she finished reading. She reported the queasiness had gone and she felt less fragile. Writing had helped her discover the personal meaning and power of the story. Her family had sacrificed her; their deeds had been hidden in the dark cave of memory. Yet, metaphorically, she had found the courage to go into the cave, to bring to light what had been done. Now she had the strength and courage to tell her story.

Later that day, while Jenny and I were walking along the rocky California coast, a huge wave washed over the boulders in front of us. Salt water sprayed the rocks making them slippery. Jenny fell, barely able to hold onto a bit of rock, her body inches from the surging ocean. As I struggled to pick her up she had a flashback so powerful she started to shake and it was all I could do to hold onto her as we crept off the rocks and on to solid ground. She was breathing with such difficulty it took a while for her to tell me what happened. She spoke in a child's voice, her eyes closed.

"I'm swimming in the ocean and I hear my mother yelling at me. She's angry that I went into the water. She told me to stay on the beach. Suddenly a huge wave knocks me off my feet and my head goes under the water. I try to lift my head above the water so I can breathe but something is holding my head under the water. Hands are holding my face in the water. I'm struggling to get away. I feel hands pushing the hands holding my head. The new hands grab me and lift me up, out of the water. A lifeguard is yelling that I'm okay as I gasp for breath. He's between me and my mother. It's her hands I felt holding my head under the water. She tried to drown me. He saved me. My mother wants me dead."

She looked at me, tears streaming down her face. "Is this possible? Is this why I've always been afraid of foaming, swirling water even though I'm a very strong swimmer?" Sobbing, she held her face in her hands. I waited; my hand on her shoulder. When she was able to talk, she said, "I feel like a piece of my life has been given back to me."

How did Jenny unexpectedly understand something that had previously eluded her? I think it has to do with symbolic learning, how we give meaning to the symbols through which we interpret our world. Jenny felt great fear every time she put her head under water even though she was a trained lifesaver and knew she could raise her head any time she chose. Her uncontrollable terror filled her with shame because she was unable to rationalize away her fear. Trusting that we have inner wisdom and knowledge beyond conscious knowing is empowering and, given the right tools, can be brought to consciousness. Spontaneous imagemaking and storymaking bypasses our inner censor and customary ways of expressing thoughts and feelings, allowing us to become aware of hitherto hidden knowing.

Not all storymaking has to do with uncovering hidden trauma or discovering important information about one's self. Sometimes it's just enjoyable, a release and an occasion for laughter. The images created in response to the story of "Caterpillar and the Wild Animals" (p. 44) were increasingly hilarious, with each storyteller trying to outdo the one who had come before. This too offers a path toward reconnecting to our inner life.

Through imagemaking and the words evoked by it, we learn to pay attention to signals, initially so faint we might well imagine we are hearing, seeing, or feeling nonsense. Perhaps, in its first appearance, the information that comes up *is* a kind of non-sense because we haven't learned to honor it, to make sense of it. We haven't thought to pay attention to, or value, what comes out or up before conscious thought. It is also true that significant trauma can cloud our ability to remember. Imagemaking helps us regain valuable access to troubling events, in as much detail as we are currently ready to process, and to recall these events without needing to speak out loud. This particularly helps those who have had difficult childhood experiences and have repressed what has happened, in part, because they have been warned of dire consequences if they tell.

What releases or recovers memory is not the same for everyone. We can remain silent for so long that the urge to speak seems lost. Sculpting or painting images helps to bypass our inner censor and jog memory, making it possible for us to become aware of feelings. Words evoked by images enable us to express ourselves with some degree of clarity and authenticity. Not only does imagemaking facilitate our ability to verbalize, it also stimulates the integration of thinking and feeling, a process that connects our inner and outer worlds. Images stimulate words that often evoke memory or experience and in turn, create new images. The stories that emerge from these images and words can improve our emotional and mental health... because when we tell stories of our lives to people in a caring community, we invite our listeners to learn more about the essential us. By integrating newly released or recovered memories into the context of the whole of our lives, we come to understand more deeply who we are and who we choose to be. Bearing witness to the stories of our lives makes us more aware of what it means to be human— always fallible yet with the capacity to make new choices that allow us to grow and develop.

2
STORYMAKING

I'm a storyteller. I'll work to make you believe me. Throw in some real stuff, change a few details, add the certainty of outrage. I know the use of fiction in a world of hard truth, the way fiction can be a harder piece of truth. The story of what happened, or what did not happen—but should have—that story can become a curtain drawn shut, a piece of insulation, a disguise, a razor, a tool that changes every time it is used and sometimes becomes something other than intended. The story becomes the thing needed. *Two or Three Things I know for Sure* by Dorothy Allinson

TRADITIONAL SOCIETIES TRANSMIT information, history and culture through stories told by elders and those entrusted with ancestral memory. People come together to hear the storyteller inform, entertain, instruct, and impart tribal wisdom. The shared experience of hearing their stories strengthens the society, teaching and enriching the next generation. Today, although we obtain information in a variety of ways, we still need storytellers to share both traditional tales as well as stories of contemporary life in the community. After hearing them, people frequently share impressions, discuss new ideas, think about old questions and, very often, share personal experience. It's as if stories beget stories, one stimulating the next.

When we tell a story, we have to choose what to say, select the emphasis we place on events, take into account the effect of our narration on our audience, and decide how we want to end our story: With questions? A wonder? What we've learned? A laugh? With a reference to what has happened in the lives of our listeners? No two tellings are ever the same, for no one can tell the same story exactly the same way each time. Memorization is not storytelling. When we tell a story we elicit constant feedback from listeners and adjust our telling to ensure attention. Noticing what we add, change or leave out provides important clues about how we are thinking and feeling at the moment. For example, when working with a group of ten-year old girls in a literacy project, I told the story of Cinderella and heard myself emphasizing Cinderella's despair and feelings of abandonment. At the time, my son was critically ill in the hospital fighting for his life. The young girls were resistant to the idea that they could learn to read and write. A few weeks later, telling the same story to another group, I heard myself highlighting Cinderella's gratitude for her fairy godmother's help. At this point, my son was recovering and the ten-year old girls in the literacy project had begun to work productively. As I reflected on the differences between the two tellings, I realized the changes were unconscious. Since then, I have come to understand that each time we tell a story we reflect our current experience as well as react and respond to those hearing the story.

Reading about storymaking sessions gives readers the possibility of vicariously experiencing some of the benefits and joys of sharing stories in a caring community. Therefore, this section includes a variety of stories, both traditional as well as those told by group members in workshops and classes. I include these examples to give the reader a sense of what storymaking sessions are like and the effect the sessions can have on participants. The accounts can be read straight through or in bits and pieces.

The Power of Speaking in Role

Stories contain characters whose behaviors run the gamut of human experience. When we talk in role, as a character, we have the possibility of vicariously experiencing life as we would likely never know it. Using our imagination, we step into the shoes of people whose choices are not ours and whose actions we may not approve. Yet, because we are not bound to a character, and can shift and change as we choose, we open ourselves up to the possibility of understanding people whose lives and choices are very different from ours. Even if we continue to disapprove, our understanding deepens and we are less likely to be prematurely judgmental.

Sharing stories and speaking in role, provide ways of talking about personal issues without revealing intimate details. For example, in a seminar in Europe, Lisa, a heavyset woman, looked depressed, but when people asked what was wrong, she laughed and waved away their concern. Toward the end of an afternoon session, she looked increasingly tense, yet the cause remained a mystery. As part of our exploration of a novel through drama, participants chose a character from the novel, made an image of their character at a significant moment in their character's life, and then wrote a brief autobiography of their character at that critical moment. Lisa chose to be the apple on a tree that is thrown away by a hungry little girl when the child realizes it is not edible. After Lisa shared her image and autobiography she said, pointing to Petra, a group member, "I am the apple you threw away. I know you said I was rotten and that's why you did it, but even rotten apples have a good smell. You could have put me on your mantle. I would have sweetened the air. I would have been useful even if you couldn't eat me." Lisa looked like she was ready to cry.

Initially taken aback, Petra, speaking in role as the little girl, nodded her head. "I see. Well, now that you tell me this, I must say that I am sorry. I hope you will forgive me. You know I am a young child and we children don't always think about our actions. All I could think about was my hunger and my disappointment that you weren't good to eat. You are right. I should have taken you into the house and put you on the mantle. Can you imagine that I now recognize my mistake and am going out to find you and bring you inside?"

"Oh yes," said Lisa, smiling. "I can. And I promise, I will make your house smell nice for many days." Her face relaxed and the group continued sharing their images and autobiographies.

As we reflected on the session, Lisa said, "I would like to speak. I was feeling really bad about myself and decided that you (the group) didn't like me. I kept feeling worse and worse and even though many of you tried to help, I felt that nothing you could do would make me feel better. When I spoke as my character and said how I was feeling, and Petra, as her child character, apologized, I suddenly felt okay about myself even though I was speaking in role."

Petra got up and gave Lisa a hug. "It's funny that you say this because I was so angry that the apple was rotten I forgot that the apple didn't have a choice; it had been on the tree too long. I asked myself, 'where is this anger coming from?' but I couldn't figure it out. As I was apologizing to you I remembered a drawing I made for my older sister when I was three or four. Although she thanked me for it, I overheard her laughing about it to her friend, making fun of what I had worked really hard to make. When she left the house, I found the picture and tore it up. I also remember I never made any drawings after that. Maybe that's why all this fingerpainting has been so hard for me."

Bengt, the man sitting next to her said, "I like your paintings. I hope you'll keep painting after the workshop is over." After group members shared a number of stories of hurtful responses to gifts, Bengt said, "It's good to talk about this. I also made a picture for my father when I was little. He made such fun of it I never made presents for anyone ever again. I gave him all my creativity and now I'm taking it back. I'm going to make a painting for my wife and for each of my kids."

Petra asked, "What if they make fun?"

"I don't think they will, but if they do, I'll tell them they hurt my feelings. I wish I'd told that to my father even if it didn't do any good. They don't have to like my pictures but it's important to me that they appreciate I made something for them because I love them."

Expressing our feelings and ideas can sometimes be

difficult because of socialization and/or personal experience. Even our place in the world may prevent or obscure our ability. We may not want to divulge what we might judge to be embarrassing or upsetting, especially with a group of people we do not know well. Yet the willingness to share parts of our lives helps restore access to previously hidden memories and experiences. There are many safe and appropriate ways to do this. For example, in the above episode, Lisa revealed nothing about what had been making her feel bad, yet in role, she was able to tell Petra she felt devalued by using circumstances from the story rather than her own life. In role she was honest, direct, and forthcoming, as was Petra. The exchange, although apparently between two fictional characters, allowed Lisa to express important and truthful feelings. Later, Petra said the episode also reminded her of a time she had pushed her younger brother too hard and he had fallen and hurt himself. No matter how she apologized, she never felt her apology was accepted. Petra told Lisa that her forgiveness had shifted and eased some of the burden she (Petra) was carrying.

Even when group members have little in common, telling stories creates a community between teller and listeners--a connection between the teller and what is told, among group members, as well as between individuals, all of whom bring history and experience to their reactions. I have never found a story that had only one meaning, nor have the events of a story been so fixed that listeners could only come up with one explanation.

One Story, Many Meanings

When we hear a story, we react according to our history, current state, and point of view. For example, if we have just had an argument with our boss, we might focus on how to deal with those more powerful than we are. If we are struggling with illness, we might pay particular attention to healing rituals. If we have suffered discrimination or injustice, we might identify with those suffering similar indignities. As our situation changes so does the issue that holds our attention in a story. For this reason, we can hear the same story at different points in our lives and extract a different meaning each time.

The following incident took place among older adults in a community center and exemplifies just how differently each person can hear the same story, in this case, a Cherokee story called, **"How Light Came to the People."**

The people were in darkness, but they knew, far away, there were people who had light and would not share it. As a community, they decided to send their biggest and strongest warrior to steal a bit of the light, but he returned without the light, burned and hurt. The community determined they would send the next strongest but he too returned empty-handed. One by one, the most powerful warriors flew to the people who had the light. Every attempt ended in failure, each suffering greatly in the process.

In despair, the people held a meeting to decide what to do. Although a tiny, weak-voiced creature kept offering to help, the community refused to listen. How could an old, powerless member succeed when those in the community who were most vital and strong could not? But, when there were no more warriors able to attempt the feat, Grandmother Spider finally convinced the community to give her a chance. She pointed out, "I am old and slow, not like the young, strong, vigorous warriors. If I do not succeed, little will be lost."

Grandmother Spider might be small and weak, but she was clever. After thinking carefully about how to steal the light, she went down to the riverbank and fashioned a small bowl of clay. She let it dry in the sun until she was sure she could safely put the ember of light into it. Then she spun a fine strong thread on which she traveled to reach her destination. Although the way was far, she took her time, resting when she grew too tired to continue.

The people with the light were looking for big, strong warriors, not someone old, weak, and small like Grandmother Spider. She entered their community unnoticed and stole an ember of light that she hid in her little clay bowl. Avoiding their scrutiny she spun another fine strong thread and traveled home, successfully bringing light to her people.

After I told the story, participants had lots to say about it. Women chortled, happy that an old woman had achieved such an important feat. Men felt Grandmother Spider had just been lucky and was not a heroine. They complained the warriors hadn't gotten enough credit for their effort and subsequent suffering, and that the "real" meaning of the story was no matter how hard men try, the women in their lives never appreciate them. The women countered that no matter how women succeed, men always find fault and denigrate their accomplishment. People described the story's meaning as if each person had heard a different account. They argued the correctness of their version with vigor and passion, using elements of the story to support their claims.

Given that a story has no one right interpretation, the arguments might have continued ad infinitum, each group defending their position, had not a frail woman named Bessie said, "What's important to me is not that she's a woman, but that she's old. It's hard to feel valued as an old person in a culture that fixates on youth."

This hit home with both men and women. The conversation changed abruptly. Stories poured forth about the difficulty of aging. Grace, sitting erect in her wheelchair, spoke first. "I'm old. I'll be 86 on my next birthday. I've been in a wheelchair for about five years since I broke my hip and it didn't heal right. Before that, I hiked in the mountains every week and kept pace with people twenty years younger than me. But when I could no longer hike, it was like I died. No one called to invite me anywhere or do anything. And yet, I'm the same person. I read the papers... pay attention to what's going on in the world. I don't think I've lost my sense of humor, although it's been tried. Lord knows it has certainly been tried." She sighed. "And it's not that I can't get about, I have help. I can go most places that are wheelchair accessible." She snorted. "Not that there are enough of them. Even places that say they are aren't always."

Franz, a refugee from World War II, looked sympathetic, yet he remained silent. His friend Simon kept poking him, not so surreptitiously, urging him to speak. Hesitating, Franz reluctantly spoke in a soft voice. "Well, I'm not in a wheelchair, but I have an artificial leg. Lost it when I jumped off a train escaping the Nazis. The older I get, the harder it is to get around, but I'm determined to keep going. They may have taken my leg, but they'll never get my spirit." He turned to Simon, "Okay, I told mine. You're the one with the real story. Tell it."

Simon, a large gaunt man with a creased face and haunting eyes shrugged. "I used to be a businessman, just an ordinary guy, no special talents or story, like Franz. We met in the hospital. He was in for surgery—I had had a stroke that affected my left side. I could hardly speak or move. I was angry and when my children came, I wasn't very nice to them. Told them to go home and leave me alone. I just wanted to die and ..."

Franz interrupted him. "But you found a way."

"Yeah, thanks to you" said Simon. Franz blushed and shook his head, but Simon paid no attention. "My kids were about to leave when Franz told them, 'Just because he says to go home doesn't mean he wants you to go. Stick around no matter what. He can blame me for your disobedience.' Then he looked at me, grinned and winked, infuriating me so bad I thought I'd have another heart attack. What gave this stupid clown who could talk and walk, the right to tell my kids to stay when I told them to go, the sooner the better?" He smiled shyly at Franz. "Then, as if he wasn't causing enough trouble, he told Mark, my son, to order Chinese food, whatever I liked, it was on him. I couldn't hold a fork, how was I supposed to eat? Use chopsticks? Had he lost his brains? That's how screwed up I was. Fortunately, Mark was smart enough to listen to Franz, not me, and while Emily stayed, he went to pick up the food. Franz talked to Emily as if I wasn't there, knowing all the while I could hear everything he said. I tell you, he got me so mad I started to move my left hand. Just one finger at first, but it was enough to stop me in my tracks. When Mark came back with my favorite dishes they smelled so good, I forgot how angry I was and ate. Thanks to Franz, my kids stayed long enough for me to recover. I wasn't old, only 52, but I felt like 102. It made me realize the importance of someone caring enough to kick you in the butt if that's what it takes. Franz and me, we've been buddies ever since. More than thirty years. Every week, the two of us go visit someone who's given up, or thinks they have. We tell them our stories and get them to tell us theirs. It always makes a difference." People nodded, talking to each other. The room vibrated with the energy and passion of people who had something to say and wanted to be heard.

The stories that followed related what it was like to grow old, to need care, to lose independence, to feel isolated and lonely. The adversarial relationship between the men and women disappeared. In its place grew a community of people sharing what they had experienced, suffered, gained, lost, and learned. One member of the group who had been following what each speaker said, sometimes writing in a small notebook, raised his hand. "I've been a lawyer for more than forty years. I'm used to people arguing and I'm used to pointing out the fallacy of positions, but I've never experienced anything like today. Here we were at each other's throats, ready to do battle, and then Grace told us her story about what it was like for her to grow old. Suddenly the adversarial atmosphere shifts and we're all on the same side. Amazing."

In another instance, after hearing "Grandmother Spider," a group of incarcerated young men painted an image of courage, writing words that came to mind. A young man, who wanted to be called Pistol, showed us his image, a huge blob of red lying on a rectangle of black. He wrote: blood, brave, no fear. "Those guys who tried to steal the light," he said, "they went about it all wrong. They had no plan. Now my guys, we go out to do a job, we take our time. We make a plan."

Frank whose physique suggested he spent a lot of time lifting weights interrupted. "Yeah? If you're so smart how come you're in here?" Everyone laughed. Pistol was not amused. He threw himself at Frank and started punching. Before any real damage was done, the group separated the two.

Pistol sneered, "Okay wiseass, let's see your picture."

When Frank said, "I can't draw good," the group responded with catcalls and jeers leaving Frank little choice but to defend his honor. Glaring at Pistol, he said, "Courage can be good or bad, depending. Like it's good when my little sister walks to school. Sometimes she hears gunshots. Once she saw a dead body but she still goes every day. She says she wants to be a doctor when she grows up so she can fix the people bleeding in the street."

"So when's it bad?" asked Sam.

"When you think you're brave 'cause you're not afraid to fight and you do stupid things that get you put in places like this," he said.

"You didn't show us your picture. Let's see it," demanded Marco.

Frank sighed, reluctantly showing his image, a tangle of red, black and yellow. The words he wrote were: smart, help, friends. When asked to talk about his image, he spoke slowly. "I was thinking about Grandmother Spider and that made me think about my grandmother. She's old and sick and it's hard for her to walk good, but she cooks and cleans for me and my sister. Since I been in here I been thinking about stuff...and that story... Sometimes, no matter how strong you think you are, there's people stronger, only in different ways. That old lady used her brains and she got what she wanted. Not like me." He sighed and looked down.

His words seemed to have struck home because the group grew quiet. The sparring and muttering stopped. Pistol asked, "So what's that mess of color have to do with courage?"

Frank spoke apologetically. "Well, as I said, I ain't no artist but I made the red for blood and the black for fighting. The yellow is for my little sister. It's all mixed up though I wish it wasn't. I wish she could go to school without worrying."

Pistol nodded. "Yeah, it's hard. My brother cries every time he has to go outside."

Will spoke quietly. "Maybe instead of finding light, we need Grandmother Spider to help us find safety."

"Fat chance," sneered Pistol. "We gotta do that for ourselves."

The two groups heard the same story and even

though their reactions were completely different, each group connected to the issues that mattered to them; their responses were equally emotional and specific to their experiences. Group members were able to find common ground among their differences, allowing them to end the session with newfound respect and, in some cases, admiration.

What happened within each group is not an uncommon occurrence. Stories have a way of finding their own level within each person and group, much like water filling the crevices and crags of a river. As a storyteller and workshop leader, I never know how a story will live inside a group, nor can I predict how the story will affect individual members. What I do know is that every story is as wide and deep as people need it to be.

Archeology of the Self

In order to recover any semblance of our true story, we need to become archeologists of the self, examining the fragments we have, exploring ways in which we can put them into a recognizable shape, even if we have no idea how to begin. One way through the maze of lies, half-truths and denials we may have been told, is to pay attention to contradictions in the stories. Few liars remember all the details of each lie every time. Logic has its uses. Memories and images inevitably reveal incongruence. Stories told by family members and friends let slip important details, even in explanations designed to cover the truth.

Discovering and uncovering our stories require that *we* decide what a story means. Only the listener or storyteller knows the personal meaning of that story.

Although its significance might not be immediately apparent, understanding why a particular passage or story seems so important may take time, perhaps more time than we have patience or faith. If no meaning comes readily to mind, this may be an indication we need to continue exploring. Group members facilitate the uncovering of meaning by asking helpful questions--those that cannot be answered with a "yes" or "no"--sharing in the mystery and offering their own unique points of view.

The group's facilitation helped Marsha, a successful pediatrician in her late fifties. She told the participants, in the initial session, that she took the storymaking workshop to explore the idea of giving her hospitalized patients an opportunity to fingerprint as they waited for or recovered from treatment. Marsha said she had loved to hear stories when she was a child and listened attentively to "**Ulu and the Breadfruit Tree,**" a story from Polynesia.

Ulu and his wife watched their son struggle for every breath. They knew the end was fast approaching. While his wife wet their son's lips with water, Ulu prayed for guidance from the great Mo'o. Upon his return, he calmly told his wife what needed to be done to save the life of their child. When Ulu was satisfied she would do as he asked, he went outside, lay down near the spring, and died. Despite her grief, his wife planted Ulu's head near the clear waters of the spring and the rest of his body near the door of their house. Then, heartsick at losing her husband, she lay near her son and waited for the sun to rise.

In the morning, she went to the place where she had buried her husband's heart and there stood a tall graceful tree, its leaves shining in the sun. She picked a ripe fruit and gave a tiny piece to her son. Immediately his pale face filled with color. With each piece his strength returned. Soon he was strong enough to walk to the place of his father's prayers and give thanks for the gift of life his father had given him. He grew up to become a warrior known far and wide for his wisdom and compassion.

After sculpting an image of "one in need of healing" in relationship to "one who is a healer," participants wrote the story of the meeting between the two sculpted images. Marsha paid careful attention to the stories people read, occasionally responding to their questions about medical conditions. When it was her turn to read the story she wrote, about a tiny ant too sick to carry a crumb, asking for help from a larger ant, she suddenly stopped mid-sentence, looking upset. "What's the matter?" asked Jean, the woman sitting next to Marsha.

"I don't know. Something in my story. Something I can't quite remember." I suggested she paint more images. Initially, Marsha refused, but her distress was so great she changed her mind, smearing huge gobs of black and red on page after page over the edge and on to the newspaper underneath. Suddenly she stopped. "I have to make a phone call. Please excuse me." Although the group carried on, we kept watching the door, waiting for her to return, wondering what had happened.

We were almost at the end of the session when she reappeared, red-eyed. Although we assured her she didn't have to tell us what had happened, we waited, hoping. "I don't know if I can talk about it," she said. "My father died when I was five, from an infection, was what my family told me. But I had vague memories of him coming to see me in the hospital when I was sick. And I was older than five—maybe six or even seven. I'm sure of this. Yet every time I asked my mother and aunt, they said I remembered wrong. Something about the story and my sculpture triggered something. I didn't know if it was a memory or what, but I could see my dad dressed in a hospital gown walking to my bed, sitting down next to me, kissing my cheek, telling me that everything was going to be okay, that I would get well." She looked at her sculpture, two figures--one much smaller than the other. The larger one had a hand on the smaller figure's head. "I called my aunt and begged her to tell me the truth. I was right. I did remember him coming to see me. I was six and a half. My dad donated a kidney to help save my life and had a heart attack shortly after the operation. When I asked my aunt why everyone lied, she told me they didn't want me to feel guilty. The story you told us is my story in a way." She gently bent the larger sculpture into a sitting position and placed the smaller one in its lap, mumbling words too softly for us to hear.

At the end of the workshop, Marsha asked where she could buy finger-paints and clay.

The Healing Power of a Story
A group of older adults participating in a workshop on writing autobiography heard the **"The Healing Water,"** a Native American story.

The village was suffering from a devastating plague. None of the peoples' prayers, rituals, or medicines was powerful enough to stop the illness. A young brave, Nekumonta, having stood by helplessly as his parents, brothers, sisters and children died, now watched his deathly ill wife struggle to breathe. He knew her only chance of survival lay in his finding the water that nourished the healing herbs the Great Manitou had planted.

The day he left the village to find the healing water was cold. Ice was everywhere yet Nekumonta walked without food or drink. Every time he encountered an animal he asked, "Can you tell me where to find the water nourished by the healing herbs the Great Manitou planted?" Each animal said no and continued on its way. Three days and three nights passed. Too tired to keep going any longer, Nekumonta lay down on the frozen earth, prepared to die.

While he slept, animals gathered around, warming him with their breath. They remembered how kind he was. How he never killed unless it was necessary, for food, clothing or shelter. How he thanked the animals for their sacrifice and nourishment. They begged the Great Manitou to help him.

As Nekumonta slept, he dreamed his wife was alive and well, singing a sweet song that sounded like a waterfall. When he awoke, he listened to the sound around him. He looked around but saw nothing. Still, he knew he was hearing the sound of water falling. Suddenly he realized the sound was coming from beneath him. Digging frantically with a strong branch, he soon made a deep hole in the snow and uncovered a hidden spring.

Nekumonta jumped into the hole and immediately felt refreshed and energized. He made a small jar out of clay and baked it in the fire until it was hard enough to hold the healing water. Moving as fast as he could, careful not to lose even one drop of the precious water, he made his way home.

He found his beloved wife close to death, barely breathing. Dipping his fingers into the healing water, he brushed her lips, and then bathed her hands and face until she fell peacefully asleep. When she awoke, she was fully recovered. Other members of Nekumonta's tribe followed in his footsteps, eventually ridding the village of the plague. For the rest of his life, Nekumonta was known as Chief of the Healing Water.

The director of the senior center warned me about Jerome. "Whatever you do, be careful. His sarcasm is biting. A number of people have complained about him, but we don't know what, if anything, to do about the situation. He's had severe heart trouble and we don't want to upset him."

It was easy to figure out who he was. As soon as the story ended, before anyone could speak, he said, in a withering tone of voice, his eyes flashing anger, "Right. That only happens in fairytales. I'm too old for happy-ever-after, not that it exists." Some people sighed. Others looked at me, waiting for my response.

I decided to ignore the outburst and gave directions for the first experience. "On the left side of your paper, paint an image of 'hopeless' and write any words or phrases that occur to you. Then, on the right side of the paper, paint an image of 'hopeful' and write whatever words come to mind. After you finish, in the middle of the paper, write a few words or paint an image of whatever helps you move from feeling hopeless to hopeful."

Much to my surprise, Jerome followed directions, all the time shaking his head and muttering to himself. When I asked the group if anyone wanted to share their response, he glared, as if defying me to call on him. Molly, a plump, cheerful woman smiled at Jerome as she raised her hand to show her images. The image on the left was a black square with the words: no way out. On the right was what looked like a red and yellow flower with a blue and green stem. Her words were: breathing deeply one finds new ways. Jerome's "humph" was audible but Molly paid no attention. "The image that helps me move from hopeless to hopeful is a bubbling stream, making its way down the mountain out to the sea."

"What if there's a drought and your stream dries up? Then what?" sneered Jerome.

"That happens, I know, but in my experience, the rains eventually come and the drought ends. I just have to remember nothing stays the same, not bad or good." She looked at him and asked, "Would you show me your images?" Her voice was kind, her manner gentle.

"Well, you know I'm no artist," he replied defensively.

"None of us are," responded Molly.

"Yeah, well your flower looks like a flower."

"Actually, it's not a flower; it's a brooch my mother had when I was a little girl. She lost it when we moved and even when she was dying, she kept asking me to look for it. After the funeral, when I was packing up her clothes, something stuck my finger. I put my hand into the pocket of an old apron and there it was. She probably took it off while cooking and forgot about it. When I feel bad, I think about finding her brooch. Anyway, what did you paint?"

"I don't know," he said. "I just 'smushed' colors on to each side."

"From here, the one on the left looks like a bird with a broken wing," said George.

Jerome laughed. "Boy, have you got a wild imagination," but he looked at his image again, shaking his head.

"Well, that's what it looks like to me, and on the other side, it looks like the bird's flying." Others nodded in agreement.

"You guys are kidding, right?" he said, looking increasingly uncomfortable.

Molly walked over to him and said, "Let me hold your paper. Maybe if you take a few steps away you'll see something too." Reluctantly, he handed her his paper and walked backwards, shaking his head.

All of a sudden he grew pale and looked frightened. He quickly sat down, avoiding the group's eyes. Molly asked, "Are you all right?" He nodded but it was clear something was wrong. Perhaps his heart condition had worsened…. We waited.

"I don't believe this," he muttered. "I just don't believe it." We continued to wait.

Molly asked, "Do you want me to read the words you wrote?"

"If you want," he said, practically whispering.

"Under the image of 'hopeless' he wrote: It's no use. It will never get better. It's broken. Under the image of 'hopeful' he wrote: maybe. In the middle he wrote: perhaps.

Jerome looked up at Molly and said, "Thank you." The group seemed stunned to hear him speak without his customary sarcasm or irony. Molly patted his shoulder and sat down next to him.

"You saw something, didn't you?" she asked gently.

"Yeah, I did. It reminded me of...something that happened a long time ago. Something I forgot until George said my picture looked like a bird with a broken wing."

"Want to talk about it?" asked Molly

"No," he said, shaking his head, staring at his picture. It was like he was struggling privately with an issue he didn't want to deal with, especially with twenty pairs of eyes watching. I thought about assigning the group a task to give him a bit of privacy but speaking felt like an intrusion. The group seemed content to give him all the space and time he needed, and since they knew each other better than I did, I took my cue from them. After a few minutes of silence Jerome looked at the group and then said to Molly. "Thanks. I appreciate your help."

The ensuing silence felt productive so I waited, wondering if anyone else wanted to share images. Soon a few hands went up. Shirley spoke first. "For 'hopeless,' what I kept thinking about was no possibility so I painted a black box. My words are: no way out. For 'hopeful,' I painted the same black box, but this time I streamed yellow through it and wrote: many ways out. What helps me move from hopeless to hopeful is ingenuity and resourcefulness. When Jerome said there were no happy endings I was ready to agree with him. As you all know, Martin's death was a long drawn out time of suffering. Where was his happy ending? Or mine? Or our children's? No healing water for us. But then I thought about all the years I had tried to get Martin to talk to me. How he was always too busy, at least that was his excuse. When he was dying, there was no busy, only pain and the fear it would get worse. Which it did. One night, he started to talk and kept talking for as long as his energy lasted. He told me how much he loved me and our sons. How sorry he was he'd never been able to say it. How tragic it was he hadn't made time for us, for what was most important in his life. We held each other and cried. He told me to call our children, to ask if they would come because he needed to apologize to them while he was still able to talk. The next day was the richest day of our lives. And when he died, a few hours later, with all of us around him, I felt at peace."

"Maybe it's not exactly a happy ending for someone like Jerome, but it felt like one to me and the boys and their wives and our grandchildren." Shirley shrugged, "Maybe healing water is just a metaphor for what makes the best of a bad situation. Martin wasn't cured but he helped all of us to heal. I took this workshop even though I didn't know what I wanted to write about. Now I know and it feels, I don't know, it feels like something I can do."

More people volunteered to share their images and words. They no longer looked at Jerome before speaking. He seemed to have lost his power to intimidate, at least for the moment. When we resumed working after lunch, Jerome did not appear. No one knew where he was. After a few minutes, we decided to begin despite our discomfort that he had not returned. People sculpted an image of one of the words or phrases they had written down in the morning. In twos, the sculptures were put into a relationship and each pair wrote a dialogue that emerged from their sculptures. Joan and Sydney were so excited they asked to share their dialogue with the group even before everyone finished. Just as they were about to start, Jerome walked in. He looked older, as if he had suddenly aged. Muttering, "I'm sorry I'm late, I had business to take care of," he sat down in the middle of the group instead of at the edge, as was his wont. I told him the assignment and gave him clay. Crumpling the clay into two pieces, he positioned them as if they were opposing armies. Oblivious to the group, he circled them around each other and then put the two pieces together in a kind of embrace. There were tears in his eyes but he said nothing to the group. Not then or later.

Although he chose not to talk about his experience, something important within him changed. His sarcasm lost its bite. When he did choose to participate, he was less confrontational. Occasionally he spoke in a kind and caring manner. The group stopped complaining about him. The next year when I returned to lead another workshop, I learned that Jerome had died. Molly told me that when she went to visit him in the hospital, he asked her to tell him "The Healing Water." When she said she wasn't sure she remembered it, he told her, "Whatever you tell me is the part that's most important." After hearing the story he closed his eyes and slept. That was the last time she saw him.

A well-attended memorial service was held at the

senior center to commemorate Jerome's life. The workshop group planned the ceremony and although Molly disclaimed any poetic ability, everyone requested she have the last word, to read what she had written about Jerome.

He wasn't tall, dark or handsome.
His voice was hard.
He wasn't kind or compassionate or caring.
His presence was intimidating.
One day he heard a story.
It wasn't about a man who lived in a box, hiding
    from the world.
It wasn't about a man who pushed everyone
    away from him.
And yet, the story spoke to him.
He wasn't tall, dark or handsome.
He was a man who found life difficult.
Yet his voice softened.
He learned to be kind.
He learned to tell stories.

We miss him.

3
EXPERIENCING THE STORYMAKING PROCESS

"A story is like the wind. It comes from a far
off place, and we feel it."

—*San Storyteller*

FINDING THE WORDS to tell our story, to speak our truth with confidence and wisdom, takes time. A few supplies--a set of finger-paints, including black and brown, (or any washable paint you can use with your fingers), a package of non-hardening clay—a few stories, and the willingness to start the journey of discovery as our own expert is all that is needed. It helps to collaborate with a small group of like-minded people, who know how to listen and respond using "I," rather than "you," who want to help us move in the direction we choose to go. Although those with whom we share our stories will not tell us what the image or story means--they usually don't know--they can respond to the painted, sculpted, or written image by sharing what comes up for them, what they notice, what our story evokes in them, questions that occur. If they are close friends, our story might remind them of an experience they know we have had. Suggestions, questions or ideas that may or may not make much sense initially also prove helpful because the group's responses are always in the service of furthering awareness. After exploring our ideas, questions, and feelings, we usually know more than we did before making the images.

The Power of Sharing

In a workshop that dealt with spirituality, I asked participants to sculpt an image of spirituality. When Roberta offered to share her sculpture, she prefaced it by saying, "I don't believe in God. I don't go to church. So, I have no idea what I sculpted or why I think this symbolizes my notion of spirituality but it does, or at least begins to symbolize it." She laughed and added, "Given, that is, that I have no idea what spirituality is."

The group looked at her sculpture and then at theirs. At first, no one said anything. Many had clear ideas about spirituality yet were reluctant to impose their meaning on her. Finally Gwen said, "I have an idea. Your sculpture is very tall and the base is narrow. It doesn't look very stable to me. If you're willing, I'd like you to put your sculpture in mine." Hers was a bowl-like structure with narrow sides. "Mine feels like something is missing but I don't know what it could be."

Roberta nodded; the two figured out how to place the tall sculpture in the bowl and then placed the new sculpture in the middle of the circle so everyone could see it. There was an unexplainable sense of satisfaction in the room. Roberta kept looking at the new creation and then spoke. "When Gwen offered me her bowl I thought, "What a stupid idea. How is putting my sculpture in hers going to change anything. But, I decided to keep my mouth shut and try it. Now I think, maybe for me, spirituality is about connection. I have to say it was an amazing experience. I feel like crying but I don't know why."

Group Contribution

Initially, the importance, satisfaction, comfort and necessity of sharing images and stories within a community of people were not apparent to me. But experiencing the responses of students, workshop participants, colleagues, and friends, in a variety of situations, helped me to understand that what we learn occurs in direct proportion to the questions, ideas, and feelings shared by group members. It is as if through group interaction we tap into a collective wisdom that is infinitely richer than that which we possess individually. The idea that the "wisdom of the psyche" (whatever people express without fear or coercion) is appropriate seems to prevail. Group members share at whatever level feels personally comfortable. No one is pushed nor prods others to confess or divulge information not readily forthcoming. Even when there are no answers to questions evoked by the stories or our responses to them, we end each session with a reflection, feeling respected, our privacy intact, and our personal awareness heightened. At the very least, we have a lot to think about.

Working in a group does not mean "groupthink." Every person writes from his or her own point of view, feelings and experience, yet when participants share their work, each contribution enriches everyone. This is illustrated by the responses of a group of European students who heard the Venezuelan story, **"The Light Keeper's Box."**

In the beginning, the people were living in a world neither light nor dark. The chief had heard there was a man who owned a box containing light although he didn't know exactly where the man lived. Thinking that having a source of light would make life so much better for his people, the chief gave his oldest daughter his blessings and sent her to find the Light Keeper. When the young woman came to a place of many paths, she didn't know which one to take. The path she chose led her to the house of Deer. She stayed with him, enjoying his company until she eventually remembered why she left home. Sadly, she returned to her father's house without finding the Light Keeper.

Her father then sent his younger daughter to find the Light Keeper and this time, when he gave her his blessings, he told her he would play his flute while she traveled, hoping this would help her choose the right path. When she came to the place of many paths she heard her father's flute and had a feeling about which road to choose. She walked on the path that felt strong and old. Her choice led her to the home of the Light Keeper and he invited her in.

She told him that her people lived in a world with neither light nor dark and that her father sent her to find the man who kept the light. She asked if he would part with some of his light. The Light Keeper was entranced with her, and she with him. The two spent many days together enjoying and sharing the light and dreams contained in the Light Keeper's box.

When the young woman decided she must return home, the Light Keeper loved her so much he gave her his box of light and dreams. Overjoyed to see his daughter with the Light Keeper's box, her father decided they must share their good fortune. He hung the box from a high pole. Soon people from the surrounding villages came to see *the light and experience the dreams. The chief and his daughters made food for them but no matter how many villagers they fed, more people continued to come.*

Exhausted, the chief decided that the box belonged to everyone and he tossed it into the sky. The light became Sun; the box became Moon.

Now, although there was light, Sun and Moon moved so quickly there was still not enough, so the chief asked his younger daughter to bring him a turtle. As Sun was going past, the chief flung the turtle into the sky. He told Sun he was giving him a friend in thanks for Sun's light and warmth. And because the turtle moved slowly, Sun stopped hurrying, and kept pace with his new friend. Moon, not wanting to disturb their friendship, kept well behind the two. Thus was light and warmth and dreams brought to the people of the world.

Group members made images of "in the beginning" and then wrote how it was, in the beginning. Some wrote stories; others discovered they were writing poems. One person wrote a dialogue between the two sisters. Joseph immediately offered to share what he wrote.

In the beginning, I was small and frightened.
Everything and everyone was bigger than me.
Even when I grew up, I was still small.
Until I saw the light and took a deep breath.
Now I'm as big as I need to be.
I can do what I want.
Mostly.

He laughed, as did the others, but then his look turned more serious. "It's interesting how I wrote that now I'm as big as I need to be since as you can see, I'm not very big."

Jenni corrected him. "You mean you aren't very tall, don't you?" He gave her a look indicating he wasn't sure. "Well," she said, "I took your words to mean that now you're grown up and you can do what you want. That's what 'being as big as you need to be' means to me."

Group members talked about what being "as big as one needs to be" meant to them until Andre said, "I'm not sure we're ever as big or as anything as we need to be, but the fact that Joseph wrote it means to me that he's made his life work for him, more than less, and that's a good feeling I think."

Johan was the next to read.

In the beginning, he had no dreams. Maybe he was afraid to dream. He told his friends he didn't believe there was such a thing as a dream but he knew there were dreams. He knew that for sure. He secretly envied people who had dreams. Even bad dreams. And what made him so mad was that he tried very hard to dream. Tried everything and anything he knew to do. But trying isn't what makes a dream happen. Dreams come and go, but not by asking or trying or pleading, which he was not about to do. At least that's what he told himself.

So there he was, walking around, feeling sorry for himself and his dreamless life. And then one day, he was walking in the meadow in the early spring, enjoying the warmth and the smells and the sight of the earth waking up. All the walking made him sleepy and he put down his pack, used it as a pillow and fell asleep. And for the first time, he dreamed. And it was so wonderful, that when he woke up he thanked the dream for coming. And he hoped it wouldn't be the first and the last. And it wasn't.

A deep sense of contentment pervaded the room until Birgit spoke. "In the beginning I didn't think any of this was worth doing. And now I ask, 'what's the point?' So we wrote some words and turned them into stories and poems and they sound nice and we feel good. So what? We're the same as we were before. Nothing's changed."

Rebecca, a woman of about thirty, with dark circles under her eyes, shook her head. "I'm not so sure nothing is different now than before we started. I was up most of the night and wouldn't have come if Gisela hadn't knocked on my door and told me she wouldn't leave without me."

"So tell me, what's different?" challenged Birgit. "Is anything better?"

Before Rebecca could respond, Anna said, "I can't speak for Rebecca, but before class, Peter and I had a big fight. When I was listening to the story and hearing about all the love between the girl and the Light Keeper I wanted to throw up. But after writing the words, 'in the beginning,' I felt something soften inside me. I started thinking about how it was with us, me and Peter, in the beginning, how much love there was between us, and I stopped being so angry. I kept thinking about what it means to love. And what came out was how in the beginning it's dark and empty. Then, a miracle happens and a bright light of love begins to shine on the earth. Somehow my anger just melted."

Birgit rolled her eyes, entirely unconvinced.

Jesper said, "In the beginning, all I could think about was how the older daughter failed to bring back the light and the younger daughter was able to do it but she had more help from her father. I kept thinking the older sister must feel bad and I felt bad for her. It reminded me how many times I could do stuff my older brother couldn't do. He has cerebral palsy and needs a lot of care. It's hard not to feel sorry for him but I also feel sorry for myself. It's not my fault he's sick and I'm well. But it's also not his fault either. So this is my story."

In the beginning, before every person is born, each one gets some good stuff and some bad stuff. That's just how it is. It's no one's fault if you have a crooked leg or a slow mind. You have to do the best you can with what you have. So if you can run fast, you need to run fast, because that's your gift. And if you can draw a picture or smile in a way that makes people feel good, that's what you have to do. And if you do it in the right way, you help people to make their lives a little better.

Birgit challenged him. "All that from a little story about a box of light?"

Jesper smiled, ignoring the sneer in her voice. "What did you write Birgit?"

She said, "I don't feel like reading it."

"Why not?" he asked.

"Because it's stupid, that's why."

"I'd like to hear your story," he said in a quiet voice. "Really, I would."

She hesitated, looking around the group, as if trying to make up her mind whether to read. She knew she could choose to pass. Shrugging, she spewed out her words. "Okay, if you want to hear it... You asked."

In the beginning everything was empty and gray. There was no life. No possibility of life. And yet, somehow, maybe it was a miracle or maybe there was a mystery but somehow, a tiny light began to glow. And no one really knows how or why but from that light, life began. And it was a light that shone in all the dark places, in holes, crevices, chasms... When the light became strong enough it began to create life. And for a while, life was good for everyone and everything. And then it wasn't. And no one knows why. But now it's good for some and not for others. And that's just the way it is.

She glared at everyone, daring them to say something.

Jesper asked, "What would it take for life to be good for you."

Birgit shot back, "How do you know it's not good for me?" He shrugged. She grinned and said sarcastically, "How about someone to dance with?"

"I'll dance with you," he said, ignoring her tone of voice as he put on a CD.

The two began to dance. Slowly, others joined them until the whole group was dancing. When the music stopped, while people were talking and sitting back down, Birgit picked up her story and started to write.

"Could we know what you're writing?" asked

Rebecca.

Birgit shook her head, her tone of voice subdued. "Not yet. I think it's going to take me a while to finish."

"When you're finished, will you share it?" persisted Rebecca.

Birgit looked at the group. The lines around her face had softened a little. She shrugged and said, "If you want."

Rebecca smiled. "Yes, we do," the others nodding in agreement.

Storymaking is not a panacea. It cannot make everything better instantly or in the long run. It can provide a possibility for uncovering feelings, exploring knowing, and perhaps making new choices. In the above example, Birgit had always felt like an outsider. She held herself aloof and used sarcasm or irony to prevent people from knowing what she felt or thought. Although she was quick to criticize, she judged herself more harshly than anyone else. The others in the group were wary of her yet most felt her unpleasantness was aimed at herself rather than them. She had difficulty believing the others cared about her and pushed away their attempts at friendship. Each morning of the workshop Rebecca asked if Birgit had finished her story and for almost a week she said she was still working on it.

The last story the group worked with was **"Ant and Elephant,"** from India. I chose it because I wanted to encourage Birgit to feel a more integral part of the group. Although there had been a slight shift in her behavior--she was a bit less sarcastic and didn't always choose to sit by herself--I felt she was afraid to trust the group's caring. I hoped Birgit could identify with Ant, the tiniest member of the community, considered to be too small to do anything to help the community. Although the group welcomed Birgit, she excluded herself—not exactly a parallel to Ant in the story, but Ant and Birgit both liked to dance. When choosing a story, it's impossible to know how people will hear it, yet I told it, imagining Birgit and Ant dancing together.

The animal community decided they needed a ruler and voted to make Elephant King of the Animals because he was the biggest and strongest, yet very gentle. But after a short time, he changed drastically, and not for the better. When he saw animal mothers carrying food for their children, Elephant grabbed and ate it without listening to their cries. He stopped caring where he walked and trampled on nests without apologizing or repairing the damage. He spewed water, ignoring cries for help from creatures trying to escape the rising waters.

The animals were upset and terrified. They called a meeting when Elephant was sleeping, but no one knew what to do or how to stop Elephant. When Ant said she had a plan that would not only make Elephant stop behaving badly, but would also make him apologize for the misery he caused, the animals laughed in spite of their misery. What could such a tiny creature possibly do to influence an enormous animal like Elephant? But Ant persisted, continuing to ask permission to take action until the community gave in, realizing they had no other ideas to remedy the situation.

Ant observed Elephant's behavior for a few days, noticing that after lunch he always took a long nap. One afternoon, when Elephant was snoring, she climbed up

into his brain and started to dance. Elephant woke up with
a terrible headache and roared in pain. Ant told him her
dancing might be causing his headache but that she would
only stop if he promised to behave.

Elephant roared his displeasure. "I am King! I do
what I want, when I want, as I want." Ant said nothing.
She just kept dancing. When King Elephant's headache
grew unbearable he agreed to all of Ant's demands. Just to
make sure Elephant didn't change his mind once she
stopped dancing, Ant reminded him, "I have lots of
relatives and we all love to dance."

Participants painted an image of "powerless" on the
left side of their paper and wrote words evoked by the story.
On the right side of the paper they painted an image of
"powerful" and wrote words that came to mind. In the
middle of the paper they wrote a word or phrase that might
help them move from powerless to powerful. Without
sharing their images or discussing the story, group members
wrote a story about someone or something that moved from
feeling or being powerless to feeling or being powerful.

Much to everyone's surprise, Birgit raised her hand.
"I'd like to start." She showed her image. On the left side
was a small dot, "Ant," she said. Her words were: tiny,
helpless, hopeless, stranger, stuck. On the right side was a
small dot. "Ant," she said. Her words were: huge,
resourceful, hopeful, energized, capable. What helped her
move from powerless to powerful? "Myself," she said, a wry
smile on her face.

"Did you write a story?" asked Rebecca. Birgit nodded. This time she read without having to be coaxed.

Once upon a time there was a creature that was very small. From birth she had been small, even smaller than her quite small parents and her rather small brothers and sisters. Because she was so small she lost every fight she ever got into and scarcely managed to escape being squished more than once. She thought life was absolutely awful, but didn't think about wanting to die because she didn't know about death. And, when her family told her it was time to leave, to make her way in the world, she felt hopeless. She was so tiny. She had no friends. How would she survive?

Just as she was walking along a path, feeling sorry for herself, she heard a sound--a ferociously, terrifying thundering sound. So frightening, she used all her energy to scurry out of the way, just in time to avoid being trampled on by a herd of deer. As she waited for her heart to stop beating wildly, she had a new thought. "I heard that sound and I acted. I saved my life." And with that, she began walking down that very same path, only this time she held her head high and whistled.

After reading, Birgit looked somewhat abashed. People clapped, some whistled. Jesper leaped over to her, picked her up and danced with her to the whistling and clapping of the group which grew increasingly enthusiastic as the two cavorted around the room, thoroughly enjoying themselves. When the whistling and clapping and dancing ended, Birgit looked like she might cry. She started walking towards the door when the tallest, heaviest man in the group got up. Speaking in his deepest voice, he moved toward her, holding his hands to make a trunk, swaying from side to side as if he were Elephant. "Oh Ant, you have helped me so much. You can't know how hard it is to be so much bigger than everyone else. I was really very lonely. Now, everything is so much better. I'm happier and all the animals are happier. And all this happiness is just because you cared. We owe you so much. How can we thank you? How can we help you?"

Birgit looked flustered, frozen in place. Rebecca moved toward her, on all fours, making what she later said were tiger sounds. Using a "roaring" voice, she said, "Thanks to you, Ant, I don't have to worry about feeding my babies."

Johann, a tall skinny man, squeaked, "We giraffes are grateful to you as well. Now we can eat the leaves of trees without being afraid that Elephant will steal our food."

Birgit laughed and said in the highest pitched voice she could muster, "Thank you."

Jesper, ever the clown, said, "Let's party. We have a lot to celebrate." And they did.

Finding Stories

Although almost every story has the potential to lead us into inner knowing, *finding* a story that resonates within us can occasionally prove elusive, frustrating, difficult, and time consuming. My experience suggests that the more we are blocked emotionally, the harder it is to stumble on one with which we want to work. It helps to read a variety of stories from cultures around the world, many books of stories (retold by a variety of tellers), and to read without judging or censoring emotional response. "Happily ever after" doesn't necessarily mean we can't relate to the story because our lives don't seem to be very happy. In fairy tales, happy endings are meant to give us a rest before new problems inevitably arise. What matters when reading stories are the issues, the ways characters deal with their problems, the kinds of help and helpers that emerge, and the way our gut responds.

At a difficult period in my life I stopped reading folk and fairy tales because I was upset by the absence of a fairy godmother in my life. I couldn't relate to princesses, wishes that come true, or pumpkins that turned into coaches. I rode in cars, trains and busses, not donkeys and horses. Turning off the stories in my head, I focused my attention on schoolwork and dealing with family problems. I can't say this made me happier but at least I wasn't wasting time and energy hoping for miracles. When I later began to teach with a children's literature specialist and had to read folk and fairy tales for the course, I read them like a thirsty person gulping water.

Making up stories has always been a part of my life. Now, I depend on reading or telling them, especially when I'm upset or facing serious or life-threatening issues. Yet occasionally, my connection to stories is challenged. There was a time when I was dealing with a lot of personal issues, making no progress, feeling grumpy and out of sorts. Not the best attitude when entering a strange classroom as a storyteller where the children were out of control. The teacher had run out of the room as soon as she saw me even though she was supposed to stay and observe, if not participate. What I thought is unprintable. What I did was sit down on the floor, my head in my hands, wishing I were anywhere but where I was. First graders are curious. Soon one sat next to me, followed by another. Before long, all twenty-two children were sitting in a circle, looking at me, quietly waiting. I knew this was the moment to take control, but my brain had stopped working; the plug to my mind had suddenly been pulled.

I was saved by the response of a little girl. "Please, Miss, we're waiting for the story."

"What kind of story would you like to hear?"

Although I asked her, a cacophony of voices quickly shouted out their answers. Too many responses are as bad as none when you're feeling miserable. I raised my hands to quiet them, but it was as if I had turned on a tap that had no turn off valve. I sighed. I looked at my watch. My brain was on hold or stop or vacation. Then a little boy sitting next to me said, "You choose. You're the storyteller." Right. A storyteller who can't remember any of the hundreds of stories she's read and heard and told. Wonderful!

When in doubt, "make something," is advice that's stood me in good stead. "Okay," I said, loud enough to stop the flow, "everyone take a piece of clay." I passed out small mounds and immediately the children began playing with it. "Sculpt a character who wants something."

The children, used to having to know the right answer bombarded me with questions: "What kind of character? Can it be an animal? Does it have to be a person? Can I make it up? Does it have to look like a person? Can I sculpt a bunny? What if I can't sculpt?"

I know what it feels like to be afraid to be wrong,

especially in school, where it seems as if there is always only one right answer to any question and all too often, not in my repertoire. "Don't worry," I told them. "It can be anything you want. Just sculpt until I say stop" Thirty seconds later I yelled, "Stop." Without being aware of it, I had also sculpted an image and when I told the children to stop, I stopped. They wanted to know what I sculpted. When I said I didn't know, they looked shocked.

"But you're the teacher," one boy managed to say.

"That doesn't mean I know everything," I said. "Tell me about your sculpture."

He looked at the two roundish balls that were connected at the middle and said, "These are apples that grew together, and if you want to eat one, you have to eat the other, otherwise it will be lonely."

This released a floodgate of stories about their sculptures; each so wonderful I wished I had videotaped the session. I was about to admit I couldn't think of a story when I took another look at my sculpture and somehow this triggered the story of **"Hummingbird and Panther,"** a story from Brazil. I told it with amazing ease but even more startling was that stories soon flooded my brain. It seems that by allowing myself to enter into one story, I released others from my self-imposed incarceration.

Hummingbird was extremely upset. She was tired of being drab, utterly colorless, unlike the beautiful flowers, the brilliant sky, and the glorious shades of grasses and leaves that surrounded her. Despite advice from many creatures, nothing she tried changed the color of her feathers.

One morning, while feeling glum and miserable, she heard a loud groaning, a hideous noise. Much to her horror, it was Panther, an animal who terrified her. His sharp teeth were almost as big she was. As he moved closer to her, his moans grew so unbearable Hummingbird blurted out, "Why are you making so much noise?"

Panther told her. "Last night, I stepped on Mouse Mother's children as I was running through the forest chasing after my dinner. When I was asleep she put mud on my closed eyes. Now the mud has hardened and I cannot open my eyes. I cannot see. I am blind. How will I ever find food to eat?" He began to wail louder than ever.

"You are not the only one with a problem," snapped Hummingbird, "I am so drab and colorless no one even notices me."

"That's not a problem. I know how to help you become more colorful."

"You do?" asked Hummingbird, not at all sure she believed him.

Panther said, "I'll make a bargain with you. If you peck the mud from my eyes so I can see, I will help you become as colorful as you like."

Although Hummingbird wanted this more than anything in the world, getting close enough to Panther to peck the mud from his eyes was almost too frightening to think about.

Yet, despite her fear, she gathered her courage and flew to Panther, making him promise to keep his mouth closed. She pecked out the mud from his eyes as carefully as possible, hoping he wouldn't open his mouth and eat her when she was finished. When Panther could open his eyes, he leapt into the air. "I can see. I can see."

Hummingbird grumbled, "What about your promise? What about our bargain?"

Panther took a long look at Hummingbird. Shaking his head, he said, "You really are drab. No wonder no one notices you." Hummingbird was about to tell him that he didn't have to try to make her feel bad, she already felt awful, when he said, "Follow me."

He led her to a clearing in the forest near a bubbling stream and told her to gather as many different colored flowers and grasses as she could find. He made a roaring fire and put a pot of water over it.

Hummingbird filled the pot with flowers and grasses and seeds and leaves. Following his instructions, she stirred and stirred and stirred. When the mixture was cool, Panther told her to jump into the pot and wet herself all over. Then he told her to fly out and shake herself off. Panther looked at Hummingbird and said, "Better do it once more."

After the third time of jumping into the pot and shaking herself dry, Panther said, "That's better. Fly to the river and look at yourself."

Filled with dread that Panther's plan had not worked, Hummingbird flew to the water, afraid of what she would see. "Open your eyes and look!" commanded Panther.

Hummingbird took a deep breath and did as she was told. "Oh," she gasped, hardly believing her eyes, amazed to see such a marvelously colored bird reflected in the water. "I'm beautiful," she said, stunned.

"Yes, you are, and I'm hungry," said Panther and he walked into the forest.

After I told the story, the children divided into pairs and sculpted images of Hummingbird and Panther who meet some time after the story ends. When they shared their dialogues, one child said, "I never could have imagined so many stories coming from the one you told us. I'm gonna ask my mom to buy me clay. It's good stuff."

Whenever I tell "Hummingbird and Panther," I think about what it takes to face and conquer fear. That afternoon, the story was still on my mind when I met with a group of returning adult students who were all at critical points in their lives, facing difficult choices. Laurie, a psychologist who closed her practice in order to find new work, looked ready to pounce. As the unacknowledged leader of the group, she often let me know she was looking for my so-called hidden agenda and took every opportunity to challenge me. This time was no different. When I asked them to paint images of "fear" and "courage" she glared at me, demanding to know, "What do you do when fear runs your life?"

"Listen to Hummingbird," I answered.

After telling the story, and before Laurie could respond with a retort or begin a discussion, I asked the group to paint an image of "fear" on the left side of the paper, an image of "liberation" on the right side, to title their work and then to write the story of the title.

Although everyone else started writing immediately, Laurie didn't even pretend to put pen to paper. Studiously avoiding my eyes, she sat, annoyed, tapping her fingers on the desk. "Write what comes to mind," I suggested, but she made no move to begin. No suggestions or words of encouragement helped. Frustrated, because a few of the participants had already finished their stories, I let my irritation show. "What's so great about your fear?" I asked. "How come you let it take up so much space? Is it so beautiful and so wonderful? Is it so much better than your liberator?"

"I have no liberator," she shot back. "And besides, what's it to you? You have a job. You know where your next paycheck is coming from. What gives you the right to say anything to me about fear?" She got up to leave but I stopped her.

"You're not the only one who has fears. I have plenty, but this isn't about me. Maybe what frightens you is that you're afraid there is no liberation, that you have no liberator." She looked taken aback. Controlling the anger I shouldn't have showed, I softened my tone and spoke quietly. "There is, I promise you. It's just that sometimes its voice is so low it's hard to hear even a peep. Maybe what you need is a professional peep liberationist." We both laughed at the absurdity of such a job title. Slowly, she walked back to her seat, sat down, and picked up her pen. She wrote without hesitation.

When it was time to share images and writing, everyone focused on Laurie, wanting to know what she had written. Shrugging, she showed her image of fear—a burly jagged black and red monster with huge sharp claws and orange fangs. Her image of liberation was a tiny yellow dot, so small it looked like she'd made it with the point of a toothpick. Her title was "David and Goliath." This is what she wrote:

In the beginning was Fear. In the middle was Fear. In the end, Fear got so fat and large it crowded everyone and everything into such a tiny space it was almost impossible to move or breathe or speak. The biggest creatures were squashed too tightly to use the little strength they had. The middle-sized creatures were scrunched into the crevices of those that were bigger. And Fear kept growing, taking more room, pushing and pressing everything and everyone into an even tinier space.

Some did their best to fight back. Others tried to bribe Fear although they didn't have much to offer. Fear laughed, knowing there was absolutely nothing anyone could do. It looked as if Fear was going to use up all the air as well.

SHE had always looked big and felt small. Inside her there was a lot of empty space so when Fear started pushing and shoving SHE shrank inside herself but it was only the empty space that got smaller. Anger and determination and rage grew inside her. SHE had always been teased for thinking differently but now, instead of giving up as everyone around her was doing, SHE grew more observant. Although SHE couldn't see very well and couldn't hear anything but moans and cries, SHE noticed that just below Fear's bloated belly was a space not covered by shirt and pants. SHE also noticed his untied shoelaces.

Pushing and shoving and gasping and reaching, SHE wormed her way toward him, tying his shoelaces tightly together. SHE saw a crumpled hat and in it was a hatpin. Although it wasn't long enough to pierce much of Fear's belly, it was all SHE had. Closing her eyes, SHE plunged the hatpin into Fear's belly, hoping it would make him mad enough to try to run away. SHE hoped that when he tripped on his shoelaces, others would rush to help her.

Instead, Fear made a strange sound and shriveled into nothingness. Suddenly there was air and space. People laughed and danced and hugged. No one thought to ask what happened but SHE knew. SHE never forgot.

Laurie smiled wryly. "Okay," she asked with a sheepishly, "how did you know I had a story to write? The semester is almost over, you can tell us. What's your agenda? What's your secret? What are you looking for?"

"I keep telling you, there is no hidden agenda. What I'm looking for is what I ask you to do. And there's no secret or trick for that matter. I have no magic powers to turn on a metaphorical spigot for stories to pour out. Everyone has stories inside them waiting to be expressed. If there is a trick, it's figuring out how to help people find a way into their stories. I think humans need stories because they help us make sense of our experience. They make it easier to connect to each other."

"But why do we have to work so fast? It makes me uncomfortable," said John. "I like to think about what I'm doing and make sure what I say is carefully thought through."

"Speed makes it difficult to agonize about what to do. It minimizes the power of the inner censor. Having to respond so quickly forces you to focus on the task at hand, but if you didn't have stories inside you, nothing I did would liberate them."

"But what if I want to submit my work for

publication?" he asked.

"Fine tuning and honing your work comes after you've written the sense of what you want to say. In storymaking, we focus on accessing and exploring first thoughts. Too often, we're taught to ignore or react negatively to initial ideas. Sometimes we dismiss them so quickly we don't even recognize we've done this. Yet first thoughts or feelings are a rich source of knowing and we do well to honor them."

"So why do you always tell us a story before we make images?" asked Jim.

"The story acts as a container for our feelings, letting us know on a deep level that everything is going to be okay. Just as Hummingbird finds the courage to peck the mud out of Panther's eyes so he can see, she has to decide to trust that Panther will keep his promise and help her transform from a drab creature to one that is beautifully colored. The story provides a kind of spiritual safety net as well as a source of psychic nourishment."

"Couldn't we write stories without hearing one?" asked Beverly.

"Sure, but hearing a story nourishes the psyche and facilitates spontaneous writing, especially when people are afraid they have no stories or feel they're at the mercy of their inner censor."

Jim turned to Laurie and asked, "What do you think about this story writing business?"

She rubbed her face, rereading her story. "I'm thinking there's a lot I don't know, about myself, let alone writing stories. I was positive there was no story inside me and I didn't want to write drivel. But once I started, I couldn't get the words down fast enough. Makes me wonder how many other stories are inside me and what they're about." She grinned, "I'm sure glad the semester isn't over just yet."

Revealing the Concealed

Storymaking can make known aspects of people that are so hidden even those who interact with them are astonished. I once led a workshop at a high school with a group of twelfth graders who met on a Friday afternoon, the last period in a week, where for five days they'd had a substitute teacher. As the students walked in, I asked them to arrange the desks and chairs in a circle. A few teachers sat in the back, ready to observe. After telling "Ant and Elephant," (p.90) I asked them to make a telling image. One young man, almost too big for his chair, quickly painted a small black dot in the middle of the paper where from all directions, arrows of different colors zoomed at the black dot. It looked like a tiny being under siege. His words were: small, powerless, helpless, and under attack. Later, when asked to sculpt a creature that was or could be in the story and to decide what it wanted, he sculpted a giraffe he named Elvira. She wanted a voice. All through the session, the young man was helpful, often encouraging fellow students to participate, even assisting an agitated, nervous male to share his images. I noticed the observing teachers looking at me strangely and wondered if my blouse button had popped open. At the end of the session I thanked him for his help and told him that since I was a stranger, teaching in the last period of the week, the session could have been a disaster. His participation definitely helped make the class the success that it was. He smiled shyly, thanked me for thanking him, and left.

As soon as he closed the door the teachers rushed up to me and asked, "Do you know who that person is?"

How would I know? It was my first time in the school. I shook my head.

"He's the school bully. Everyone's afraid of him."

I was flabbergasted. I couldn't believe it. He had been so kind and caring. "He might be the school bully but inside there's a shy, hurting human being who cares about people and feels he has no voice. Isn't there anyone who can build on what happened during the class?"

The drama teacher nodded. "I'll try. Maybe I can help him write a play about how Elvira found her voice."

Storymaking is one way to find our voices. Through hearing and telling stories we replenish our inner resources so we are more likely to experience being reconnected to our essential selves. How do we know what our essential self is, much less whether we're connected? I have asked this of many workshop participants. These are some of the answers they gave me: "It feels different." "It feels right." "It feels powerful." "It feels like I'm opening up a part of myself I didn't know was there." "It feels like I'm writing something I've always known but didn't know how to express it." "It makes me feel huge." "There was a lump in my throat that wouldn't go up or down and now it's gone."

Dancing With Wonder: Self-Discovery Through Stories contains myths and tales from around the world. Perhaps one or more will attract your attention. If you have trouble finding a story, just keep reading a variety of collections of traditional stories from as many cultures as you can. Eventually the stories you have read will rise in chorus and the one you need to explore will find you. It's also possible, in a storymaking session, to use a dream, an incident from daily life or a vacation, a memory, or a particularly powerful image from a film or book—anything that makes a lasting impression--something I call a "very" experience. Ultimately, what matters is that we pay attention to what we notice, how we feel, and the energy with which we act and react when reflecting on what we have chosen to explore.

4
STORY JOURNEYS

I will tell you something about stories,
(he said)
They aren't just entertainment.
Don't be fooled.
They are all we have, you see,
all we have to fight off
illness and death.

You don't have anything
if you don't have the stories
Ceremony, by Leslie Marmon Silko

STORIES LIVE INSIDE us, ready to be expressed and explored. *Dancing With Wonder: Self-Discovery Through Stories* is a book designed to help readers enter into and connect to a story through active participation. All we need to do is listen, make images, notice what captures our attention, and tell or write what comes to mind.

Traditional stories, retold by generations, across cultures and time are a wellspring of wisdom, enabling us to ask and answer age-old questions from our own continually changing perspective. Although the myths and tales have been retold, there is no authorial voice to shape the impact or bias of the reader, especially if we can read more than one version of the same tale and discover what is central to the story and what has been added. For example, in "Little Red Ridinghood" there is always a young girl going into the forest to see her grandmother and a wolf she meets on her way. In some versions the wolf eats her, yet in others, hunters save her or she outwits the wolf. Every time a story is retold, the teller adds something personal but what matters is that core contents are honored and respected. Therefore, the more versions we read of a story, the clearer we can be as to what the reteller has added. What if we can only find one version? We do the best we can.

Traditional tales, personal narratives, and created stories are like beacons, shining light on what lives inside us. When we give voice to our stories we begin a powerful and unpredictable process that takes us on a journey we can neither foretell nor control, yet one that enables us to reap unexpected and insightful benefits. In traditional stories, like life, there are gaps in the narrative. Often without explanation or description, the action shifts and characters surprise us. Storymaking helps to fill in the gaps and in doing so, we put something of ourselves into every story we tell or write. Although why and how storymaking can be so potent is still a mystery to me, I have repeatedly seen significant changes in mood or self-awareness in people and groups as they create stories they didn't know they knew. Perhaps making a story enables us to use the energy of the feeling of what is happening to us in much the same way we make bread out of flour, water, yeast, sugar, and salt. The ingredients in no way resemble the final product, yet out of them we create a nourishing and satisfying story.

The story journeys described in *Dancing With Wonder: Self-Discovery Through Stories* have been chosen to give readers a sense of what can be discovered when we allow ourselves to enter into the world of story without bias, pre-planning or judgment. I use the term story journey to express the idea that a story is a journey into the self, as well as a journey of the group. We can take many story journeys into the same story--it isn't necessarily a one-time sojourn. We begin by noticing what holds our attention, the sticking places to which we constantly return, and the questions that come to mind. When we are troubled, but don't know what is causing our discomfort or where to look for possible causes, reading and telling stories can provide clues and information not easily obtained from other sources as we identify with particular characters or situations and not with others. Spontaneous imagemaking and storymaking are significant precisely because we don't know what we're looking for and, therefore, we can't control the search. In a sense, when we are willing to give up searching for answers and encourage our unconscious knowing to become conscious, the spontaneous expression often reveals what we want to know.

Hidden in Plain Sight
When working with a group of teachers who made images of themselves before and after the workshop, one teacher noticed that her first image was of a brown figure with an extremely swollen knee. Her words were: afraid, anxious, uncertain, tired, fearful. Her second image showed the same figure with a normal-sized knee. Her words were: happy, relaxed, amused, curious, interested. When asked what happened to the swollen knee and fear, she looked surprised. "I don't know, but it's gone right now." After studying her image, she decided the swollen knee was triggered by her anxiety about upcoming knee surgery, but she wasn't sure why the second image, made at the end of the session, but before the surgery, should show a normal

knee. After further reflection on the story with which we had worked, (Ant and Elephant, p. 90) she said, "I guess if Ant could vanquish the tyranny of Elephant, I can recover from knee surgery." She laughed. "It's good to know my unconscious is so positive.

Stories, like music, have an effect on our mood. Just listening to a tale of someone overcoming great odds can cheer us up even though folk and fairy tales are sometimes thought to be predictable and sexist. If they are looked at strictly on the surface, these assertions might appear to be true. But if one considers patterns, the issues become more complex. No matter how beautiful or handsome you are, if you push too far too fast, or if you ignore the needs of others, you seldom get what you are after. Even if the character is an intelligent, strong female, when she doesn't take appropriate advantage of an opportunity, she usually doesn't succeed. Macho males, such as those who pay no attention to anyone and forge ahead, unwilling to be "sidetracked," generally fail to win what they want. Sometimes characters have a second or even a third chance but only when the hero or heroine recognizes the truth of a situation, and accepts and gives the requisite help, does he or she get what is wanted. If we read a lot of traditional tales, patterns become more obvious, and we realize that in almost all cases, the heroes and heroines who succeed are those who integrate both the "feminine" side—caring, intuitive, nurturing, with the "masculine" side—knowing, taking charge and doing.

Stepparents, stepmothers in particular, get a bad rap, yet even though the evil parent or stepparent makes life at home so intolerable the young person has to leave, if home were so pleasant and so cozy that young people had all their needs met, how would they get on with their lives? How would they find the wherewithal to leave the safety and comfort of home to make their way into the world? Finding the courage to leave an unhappy situation is a source of strength and comfort when the inevitable disappointments and setbacks occur.

Although some contemporary critics deride the "happily ever after" endings as being too pat, these endings are one way of saying, "For the moment, all is well. Rest. Tomorrow the sun will come up and there will be more challenges." If there were no "happy endings," how could we take a full breath or sleep peacefully? How would we nourish ourselves to prepare for the next challenge that will inevitably appear? How could our psyches develop the wherewithal to keep us going if they had no chance to rest and replenish?

Read but Not Written
How we read or hear a story depends on who we are and what is happening to us at the moment. **"The Fern Girl,"** a Yakut tale from central Asia, provided a participant with an opportunity to explore the difference between what she read and what she thought she read:

> *Early one morning, as usual, an old woman went to the field to take care of her cows. While there, she saw a horsetail fern with five shoots and pulled it out without damaging the roots. She carefully brought it home, put the fern on her bed for safekeeping, and went back to the field to finish taking care of her animals.*

At sundown, the woman returned home and decided to lie down for a little nap before making dinner. There, just where the fern had been, sitting on her bed, was a lovely young girl.

The old woman was almost too overjoyed to speak but she managed to say to the girl, "Stay with me, please. Be a daughter to me." The girl agreed and the two lived together happily.

One day a hunter came by and shot many arrows without hitting anything. One of his arrows fell into the smoke hole of the old woman's yurta. He demanded that she return his arrow but the old woman did not respond. Angry, the hunter stormed into the yurta, saw the young girl, and was so taken with her beauty he left without saying a word.

Soon after, his parents visited the old woman and asked that the young girl be given to their son in marriage. The girl was willing so the old woman readily consented. For the bride price, she asked that the parents give her as many cows and horses as her field could hold. They agreed and all proceeded as was promised and approved.

The hunter and young girl, dressed in new clothes, were on their way to his home when the he saw a fox. "I will ride after the fox. His coat will make a fine hat. Follow this road and when you reach the place where it branches off, take the road where you see the sable skin."

The girl did as she was told but when her husband-to-be had gone, she forgot his instructions and took the wrong road. After only a few minutes a hideous hag blocked her path and forced the girl to change places with her. The hag made her way back to the right road and when the hunter caught up with his bride-to-be he did not guess that something was amiss.

His kin welcomed them and said, "The bride has only to open her mouth and beautiful beads will drop out." Yet when the bride opened her mouth, frogs greeted those who had come to meet the couple. They were unpleasantly surprised but said nothing and prepared for the wedding. No one guessed the bride was an imposter.

The old woman sadly resumed her old life, hoping her daughter was now happily married. Imagine her surprise when she returned home one evening and saw her daughter slumped on the bed. Sobbing, she fell into her mother's arms and told her what had happened. The old woman comforted her. "Do not cry. I am sure he will come to his senses and return to find you."

And so it came to pass that the horse on which the young girl had ridden whispered the truth of what had happened to the hunter's father. As the father told his son what he had learned, the hag overheard and her face turned red with fear and rage. The hunter grew so angry he grabbed the hag and tied her to the wildest horse he possessed. Then he quickly made his way to the yurta of the old woman.

When he arrived, the young girl cried out, "Why are you here? You left me to ride by myself. Look what happened. Go away. I never want to see you again."

The old woman took her daughter in her arms and dried her tears. "Hush my daughter. Think on what I say. You were lost but you found your way home. Now your beloved has come for you. Why is it you do not rejoice? Can you not love each other as you did before?"

The young girl looked at the hunter and saw the sorrow in his eyes. "You are right, mother." Overjoyed, the hunter took her into his arms and they held each other, healing all that had been torn and broken.

This time, the hunter made sure he rode all the way home with his bride where they were joyfully welcomed by his family and friends.

After the class painted an image of a telling moment in the story, Jessica painted a green stream trying to push its way toward a garden of brightly colored flowers, blocked by blobs of black, brown, and purple. She wrote the following story in response to her image and the story of "The Fern Girl."

There was once a young girl who grew up in the care of a kindly old woman. The girl loved her and would have been content to stay with her for a very long time, but when the girl reached her 18th birthday, the old woman told her it was time for her to be married. The girl protested. "I do not want to leave you. I am happy here, tending the garden, caring for the goats."

"I have found a good and caring man for you to marry. He will come next Sunday for the two of you to meet."

"But I do not want to marry. Why can I not stay here with you?"

"It is time that you are married. It is right for you to be his wife. It will happen as he wishes."

And so, hiding her tears and misery, the young girl married the man of the old woman's choice and that was the way it was.

Jessica read her story to the group. "I identify with the girl who is pushed out of her house to marry a strange man and live with people she doesn't know. My family forced me out of my house, away from the people I love, just because I got a scholarship to go to this university. My parents tell me it's for my own good and probably that's exactly what the old woman told the girl in the story."

When asked to show where in the text the old woman forced the girl to marry against her will, Jessica reread the story several times but couldn't find even a suggestion that the old woman had either pressured the girl to marry or to leave her home. She asked, "How is it possible to read what isn't on the page?" In response to suggestions from the class as to how and why this might have happened, Jessica connected her not wanting to leave her family to go to a university far from home, with the bride's unhappiness. Jessica imposed the reason for her misery onto the girl without being aware she had done so until class questions and discussions helped her understand what she had done.

The spaces in the story free us to fill them in according to our need and imagination, but because we bring the whole of who we are to a story, it's not difficult to unconsciously impose our issues on the story. The wonderful thing about writing new stories from old is that we have many opportunities to look at our original interpretation and compare what we thought we read or heard with what was actually told or written. And, this process not only happens immediately after hearing or writing a story. Our thoughts may change as new life issues emerge. This doesn't mean our earlier interpretation was wrong, rather, it suggests we have outgrown our previous response or that our issues have changed or transformed.

How does an issue transform? Attached to any issue is energy. Jessica was angry with her parents. She felt they were forcing her to leave home against her wishes and identified with the girl when she was weeping on the bed. When Jessica recognized the source of her anger she found herself paying attention to the old woman's words at the end of the story.

"Think on what I say. You were lost but you found your way home. Now your beloved has come for you. Why is it you do not rejoice? Can you not love each other as you did before?"

Jessica decided to call her parents and tell them of her unhappiness. Much to her surprise they told her they did not want her to be miserable, and even though she had a full scholarship to attend the university, she was welcome to come home and attend a local college if that would make her feel better. After thinking it over, she chose to stay for the rest of the semester and sort out her possibilities afterward. It seems that moving from "I am forced to be here" to "I choose to be here" transformed the energy of her anger into the determination to do well.

Working in a group provides the possibility for interesting and various ideas about what matters in a story. Ben heard Jessica tell the story of "The Fern Girl" but what caught his interest was the transformation of the root into a person who is then treasured and loved. The image he painted was of a colorful rainbow-like waterfall arising from a mess of black and brown swirls. His words were: magic, luck, hope. He wrote the following in response to his image and words:

In the time before time, there was the possibility that every living thing would have enough food and water and love. Maybe this would have happened had the sun been a little more generous, the winds less ferocious and the rains more plentiful.

The transformation of the root into a girl did not happen overnight. In fact, it took lifetimes of misery and hunger and violence without end. Oh, there were respites; sometimes there was enough food and rain. Sometimes people forgot their hatreds and feuds long enough to reproduce, for children to grow. But in the end, violence and misery, hunger and drought returned.

So how did the root come to transform into a child? It came to pass because one little tree was tired of being trampled on. Instead of growing up, it figured out how to grow down, deep into the earth. While drought and war and famine raged, the little tree grew strong, determined to find a better place. It sent its roots in all directions.

Some of the roots crashed into boulders and died. A few roots reached into rivers and drowned. But one root, small and spindly, yearned for something it could not define. As it grew, it searched for good smells, soft nestling places, and kind animals that burrowed out compacted soil. It kept growing, gingerly and carefully until it found a place of sunshine and rain and kindness. A bit of garden cared for by an old woman who nourished the earth without thought of reward, toiling year after year, accepting her loneliness, uncomplaining about her lack of goods, grateful for the blessings of health and the abundance of life around her. And it was to this woman the root grew toward, nurtured by her love.

Unanticipated and unplanned, when the root broke through the earth's crust, it took the form of a young girl. And for this too, the old woman was grateful all the days of her life.

After reading his story, Ben said, "The story sort of wrote itself. I have no idea what it means. Do any of you?" he asked the group. No one responded. Josh asked him to read it again.

The person who finally ventured to speak was a returning adult student who had never volunteered to share his work or to comment on the efforts of others. "Well," said Ray, looking embarrassed when he noticed everyone staring at him. "I was listening to the news this morning and I got really depressed. It's as if nothing good is happening anywhere. Social activists hung in Nigeria. Rampaging floods in India. AIDS killing whole populations in Uganda...yet if that's all there is to life, what's the point? Something good has to happen some time, somewhere. When I heard Ben's story it made me think that it's like inside each of us there are lots of roots and we have to believe that at least one of them is going to go to a good place where it can help to make something positive happen.

"Humph," said Ben, pausing to take in what Ray said. "Maybe I do know where the story comes from. We waited while it seemed as if he was deciding whether to say any more. When he spoke his voice was unusually soft. "My mom's been battling breast cancer for the past year. It's been really hard, especially because I can't go home very often. This morning I got a call from my dad. He says the doctors gave her a clean bill of health. I know that the cancer can come back, but right now, I just feel grateful. Like the old woman."

Josh nodded, "I know what you mean. My brother was diagnosed with leukemia when he was five. My mom and dad were either at the hospital or on the phone. One day I got so mad I threw a glass and it broke into a zillion pieces. I expected my mom to be furious but instead she gave me a big hug and said she was sorry everything was so difficult. I don't know why, but that one hug changed everything. Sort of like a root finding its way to a good place."

Ray nodded. "I admit I took this class 'cause it fit my schedule and I thought it would be an easy A." Everyone laughed knowingly. "I've been ready to drop it for the past two weeks but something kept me from signing the drop/add form. Now I think I know why. It's the only class I have where I don't feel I need to be perfect or always have the right answer. It's such a relief."

Sharing impressions and responses to stories is helpful and interesting. Not only is it possible to learn about our selves, we also get to know the people in our group more deeply. However it's important to distinguish between entering a story to explore one's responses, ideas and reactions, and listening to a story to analyze or critique it.

Although the differences are profound, one is not better than the other. When we explore our reactions to a story we are looking at it from the inside, when we analyze or critique it, we look at it from the outside, more often focusing on structure, authorial intention, technique, and place in the canon than on what it might mean to us. While one can analyze and critique traditional stories, and many do, storymaking has nothing to do with analysis or critique. We focus, both individually and as a group, on how the story lives in us and how we live in the story.

Each story has a wholeness that must be respected. It's not only useful to be egocentric when reading or hearing a story, it's necessary if we are to let it resonate within, to discover the personal symbolic value the story contains at the moment. With stories, there is no such thing as a fixed symbolic meaning that serves for all time, for all people. Symbols by their nature are fluid. A flag may be a symbol of a country but the symbolic meaning depends on who is looking at the flag and his/her experience of that country. A political exile may see her country's flag and feel relief she is no longer subject to police persecution. The same exile may see the flag of her host country and feel grateful for the safety and shelter this new country offers her. The symbolic meaning may be difficult to express verbally, but painting or sculpting the symbol often uncovers an emotional connection that makes it easier to articulate thoughts and feelings, especially when sharing the painting or writing with a group.

Popping-out Stories

Once we begin to make images and write stories, patterns emerge, helping us to better understand our current personal symbology. Because the characters and events in our written stories can feel as if they came from nowhere, I call these stories 'popping-out stories.' They pop-out spontaneously, without prior thought or planning. By allowing situations and characters to reveal themselves, dictating to our fingers without conscious interference, we encourage the hidden to be revealed. When we write spontaneously we never know where we are going or how the story will end until it ends. Each time we create a story, the energy of whatever we are feeling fuels imaginative characters and situations that often make us feel better after writing, even if we initially cannot find ourselves in the story or specifically relate to it.

As a child, the first fairy tale I read was "Cinderella" and then refused to read any more because in so many of them, young children had some kind of ally or fairy godmother to help them. Where was mine? I didn't want to believe I was too bad a child to deserve help. Then, more than forty years later, when co-teaching a university course in children's literature and drama with a specialist in children's literature, my colleague was so aghast when she discovered my lack of familiarity with the fairy tale genre, she sat me down with stacks of books and ordered me to read. Once started, I found it difficult to stop. The various characters' energy and drive to find ways to resolve bad situations, stop evil people, and answer the question, 'who am I' overcame my residual reluctance. When the first spontaneous story I wrote turned out to be a fairy tale, I decided to honor the form in which the story emerged. If it wanted to be a fairy tale, who was I to say it should be something else?

The initial popping-out story was fueled by a conversation so frustrating I hung up the phone, furious. Once again I was being blamed for everything and couldn't defend myself in a way that felt satisfying. I reached for the finger-paints on my desk, overwhelmed by anger. After painting amorphous shapes of bright colors, I immediately covered them over with black until it was almost impossible to see what I had previously painted. After writing: curse, blessing, hope, the story poured out, titling itself.

"The Black Patch"

There was once a king and queen who had been married for many years yet remained childless. Although they consulted doctors, wise men, even witches, the queen did not conceive.

One night she had a dream in which she was walking in a garden and was stung on her arm by a strange looking bee that remained on her arm, its bright eye staring at her. She was tempted to kill it but the bee was so extraordinary looking she refrained. Instead, she asked the bee what it wanted. The bee told her if she would willingly let it drink from her blood, she would conceive a child. The queen agreed.

When the queen awoke the next morning she decided to tell no one about her dream. Instead, she spent many hours working in the garden, planting, weeding, and caring for the flowers, grasses and bushes. When the king objected to her spending so much time doing work their gardeners could do, the queen laughed away his objections and changed the subject. As promised, she let the bee drink as it wished despite the intense pain.

One day the queen took the king into the garden and told him they would soon have a child. Both were overjoyed for they had feared they would remain childless. As they strolled down the paths filled with the scents of brilliantly colored blossoms, they avoided one area, an arid place in the center of the garden where no one was allowed to go, where nothing could be cultivated. It had always been a strange dark patch of earth. Although no trees kept the sun from shining on it, nor rain from nourishing it, not even the hardiest flower or grass could transform the black to green. Even the birds refused to peck at the hard black dirt. None of the wise men and women in the kingdom could explain the presence of the dark earth in the bright sun, nor could they say why nothing grew there despite the best efforts of the most experienced gardeners.

The king had the patch fenced in but the fence always fell down within the hour. The queen planted bushes and flowers around it but none lived more than a day. Although as problems go, it wasn't their biggest, the king and queen were used to getting their way. It irritated them that they could neither hide nor do away with a small black patch of dirt.

To celebrate the birth of their child, the royal couple invited all the important and intelligent people of the kingdom to come to their garden to mark the joyous occasion. First the important people gave their blessings and then each intelligent person bestowed good wishes on the princess until only one person remained, the oldest and wisest of all.

She spoke softly and kindly. "I wish for you, my little princess, a shovel that never fills with dirt." The king and queen were appalled. What kind of wish was this for a royal baby? All of the important and wise people gasped, waiting fearfully to see what the king and queen would do.

As the king considered his response, the queen spoke. "My

good woman, surely you can wish our beautiful new daughter something better than a shovel?"

The wise woman spoke without fear or apology. "I wish for her what she most needs." She kissed the infant on both cheeks and left, giving the royal couple no chance to protest further.

Time passed and the princess grew into a lovely young girl who spent many hours playing happily in the garden. Her parents took care to see she was never alone, nor was she ever allowed to go near the black patch of earth which was neither larger nor smaller than on the first day it appeared, a day no one, not even the oldest people in the kingdom could remember.

One day the princess saw something brilliant and beautiful on the far side of the garden, a place she knew she was not permitted to go. Fascinated by the vision and unnoticed by her serving maids, despite the prohibition, she crept into the area, covered with brambles and thorn bushes. The vision disappeared as quickly as it had come. Tired, bleeding from scratches, and a bit frightened, she tried to leave, but could not find her way out.

As she struggled to escape, the princess began to slowly sink below the surface of the earth. She called out for help but no one heard her. Much to her surprise, a shovel appeared. Without thinking, she grabbed it and began to dig, as if her life depended on it. Although while she dug she stopped sinking, she was unable to get out of the patch. Fear gave way to curiosity and she started digging again, this time noticing there were sights to behold.

Instead of the familiar garden she saw a grove of trees overflowing with purple flowers and huge bushes covered with yellow and blue blossoms. In each tree were hundreds of red birds, chirping with orange and green singing birds nesting in nearby bushes.

The princess continued to dig, and the more she dug, the

more she saw. Flowers, bushes and birds changed colors as the princess watched, entranced by the beauty before her. Suddenly, she uncovered a pair of shoes like none she had ever seen before. As she was examining them she heard a loud voice growl, "Thief, return my shoes!"

The princess froze but soon recovered her wits. "Excuse me sir, but I haven't stolen your shoes, I merely uncovered them. I shall be very pleased to return them to you if you will prove to me they are indeed your shoes."

"Prove to you my shoes are mine! I'll do no such thing."

"Then I will not give them to you," explained the princess calmly. "How do I know they belong to you?"

The booming voice turned ominous. "If you do not give me back my shoes I will cover you with dirt forever." Since the princess could not imagine 'forever' she was not afraid.

"I do not think these shoes are yours. I will not give them to you," she replied. With that, she began to dig furiously. Soon the bellowing voice gave way to an unpleasant echo, and in time, a comforting silence.

It was hard to dig while holding the shoes but the princess had no pockets and there was no place to rest. If she stopped digging she discovered she fell so fast it was difficult to stop yet she was unwilling to let go of the shoes. She was curious as to why the threatening voice wanted them so badly. Perhaps if I dig a little more I'll find a place where I can sit, she thought.

The dirt, which had been black, turned a deep brown. She smelled air filled with a sweet scent and looked up to see interesting shapes of dwellings glimmering in the sunshine. She wondered who lived there. Timidly she called out, "Hello? Hello?" but no one answered.

Soon the colors disappeared into a gray fog. The air grew

colder. Hungry and lonely, she felt the shoes growing heavier by the minute yet she continued to hold them as she dug, yearning for a bit of company. Then, her shovel hit something soft. She dug more slowly. The softness gave way to a moving shape. Amazed, the princess watched the shape shake itself. A woman emerged, covered from head to foot with brown earth.

"Who are you?" asked the princess.

"I am an old woman. Surely you can see this for yourself," she replied wiping the soil away from her eyes.

"How did you get here?" asked the princess, too astonished to mind her manners as she had been taught to do.

"A sorcerer condemned me to this place forever because I stole the source of his power."

"Why did you steal it?" asked the princess.

"That is a very long story my dear, and we have no time to stop and talk. We must hurry. Perhaps the shoes you are holding will help us, if you command their power."

"Are these his shoes?" gasped the princess.

"Yes my dear they are," smiled the old woman ruefully.

"I have troubles enough without these shoes; I gladly give them to you." The princess held out the shoes to the old woman, hoping she would take the heavy burden from her.

"I want those shoes more than you could possibly imagine but you cannot simply give them to me. Try! You will see I speak the truth." The princess held out her hands and tried to put them in the woman's hands but the shoes stuck fast. No matter what she did, the shoes remained tightly grasped by her fingers.

"Oh no, what shall I do now?" wailed the princess, not used to having to think for herself. Not only that, since she had stopped digging, she found herself falling again. "Help!" she cried, digging to stay in place.

"Put the shoes on," commanded the old woman, which was easier said than done. Falling in a narrow tunnel, holding a shovel, and at the same time, trying to put on shoes, seemed impossible. After a few tries the princess was ready to give up but the old woman shouted at her furiously. "Put those shoes on now!" The princess gasped at being spoken to in such a tone and was about to say 'How dare you speak to me like that, I am a princess you know,' when she made an extra effort to put on the shoes.

No sooner were they on her feet than she felt rested and satisfied, as if she had eaten and slept to her heart's content. Best of all, she was no longer falling but standing on a ledge, face to face with the old woman. "Well done my dear," said the woman, pleased. "There is more to you than you might think." The princess was not sure this was a compliment but decided not to complain. The shoes made her feel strong and smart; ready to do what needed to be done.

The old woman turned and moved toward a dark opening. "Follow me and do not stop moving or you will never get out. Hold on to my skirt and make sure you do not let go. I will take us where we need to be" Without waiting for the princess to agree, the old woman led her into a dark, dank, cold cave. The princess was very glad she had the woman's skirt to hold as they crept through tiny passages and waded into pools of water. The princess worried whether the shoes would be ruined but she had no choice, the woman was moving too fast for her to look or object to the pace.

Then, in the distance, the princess saw a bit of light. As the old woman walked toward it, the space inside the cave grew larger. Soon, they could stand without bumping their heads. When the old woman and the princess walked to the opening of the cave, the sun was so bright they had to close their eyes to stop the brilliant light from hurting their eyes.

Suddenly, the princess felt hands guiding her, leading her to a place she could not see. Her eyes would not open. Although the princess continued to hold the old woman's skirt as tightly as she could, she felt it slipping out of her grasp. She tried to cry out but had no voice. Her eyes remained tightly shut. Still, the hands guiding and leading her felt friendly and she did not resist. The hands pushed her into a pool of warm water and all her dirty, soggy clothes fell off. As she walked out of the water she felt herself dressed in fine new clothes, still wearing the sorcerer's shoes.

"You may open your eyes now," said a soft voice. Slowly, almost afraid to look, the princess opened her eyes and gasped. She was in a large palace, much grander and more richly decorated than her own. On a couch, covered with finely embroidered quilts, lay a small boy, pale and sickly, too ill to move, barely able to breathe. Feeling pity for the troubled child, she went to comfort him. As soon as she sat down near his bedside, the shoes flew off her feet and onto the feet of the boy. Immediately, his cheeks turned a healthy pink color. His body grew strong as he breathed deeply.

Suddenly, he was no longer a sickly boy, but a handsome man who stood up and took the hands of the princess in his. "You have saved my life. A very long time ago my mother challenged the sorcerer who kidnapped me by trickery. She was not strong enough to win and so he turned her into an old woman, burying her deep beneath the earth, taking away my life spirit, breath by breath. Had you not returned with these shoes, I would have died at midnight. My mother would have lived for all eternity as she was when you found her."

"I am happy I could help you but I wonder how it was the shovel found my hands. Had it not been for my digging I would still be falling."

The woman, now bright and vibrant, smiled as she spoke.

"At your birth, my sister who foresees the future blessed you with a shovel, to use when you most needed it."

"So all my hard work was nothing more than magic?" asked the princess, forlornly, thinking she had worked rather hard to help.

"Not at all my dear. You were given the shovel, but no one forced you to dig. You could have obeyed the sorcerer and returned his shoes to him. Had you done so, my son would now be dead and I would still be buried in dirt. We are very grateful for your help."

"So grateful, we wish to reward you," said the young man. "Ask for what you wish, it will be granted." The princess was silent, wondering what to ask for, unwilling to waste her wish. After all, she was a princess and already had everything she could think to want. "Take your time," he said. "Take all the time you need. Your answer is more important than you might imagine."

Finally the princess spoke. "I would like to be seen for who I am when I return home."

"Are you sure?" he asked, in a tone of voice that made the princess shudder and his mother smile.

She hesitated and then laid aside her fears. "Yes, I am quite sure."

"Very well," said his mother. "Close your eyes. When you open them you will be home, seen for who you are." And she was.

Thinking about the shovel and the shoes and the old woman who brings the princess to the boy so she can heal him and release his mother from burial beneath the surface of the earth made me wonder what, if anything, any of it had to do with me? Although I didn't identify with the princess who was so privileged and well loved by her mother and father, her cleverness in asking the sorcerer to prove the shoes were his, pleased me, as did her forthright decision not to give them to him. I liked her willingness to keep digging and the courage she had to follow the old woman. I thought it interesting that she couldn't give the shoes to the old woman but had to wear them until she met the boy. Was there something more personally symbolic about any of this? A hidden meaning that would change my life? Not that I could say at the time of writing. Mostly, I was curious about the process and felt pleased to have written a whole story, in one sitting, which somehow made me feel better about myself.

The image of the black patch continued to hold my imagination hostage. Why did no one know how it came to be in the royal garden? Why did nothing grow there? What made the fences fall down? How was it the princess saw something brilliant and beautiful that led her to the neglected garden, despite the prohibition against going there? What made her sink so quickly she had to keep digging in order to slow her fall? And how did the wise woman know to bestow a shovel upon the princess when she was newly born? Most of all, I wondered why the black patch preoccupied me.

One of the benefits of writing stories is the possibility of rereading them at different points in our lives when we may know more about ourselves or have new questions. Thinking about the black patch some time after I wrote the story made me wonder if it was an outward sign of trouble covered over, a visible referent to an obliterated past. I decided to write a new story using the same title, revisiting whatever the black patch represented, knowing that this new story was made from my reflection on the original.

Using the same process, finger-painting an image of the black patch and then writing what came to mind, I painted a bleeding female figure draped in purple, arms outstretched, mouth frozen in a scream. Before the image could dry, once again I smeared black all over it, obscuring the figure until my image was mostly a mess of black, with streaks of red and purple showing through. The words that came to mind were: A deed most foul. No witness but the earth. Once again, the story wrote itself.

"The Black Patch Revisited"

Once upon a time a husband and wife lived together uneasily. The woman yearned for wealth. The man was content with what he had yet wanted to please his wife. He could not easily bring himself to do the things she asked but, in the end, he loved her so much he did what had to be done. What she demanded, he gave to her even though it meant working from sunup to sundown. At first he felt shame and guilt and misery but soon, he was so busy pleasing her he had little time to think.

When she decided it was time for them to have a child, the man grew frightened. How could he work any harder? And, though he tried not to think about it, he worried about his wife. What kind of mother would she be? He knew at times she was not loving or caring or kind. But, as always, he gave in and a child was born. Not the son his wife had hoped for, but still, a child, a healthy bright-eyed daughter.

The birth of her child did not please the woman as she thought it would. The child cried, demanding attention the mother did not want to give. The woman could not stop the sound. She complained to her husband, "You were the one who wanted this child. All she does is cry. You care for her. I need to rest." The woman who was wife and mother thrust the child into his arms and left the room.

The man, who was husband and father, caressed his child, touching her soft cheek with his finger. The longer he held her the more he loved her. He began to feel she was his and his alone.

The more he held his daughter, the more he yearned to hold her. He found that he could not bear to see his daughter without cradling her. Fondling her. Touching her with all of him. And then one day, his wife saw him loving their baby girl. Her rage was so great she seized the baby and smashed her to the ground. The bleeding child cried out in fear and pain.

Choking her daughter, wanting to rid herself of her rival, the mother screamed. "You will not take my husband from me,"

The husband raced to the baby and tore his wife's hands away from the child's throat. When he had comforted his wife, the husband and wife made a bargain. What had happened would remain a secret between them. They buried the child's bloody clothes in the garden and covered the earth with rich soil in which they planted flowers and grass. They moved, far away.

New people have come to live in the house yet no matter how they tend the garden there is one bit of earth where nothing grows. Not grass or flowers or vegetables or bushes, not even a tree. No one knows why.

As I read what I had written something stirred inside me. I felt an excitement I could neither define nor explain. The idea that an act could be buried, but not completely hidden, made me feel that I had discovered an important truth about my life. I felt strangely comforted, as if I was being given evidence that had previously eluded me.

I kept "digging."

The image of the shovel, the last gift bestowed by the guests, given to the newborn child by the oldest and wisest of all, preoccupied me. The wise woman knows what the princess will need at a crucial time in her life and lovingly bequeaths upon her, a shovel, a most un-royal gift. Although this will help to save the life of the princess if she is willing to dig, the shovel is a gift, not an action. Even the wisest of the wise cannot force a princess to dig or make a princess depend upon herself.

Was I given a gift at birth that would help me survive when my life was in danger? Was there a metaphorical shovel in my life? I decided to write another story, making a reference to a shovel in the title to see what emerged.

"Digging Out from Under"

Once upon a time there was a child who had no friends. It wasn't that she was ugly or stupid or misshapen, it was her eyes; they made people look away. They were filled with an unbearable sadness that pierced even the most hardened mask. She saw people look away from her and felt bad. She distanced herself from them. Yet she was a child. She had no place to go. When she asked why, her mother ridiculed her questions. Her father avoided her questions. She learned not to ask. She taught herself to become small, learning to breathe so shallowly, her breaths made no sound and little movement. She even tried to become invisible, watching children play from a safe distance, envying their camaraderie, their easy laughter. Feelings she couldn't define strangled her voice. She wondered about dying and death.

As soon as she could, she left home, yet she could not leave herself behind. Her eyes asked questions no one could answer. She might have lived her whole life waiting, hoping, watching, wishing, except that one night, as she was looking at the night sky, a star dropped down, curling itself around her body, snuggling against her heart.

"Ask me anything," said the star. "Ask me your hardest question."

"Are you real?" asked the woman?"

"As real as you are," replied the star.

"What is your name?"

"Mara."

"That name means bitterness."

"True, but am I not beautiful? Do I not give off a lovely light? Do I not comfort you?" The woman nodded. "What is your name?" asked the star.

"Amina," replied the woman.

"A name as lovely as you are."

"Everyone knows I am not lovely," said the woman bitterly.

"Not everyone. Not even almost everyone. Just a few people who convinced you of this when you were young. They were wrong," said the star.

"You are the only one who has ever found me lovely," responded Amina, looking at Mara with her sad eyes.

The star did not look away. Instead, she returned the look with a hug and a sigh. "Reflected light is too dim to see properly. I will show you what you really look like."

The star shone so brightly she created a wall of light. "Look. Look at yourself. See yourself as you really are." When Amina hesitated, the star said, "Go ahead, I promise it will not be as it was."

The warm light caressed Amina like a hug. She could not help herself. At first she looked and then quickly turned away, but even the glimpse was intriguing. The light felt so comforting she looked again, this time long enough to see herself, to see her sad eyes. She looked away. She knew she was not what she saw. "Take a good look," said Mara. "Do not be afraid."

She turned Amina around and held her as she looked at herself. Really looked. And slowly, the laugh that was forming inside Amina burst out without permission.

So much for shovels.

What comes to mind when thinking about the shovel is my willingness to ask questions, an indication that I sensed further excavation could be done, that there could be more to a situation than meets the eye. The shovel story started with my wanting to continue exploring what the shovel might represent, yet what emerged was my need for comfort, to be told I am worth seeing and being seen. What remained were the ideas that digging is difficult and in order to keep going one needs an ally, a person who is not afraid to be real, to help heal festering wounds.

Variations on a Theme
I shared the story of Mara and Amina with a friend and his immediate response was, "Boy, that star had to work really hard to get the woman to look. What kind of person would have that sort of patience and persistence?"

His words took me aback. Certainly it wasn't an idea that occurred to me. Wondering how other people might interpret the story, I read it to three more friends who volunteered to participate in a storymaking session. Laura was quick to respond. "That part about the way people reacted to the girl's eyes reminds me of a time when we moved and I had to go to a new school where I didn't know anyone.

"What was it like?" we asked her.

"I'll show you," She sculpted an image of a tightly knit group of figures interacting, all facing each other. One figure stood alone, outside the circle, small and isolated.

"That looks really painful," responded Beth.

"I know that feeling," said Susie. "I remember high school. It was horrible. And when people said it was supposed to be the best time in my life I thought about jumping off a bridge."

Beth snorted. "I heard college was supposed to be the best time of your life. Thank goodness it wasn't true. Now is the best time of my life."

Laura looked far away, as if she was once more back in the time of no friends.

"Let's paint an image of Laura and the star," I suggested.

Laura painted black spirals that almost covered the page. In the lower left hand corner was a tiny blob of yellow, so small it almost looked like an accident. Beth painted an image of a small figure in purple surrounded by a yellow circle that radiated light. Susie's image was dramatic and covered the whole page. Streaks of purple and blue and red bisected a small yellow dot. My image showed the circle of figures and the lone figure of Laura's sculpture but approaching my lone figure was a yellow figure.

The four images were so different we decided to

write popping-out stories using each of our images and words as our way into our story. Although only one of us was a writer, we all wrote steadily for quite a time. After we stopped writing, we reflected on what we had written, not quite ready to leave the worlds we had just created.

Laura volunteered to go first. Her words were: alone, misfit, unwanted, no hope. At first she read stoically, but toward the end, her voice filled with energy and power.

Everyone said it would be okay, but no one said what "it" was, or how anyone knew it would be okay. In any case, I didn't believe them. I had tried. I joined clubs. Stayed after school to tutor elementary school kids needing help. Even volunteered to plan activities for a freshman dance. But after each meeting I went home alone, watching groups of kids laughing. I thought about running away but where would I go?

Then one day in school, I was walking alone in the hallway and saw that one of the "popular" girls had blood running down her leg. I knew she'd be embarrassed if people saw it so I took a deep breath and walked up to her. "Could I talk to you for a minute? I need to tell you something important."

She looked at me, wondering what I could possibly tell her but maybe the way I looked convinced her she should listen. I stood behind her so no one could see and told her. I offered her a tissue. She took it, wiped off the blood, and walked to the bathroom. I didn't see her for a couple of days. I wondered if she was mad at me or too embarrassed to say anything. During second period I saw her and then she saw me. When class was over she walked up to me and said, "Meet you at lunch. Okay?"

"Okay," I said, my heart exploding in my chest.

It was the best lunch I ever ate.

After reading what she had written, she grinned. "I forgot about Carrie asking me to have lunch. Just sitting with her instead of by myself changed everything. Girls started talking to me and in a few weeks, I even got invited to a party." Laura went to her sculpture and opened up the circle, moving the lone figure into it. "It's strange...before writing the story, all I remembered was my misery. Now what seems most important is that Carrie asked me to have lunch and things got better."

Beth looked sheepish. "My story isn't a memory. Is that okay?" Of course it was okay.

"Well, after making my image, I kept thinking that Mara was so nice and so beautiful but her name meant bitter. The words I wrote were: bitter, danger, and attack."

"Yes, it's true. My name is Mara, and it does mean bitter, but it wasn't always my name. At birth, I was given the name of Marina, a pretty name to be sure. The transformation took place when I was fourteen, a time of change, of ritual celebration. It wasn't my fault that I was pretty, that my long hair was golden, and that everything I wore looked better on me than on the other girls. I was blessed at birth with gifts but they were of no consequence. I knew that in time my face would age, as had my mother's, that my body would droop and sag like my aunts.' No, what mattered to me were the stars, the bright beautiful objects that visited my bedroom every night.

I discovered the stars also fascinated astronomers and that they even had objects with which to bring them closer. I yearned to have one. The more I looked the more I craved such a wonder. When it came my time to marry, I waited; hoping one of them would have me for a wife. I waited in vain. They wanted wives who asked no questions, who posed no challenge to their lofty theories. Time passed.

One day I overheard a group of women giggling, talking about me. "She's not Marina, she's a Mara. No one wants to marry her." Their laughter was neither kind nor pleasant. I pretended not to hear and walked past but one called out to me.

"So Mara, what will you do with your life now?"

My answer came from a voice inside me that I did not recognize. "My life is with the stars. I welcome it." Their laughter no longer touched me. And that night, when the stars were at their brightest, they welcomed me to their midst. They spoke my name with such love, Mara no longer meant bitter; it had become my star name."

Beth looked at the three of us and laughed. Of course we wanted to know what was so funny. She kept shaking her head, laughing, shaking her head. Her hilarity was contagious. When we were able to stop, Beth told us the reason for her laughter. She was an architect, working for a demanding, high-profile office boss and had become increasingly dissatisfied with her work situation. Just the day before, she had been offered a position with a small group, a collaboration of an architect, a landscape designer, and an interior decorator. They had just won a design competition, and were looking for a second architect to work on the project. "They asked me to work with them because I have a reputation for being a visionary." She laughed again. "I guess wanting to look at the stars is pretty visionary." She shook her head. "What I get from my story is how important being a visionary is to me and how much I want to work with the group even though it means less money and perhaps less prestige."

Susie looked at her image for some time before telling us her words: power, danger, frustration, attention. "My story isn't a story, it's sort of a poem," she said apologetically.

"So what?" challenged Beth.

"Read it," said Laura.

"Okay," sighed Susie, taking more than one deep breath.

In the beginning, she was small and ordinary, or so
she thought.
Why not?
No one noticed her.
No one heard her.
No one knew her.

She accepted her nothingness.
It was all she knew.

But, she hated it.
Hated being small.
Hated being ordinary.
Hated being overlooked.

Her hatred grew so large and so powerful it filled her
up.
Her hatred filled her up so tightly there was no more
room inside her.
She exploded.

She never looked back.

"Wow!" said Beth.

"What triggered that?" I asked.

"Are you okay?" asked Laura.

Susie's face was beet red. It was hard to tell what was going on. After looking at her poem once again, she shook her head. "I have no idea where that came from. It just poured out. The form. The words. The feeling. It's almost like someone else wrote it for me."

"How do you feel now?" we wanted to know.

"Weird." We waited for her to say more but she just shrugged her shoulders. We decided to take a coffee break. Sometimes it's better to let ideas and feelings simmer and percolate rather than to force an explanation. Trying too hard to decide what something means can obscure the actual meaning which usually reveals itself when we are ready.

Just as we were about to leave, Susie said, "I think I know what my poem is about. Yesterday I got a letter from my mother. My stepfather is in the hospital. She thinks he's dying and asked if I would come home even though she knows there's no love lost between me and him. I was eight when my father died and for about five years, it was just me and my mother. Then she married Joe and everything changed, including my mother's name. I refused to let him adopt me legally and I flaunted my birth name at him whenever I could. He used to tease me but it wasn't fun or funny to me. He complained I had no sense of humor and that I better 'lighten up.' When I told my mother, she defended him and said it was just his way; that I shouldn't be so sensitive. Well, I was sensitive and I felt betrayed. She was my mother. She should have defended me." Susie shook her head. "It wasn't all bad. I worked extra hard, finished high school in three years and won a scholarship to a school half way across the country. I might not have done so well in school if I'd been happier at home."

There it is, like in so many fairy tails, the evil parent syndrome forces the young person out of the nest and into the world.

She smiled. "I guess in some way I have to thank him. I love teaching art. Come to think of it, he did buy me a pretty nice graduation present."

"What did he give you?" asked Laura.

"Well, actually he and my mother gave me a check, but during the graduation party, he took me aside and said he had a special present for me. I'm afraid I wasn't very gracious but I followed him out onto the porch, mumbling to myself that I ought to be inside with the guests. When I opened his present, my jaw dropped. It was a set of paints and brushes. Expensive paints and brushes. The kind I'd been coveting for years." She sighed. "Maybe my mother is right. Maybe it was just his way. Maybe I'll go see him and read him my poem. See what he says." She laughed. "Maybe I won't ask him."

"It's amazing how different our stories are, from each other and from the original story about the star," said Beth. "And they seem to come from such different places. What makes them pop out? With no thinking or planning or figuring out what you want to write about..."

Stories are metaphors. Only by allowing images to

float into our consciousness can we begin to decipher what a story means for us at a given moment. Meaning changes as our lives change, as we experience and challenge and enter into our fears.

Jesse, who had been dealing with what seemed like a collision of issues, decided to write a popping-out story because he felt besieged by questions and choices and possibilities and didn't know what else to do with all the various feelings he felt were crashing together inside him. After writing it, he called to say, "I wrote a story but I don't know what it means. Even the title is weird. Can I read it to you?" Here is what he wrote:

"Dynamite Pretty"
Once upon a time there was a prince who had pants with no pockets. Everywhere the prince went attendants followed him to hold his things—things that could have gone into his pockets. Still, the prince was happy, until one day when he called to his servants, "You! Come here. Hold this key for me until I need it."

The servant startled the prince because he replied, "I'll do no such thing you big stupid oaf! Get some pockets in your pants and you won't need us servants following you around like stray animals! Don't you ever crave privacy? How about self-sufficiency? You big oaf! If you were my son I'd tell ya the same, like a father should. Now hold the damn key yourself!"

The prince was flabbergasted. He walked away from the spot in a hurry, crossing a hill, over a stile, through a river, and into the forest beyond. "What am I doing here?" he asked out loud.

A voice answered from the gloom. "*Exactly what you want to be, I'm sure.*"

The prince turned. "*Who said that?*"

"*The one you must speak to the most, I'm sure!*" said the voice again.

"*How do you know who I must speak to? I will not accept such a claim.*"

"*I'm sure you will,*" the voice patronized. "*Why don't you use the key you've brought? Now there's a good idea, I'm sure.*"

The prince was about to demand further explanation when he turned and saw before him a tombstone. Curious and uncertain that this grave had even been there moments before, he walked toward it, bending to read. He had almost made out the inscription when his gaze fell upon a keyhole cut right into the stone. Reaching carefully, he inserted his key and opened the lock.

"*Where am I?*" uttered the prince into the darkness that engulfed him.

"*Exactly where you need to be, I'm sure,*" said the voice, along with the body that spoke it. Suddenly the prince saw that he was in a room full of dolls and marionettes. Looking around, he realized the voice that spoke to him, who had been speaking to him in the forest, was coming from a figure that looked exactly like himself. The prince stood in amazement and reached forward, as though to touch a mirror, but no such mirror existed. "*What did you expect? Some sort of trick?*" spoke the prince to the prince.

"*I...I...*"

"*Well, you won't find trickery here, I'm sure. If you would be so kind, please remove your clothing.* The prince was too awestruck to protest. He began undressing.

"*Now put these on quickly, I don't have all day.*"

The prince put on the garments as he was told. They were

coarse and hard. Clothing that needed to be broken in.

"There! Now isn't that fine?" spoke the prince to the
prince.

"What do you want from me?" uttered the prince to the
other prince in what felt like a growing terror, like the suffering of a
bad dream.

"I want what you want, I'm sure."

"And what is that? What could that possibly be?"

"For you to be comfortable," said the prince to the other
prince, "just comfortable."

"And what if I am not? What then?" protested the prince.

"You will be, I'm sure. For the clothes you wear will be
yours always. You will never have another garment. It will change
with time, fitting your body better and better every day. Eventually
you will think of it as a second skin. Perhaps one day you will not
want to take them off."

And saying this, the prince held up a mirror so the prince
could see his new second skin. It was covered in pockets. Pockets
with zippers. Pockets with buttons. Pockets on sleeves and legs and
backs. Pockets of all colors. Pockets of all sizes. Pockets from head to
toe.

"Now I am a walking pocket," said the prince who found
himself back in the castle.

Jesse remained puzzled by the story and when I
asked him to write what came to mind, this was his response:

Sometimes my life seems to live itself, guided by structures
and principles beyond my ken. It feels like I am at the mercy of a
terrible storm, being thrown up and down and inside out. Finding

bearing in this mess can be a daunting task but one necessary for more than just survival. At the time of writing "Dynamite Pretty" I was in such a storm and had little control. I sat down to write because I needed an outlet for all the stuff inside myself, the unsettling feelings and intuitions that were as yet indescribable. What I produced was a thought picture, like a fingerprint, of my subjective life. By analyzing that picture alone and with others, I came to an understanding of my struggle and its potential. This gave me power to use the storm.

Many ideas were brought up as we talked about his story. Perhaps the pockets represented personal responsibility or the possibility of space in which to put new ideas. When the prince had his own pockets he didn't have to depend on other people to carry his load. The lack of pockets in the prince's normal clothing could symbolize his status, beholden to his father the king, his mother the queen, his allegiance to a state where he is not at liberty to be independent. The prince does not speak kindly to his servant, nor does the servant speak kindly to the prince. Why the harshness? Why doesn't the prince remind the servant that these clothes are princely clothes, designed for a person who is dependent on others to take care of his needs? What gives the servant the courage or ability or anger to speak to the prince as he does? And how does the prince feel about having his own pockets, so many pockets, in a garment that will become like his skin if he so chooses? What if part of him is like the servant, having to be at the beck, call and whim of a person he is told he must serve?

What about the key, keyhole, and tombstone? Is he opening a door to a better life by taking the initiative and unlocking something that was previously unavailable to him? Is developing a new self analogous to a kind of dying—hence the tombstone? We also talked about the title, which came before the story. Some of the ideas we tossed around had to do with the coupling of dynamite and pretty, especially since his image of dynamite was explosion, not the colloquial expression of great. One idea that stood out was that the tension between the two words was similar to that between the prince and the servant—between privilege and effort. We also talked about the expression, 'deep pockets,' a metaphor for an unusual amount of resources. A person with deep pockets has the resources to accomplish what he/she wants to do without having to ask others for help.

When the title of a story comes before the writing, it can serve as a beacon, pointing the psyche to the story's source and content. Many times, the story becomes the explanation of the title although not necessarily as clear as a theatre marquee. In the case of "Dynamite Pretty," the apparent obscurity of the title kept the writer thinking about the title and the issues it generated. One idea that came to mind is that of dynamiting the old structure to find what is pretty, or usable or different from what has gone before. When we are "sitting pretty," we are in a good position to enjoy what we have and to do what we want.

Writing stories may not be the most direct way to find answers to life's questions and issues, but if the front door is locked, it may be possible to find a back door or basement window, more easily opened, through which one can enter. The story made Jesse wonder about his emotional and financial independence. Although he didn't come to any final decision about what the story meant, a few weeks after writing it, he made a career choice that will, in the future, help him to be independent in all the ways that are important to him. As he thought about the story he decided he was all the characters; the prince and the servant, the tombstone and grave, the keyhole and the key, the prince inside the tombstone and the dolls. The harsh tones of voice are the result of their never having talked to each other. One was forced to give too much and the other expected to take too much. To achieve a sense of closure, he created a dialogue with the various parts of himself to explore and develop his inner sense of relationship and balance.

Moving through Nothingness

The connection between writing the story and Jesse's subsequent significant life decision is not coincidental. Many people participating in storymaking workshops discover that attitudes, choices, even feelings about work or relationships change as they read, write, listen and tell their stories to group members. One particularly powerful example occurred in a workshop on myth and meaning open to returning adult students at a university. The fourteen group members were as different from each other as they could be in terms of age, race, occupation, stage in life—even their reasons for taking the course. Some thought the material looked interesting, others wanted an evening course that was recommended by their advisors. A few admitted they enrolled because they needed a three-credit university course or something in their lives but didn't know what. Almost none of the participants had read any traditional stories and knew little about myths except for the

Greek myths they were forced to read in school.

One member, a lawyer, had enrolled on a dare. A friend of his had seen the course description and challenged him to take it, the talk occurring when they had both had too many glasses of wine. When he introduced himself at the beginning of the course, Marvin admitted he knew little about stories but subsequently, was quick to judge, advise, comment, and question, often appearing as lawyer and judge. Although he made jokes about returning to kindergarten when he saw the finger-paints and clay, and continued to denigrate their use for the first few weeks, his comments were generally good-natured and he readily participated.

The fifth class session dealt with Trickster, an archetype many people find frightening, intimidating, or off-putting. When more than a few class members expressed trepidation, Marvin laughed at their fears good-naturedly. "It's only an archetype, nothing to worry about." The participants were assigned the task of making their Trickster mask at home, allowing what they created to be filtered through their idea of Trickster. As part of developing their Trickster, participants gave it a name, a way of moving, and imagined experiences their Trickster might have had as preparation for writing their Trickster's autobiography when they got to class.

Some of the masks were spectacular. One was made of black velvet with sequins and drips of sparkling tinsel. Almost two feet tall, the mouth was lined with purple silk, the head had peacock feathers that waved as the wearer moved. Another was made of ribbon cascading down from a gold-dusted face. Although each mask was different--some were made from paper bags, others from scraps of material, plaster casting or bought in stores and then "customized" to fit the requirements of their Trickster--what they shared was a liberal use of color.

In contrast, Marvin's mask looked like a death mask. Totally white, with no distinguishing features, he had made it by pressing plaster-coated material over his face and then distorting it when he took it off so it didn't look exactly like him. When we sat around the circle, each person's mask in front, Marvin looked uncomfortable and was uncharacteristically quiet. When students were asked to "Write the most amazing experience your Trickster has had recently," he sighed audibly. When he heard the next instruction, "Look at your Trickster mask as you write, to be sure you're using it as your inspiration," he shook his head sorrowfully. After a few giggles and groans, everyone except Marvin started to write. Looking as pale as his mask, he picked up his pen, knowing from previous class experience he needed to start any way he could. He held it, suspended in air, until he began writing slowly, with no enthusiasm.

As people wrote, some laughed, a few shook their heads, others nodded with excitement. Afterward, the class decided to read what they wrote wearing their Trickster masks. Easier said than done. Tricksters have their own agenda and eventually, people gave up trying to read and just said what came to mind. We heard about amazing feats of cleverness, bouts of bravado, acts of guile, and scenes of sly manipulation. Only Marvin, wearing his mask, made no effort to share his Trickster's amazing experience.

Sally, who had been filled with trepidation before

we started was now relaxed, enjoying the sassiness of her Trickster. She walked by the lawyer's Trickster and teased him. "What's the matter big fella, you're looking mighty pale. Someone run away with your courage? Weren't you the one who told us we had nothing to worry about? C'mon, join us, if you dare." She laughed and kept motioning him to get up and join the group. Others collected around her, reinforcing her invitation. It was their turn to poke fun of him as he had so often done to them. They gave him outrageous advice and made outlandish suggestions. Marvin tried to stand up, with no success. He seemed paralyzed. Although we didn't know at the time what he had written, it looked as if his Trickster had lost all its energy and life force.

When the group sensed something was wrong they backed off. Although he looked relieved, Marvin's eyes followed their cavorting as if his life depended on it. After group members had removed their masks, and we were processing the experience, Sally asked, "What happened to you?" Marvin moved his mouth but no words came out. "Couldn't you at least read what you wrote?"

"Okay," he sighed. "I guess that's only fair."

I've forgotten my name. I'm pale as death and it's a struggle to breathe. I can't move. I wasn't always like this. There was a time when I had plenty of color and lots of energy. In fact, I could change my color any time I wanted. I was particularly fond of purple but the intensity sometimes got in my way so I generally settled for sea foam blue with green hair and hazel eyes. I had plenty of adventures; some are still talked about in the village where I was living. I used to be able to run for hours without losing my breath or chase Coyote for miles until he gave up, exhausted, with me as fresh as I was when we started. Look at me now. I'm a nothing. A zero.

I know. I'm supposed to write about my most amazing experience but what's amazing is the change in me. I don't even know how it happened. I woke up one morning and everything I thought I was had changed. No color. No energy. No laugh. I was so ashamed of the way I looked I crawled away from my village in the middle of the night. I didn't want anyone to see me. I didn't know who I was. All I knew was who I'd been.

I can write this because you never knew me before. You probably think that how I am now is normal, the way I've always been, but it isn't. I don't know how to find who I used to be. I don't even know if it's possible. All I know is I can't stand the way I am. I've got to figure something out. What good is a Trickster who's run out of tricks?

Sally was the first to speak. "I'm sorry. I didn't know..."

"That's all right," he said, "I didn't know either." The silence felt productive and friendly. Any resentment at his "know it all" attitude seemed to have vanished. Marvin picked up his mask and studied it. "This is better than looking in the mirror." Although it was time for class to end, people didn't leave.

Sally grabbed her Trickster mask, put it on, and sidled up to Marvin. "Hey big fella, what you need is a transfusion. Get some life back into you. Why don't you come up and see me some time." She did a Mae West vamp, giggled as she took off her mask and left, giving him a wink as she opened the door.

In the weeks that followed, Marvin was subdued, seldom offering the judgment, advice and suggestions that had flowed so freely before. He watched intently and listened more carefully. Toward the end of the semester class members suggested we have a party to celebrate. Marvin hesitated, then stood up and volunteered his house, an offer immediately accepted.

At the party Marvin announced, "I have something I want to tell you." People stopped eating and drinking, curious to hear what he would say. "I'm going to do an Outward Bound week. It's something I've been wanting to do for years but could never make myself do it." He grinned. "I've signed the contract and paid my money. Nothing to do now but meet the group in Colorado in two weeks." Everyone cheered and clapped.

Sally, always ready with a response, lifted her glass and said, "Here's to Marvin. Seems his Trickster's got himself a whole new bag of tricks."

Marvin mimicked her Mae West tone. "Or will have." As everyone drank, he looked around the room. "Thanks guys, I'm really glad you're here." They drank to that as well.

How is it possible that writing a few paragraphs could foment such change? Obviously it isn't just the writing, one has to be ready. The willingness to take in a story, to let it resonate within us--interacting, intersecting, and reconnecting disparate pieces of ourselves can have powerful repercussions, bringing to consciousness new ways of thinking about old issues and questions. One person told the group, as part of our discussion about the semester's course in myth and expression, she felt as if her personal mirror had been cleared of fog, and she could see herself more clearly than ever before. A participant asked, "Is that good?"

"I don't know," she replied, "it just is."

Character Autobiography

One way of becoming aware of our issues is to select a story, choose a character who is or could be in the story, and to write an autobiography of that character a few years before or after her/his presence in the story, at a moment of crisis, with the writing fueled by a burning question. Not only does this help us to notice concerns that may not be conscious, it also releases unexpected sources of tension and stress.

"Macha the Red"

Tired of innuendos, sexist jokes, gender discrimination, and having to work twice as hard as the male students in her class, Debra, an engineering student, was considering quitting the university. Her participation in the myth course was above and beyond her required engineering courses, but she felt she needed to find a way to express her anger or she was going to explode. Making her way through a sea of stories, she found "Macha the Red," an Irish legend which begins with three kings reigning alternately in Ireland for seven years. When one king dies, leaving his throne to his daughter, the other two refuse to entrust the royal power to her. Enraged on behalf of her mythical sister, the student wrote the following memoir of Macha the Red, titled "The Power of the Just."

"This is the way it is and this is the way it shall always be," spoke the King to the woman in front of him.

She stood, head unbowed, refusing to accept his verdict, aware that guards were closing in behind her. "And I say no! There is much that was and is no longer. Your argument holds no truth. I will fulfill the legacy of my father. I will rule as queen."

"And now it is I who say no. You are your father's daughter, but he is dead and cannot speak. I am King and I decree my son shall rule as king."

"Willem, your son Erich is barely five years of age. He knows nothing of right and wrong. He says yes to the hand that holds the biggest sweet."

"No matter. He will have counselors to advise him."

She laughed bitterly. "And who will guarantee the advisors will not use him for their own purposes? I thought you wiser than that. You, who know all about palace coups. You, who..."

"Enough. Guards, take her away."

She turned to face the approaching men with no hint of fear. "Touch me and you shall die for your insubordination. I am the rightful ruler of the land and you know it. You may put me in prison today but I will emerge tomorrow and then it will be your turn to languish in a cold dark cell, with no one brave enough to speak for you."

She turned toward one man, older than the rest, his beard graying. "You, Malich, you knew my father. I was there when you stood at his bedside, hearing his last will and testament. I heard you swear loyalty to me, his daughter. What new-made promise makes you set aside a deathbed vow?" He grew pale and turned away. He could not bear to meet her steady gaze.

"And you, Menasus, where is your loyalty? My father found you in a gutter and raised you up to be a captain in his army. Is this the way you thank him? Turning against his daughter and only heir?"

"Do not listen to her," commanded the King. "She is a traitor. She belongs in prison. Let her go and she will lead the country to rebellion. Take her away."

The young woman held each guard in her gaze. They did not move.

Once again the King demanded they take her to the dungeon but the men stood, transfixed.

"I am your rightful leader. I will treat you as the men of honor I know you to be. Come! Kneel before me. Swear your loyalty to me and your courage and allegiance shall be rewarded. I will return to you the lands that once were yours. Speak truth to justice. Choose between us. Now!"

The King watched as one by one, each soldier knelt before the young woman. Only then, when the last man had knelt, did the woman release her gaze. She turned to the King. "I will not rule as you have done. I will be just. There will be a trial. Let those who claim to be wise decide your fate."

"Guards, take him away."

Tentatively, the men stood, then gathered their courage and walked to the King who seemed to shrink before their eyes. The woman watched, her eyes betraying no emotion. When the King had been removed, she walked slowly to the throne and sat down. "Thank you," she said to those who remained. "I know how to show my appreciation to you for remembering who you are and for acting according to the allegiance you swore to my father, the man you loved."

Fourteen years passed. The country prospered. But now, a new danger loomed. Macha called a meeting of her most trusted advisors.

"Erich, the son of Willem has risen against me, charging that I bewitched his father into giving up the crown that is rightfully his. His words find approval among those who wish to be ruled by a man. I have gathered you here, my most trusted advisors, to ask for your support. There will be a war unless I make a plan to unman Erich whom I know to be a coward.

"How is it you know this for certain?" asked Menasus.

"At the royal combat practice, where we were all masked, none but me knew his identity. When I approached him, isolating him from his men, he gave a shriek and galloped off, retreating to the safety of the common area. He covered well, pretending that his horse was injured, but when we looked, eye-to-eye, he turned away. He is a skilled speaker and that is where our danger lies. His tongue is smooth and clever, most persuasive."

"Knowing you my Queen, I am sure you have a plan," teased Malich. "Even when you were a little girl, your wits were fast and your speech intriguing." The others permitted themselves a laugh, knowing this was true

"Aye, Malich, you have indeed known me before I knew myself. And you are correct, I have a plan, but it is one that carries with it much danger, for you, for me, for all of us.

"Speak my Queen, we are not schoolboys, unseasoned and untried. We have faced worse threats before. Lay out your strategy. We will listen and respond accordingly."

And so Macha told them of her plan and it was as fraught with peril as she had said. The men before her grew pale and still. Each was thinking of what might happen. And yet, the woman before them had never let them down, had never run or hesitated when it was time to lead.

"I will ask you one by one. Are you with me or against me? No harm will come to those who think my plan is folly. All eyes will close save mine, so none among you shall know who chooses to stay and who to go."

And one by one, all the men assembled, with their eyes closed, as one, lifted their arms in solidarity.

Macha raised her sword. "Open your eyes my brave and loyal councilors. You have all agreed to join with me. We shall be successful for we have wit and bravery on our side."

After students write their memoir, each in turn, appears before the rest of the class, acting as a council of wise elders, to share what has been written, ending with a question addressed to the council. After telling her story, Debra, in role, asked:

"And so my wise elders, we carried out my plan.

Although we were successful, many did not leave the battlefield alive. I am haunted by their absence. Did I do the right thing? Should I have found another way to counter Erich's false claims? Was it my anger that chose the path we took?"

After conferring as a group, the student acting as council leader spoke. "We are convinced you had no choice. Not to counter Erich's acts of violence would be to condone and encourage them. Your plan was well thought through. You acted out of love for your people. We commend your wisdom and courage. Erect a memorial to those who fell and set aside a day of fasting and commemoration so that those who lost comrades and loved ones may begin their healing, recognizing they are not alone, knowing they are not forgotten. So be it."

Debra responded, "Thank you. Your judgment eases my heart. I will do as you suggest."

After the council has spoken and the speaker responds, there is a debriefing where the student is asked to talk about how the story was chosen and to share with the class, something about the story's meaning. Debra had clearly thought about both of these issues.

"The tale of Macha appeals to my inner vision of myself. I always had an inferiority complex. I kept thinking I wasn't as talented or smart or attractive as other girls. Writing this story made me feel good, like I can be a respected woman who is able to stand up for herself, even do battle if she has to. I can challenge people who are in power. I like that Macha doesn't fret about other people's opinions although she does consult when it's appropriate. She takes charge of her life and stands up for her rights. I want to keep reaching out and trusting in myself. Macha's assertiveness illustrates that I don't have to be passive around my peers or so-called betters. Being myself doesn't mean people will dislike me. If I'm truly myself, people will like me for who I am and if they don't, they don't. It's not the end of the world."

Then she turned to a young man sitting opposite from where she was standing, a wry smile on her face. "Jerry, I helped you with your homework. You got an A and I got a B, yet you never said a word to Professor Hodgson. What kind of loyalty is that?" Jerry squirmed but she kept staring at him. Her story was being re-enacted right before our eyes. Eventually, he nodded. She stared at two other classmates who had been given A's although their answers were no different from hers.

One of the young men looked embarrassed. "You're right. It isn't fair."

"Will you help me?" Debra asked them.

Red faced, squirming more than a little, each in turn said, "Yes."

Just before commencement the following year, Debra came to my office. She said she wanted to tell me what happened after the course ended. "Although I liked the story of Macha and what I wrote for class, it was after all, just a story. Or so I thought. Every time I decided to quit, Macha leered at me, as if to say, 'And you call yourself a woman. You're nothing but a panty-waisted, chicken-hearted fool who expects men to treat her right. Use your brains, girl. Fight for what's rightfully yours and don't forget about the women coming after you. You can make a difference for them too, you know.'" She laughed. "Macha invaded my dreams, my thoughts, even my sense of what's possible. I finally had to have a conversation with her. I said, 'Macha, if you promise to leave me alone, I'll stay in school.' I thought that would end the matter but it didn't. She kept after me, teasing, pushing, scolding, laughing... "

She looked embarrassed. "I began to wonder if I was going crazy. I finally wrote more stories. I had to. It was the only way I knew to keep her quiet. I even used my finger-paints when I was angry or upset. I have a whole collection of Macha stories." She handed me a loose-leaf notebook filled with paintings, poems, and stories. "What I came to realize is that Macha is a part of me, the best part of me. And I wouldn't have met her if I hadn't had to find a story that spoke to me."

Debra graduated with highest honors in engineering and was given awards for academic excellence and achievement as a class leader.

"The People Could Fly"

It's possible to be upset and not know why. Uncovering the cause can be difficult, complicated by defense mechanisms and lack of information. Amazingly, when we pick a story with which to work, no matter the reason we choose it, we generally select one that contains the issue needing our attention.

"The People Could Fly," is an African American folktale about slaves who discover they can fly and escape from slavery. When he read it, Jason imagined himself as one of the people who fly away, leaving his family behind him. His character autobiography was fueled by the question, "Should I have flown off and left my grandson to endure slavery without my counsel and comfort?" He chose to write it on the occasion of his grandson's 21st birthday, not knowing if the young man was dead or alive. Jason read his words, addressing them to the grandson he wished was with him.

"Beloved child, I want to imagine you alive, a free man, with a free wife and a free child. Free to choose the work you do, the place you live, the life you want. But the picture will not come. My heart is pain. My head is agony. I abandoned you to save myself. I could not bear my life and flew away. Now I must live with the consequences of my thoughtless choice.

"Beloved child, I cannot even tell you my name for it was lost in the turbulence of the journey, crossing the sea, to a land as different from my own as day is to night. Yet day needs night and none of us needed that journey. My mother named me but lack of food and water and air affects memory. Perhaps she chose not to remember, for memory served only to increase our pain. Perhaps in time she might have told me had we not been sold to different people. I cannot utter the word master for they were not masters. Mastery implies excellence and these were not excellent men and women.

"Beloved child, your birth was a source of pain and joy to your mother. Joy because you were beautiful and your smile warmed the hearts of all who saw it. Yet children born in such conditions are mere pawns to the needs of men with the power to determine fate. And so our tears mixed happiness and agony.

"Beloved child, the day I flew away was a day like any other. I paused from my labor to smell the new grass and was beaten for my effrontery. In that moment I remembered the voice of my grandmother, the story she told me about flying. I closed my

eyes, uttered her words and flew. Flew far away from my misery, high above the foreign soil, to a place where my soul and spirit and body could finally rest.

"Beloved child, it shames me to admit that at that moment I did not think of you. I have no excuse. I do not ask for your forgiveness. I saved myself but left those I loved behind. What good is my salvation at your expense? Perhaps I could have helped you. We were still together though your mother had been sold.

"Beloved child, in my dreams you are alive, strong and whole and true to the spirit of those who love you. May this be so for you and all our people.

After his presentation Jason repeated his question. "Should I have flown off and left my grandson to endure slavery without my counsel and comfort?" There was a long, uncomfortable silence. Then a council member slowly stood up, deliberately focusing on the presenter. With no chance to prepare a text or her thoughts, she spoke when she had everyone's attention.

"You were given the ability to fly. You chose to act on this gift. Your grandson takes comfort from your freedom. He speaks to a woman named Harriet Tubman. They talk in symbols and sing, 'Do lord deliver me.' They are finding their own ways to fly. Your spirit gives them courage. Rejoice! Your act gives them hope. They will live and die as free people."

As part of the debriefing, the class processed their experiences. Jason, the presenter, an African American chemical engineering major, talked about feeling he had abandoned his family to come to the university. He thought he was letting them down because he could no longer contribute money to the family as he had done all through high school.

Class members were of one opinion—when he graduated he would certainly get a good job and then he could not only help his younger brothers and sisters financially, he would also serve as a role model, reminding them of the importance of following their dreams. The solemnity and caring with which the class responded to their classmate's lonely and painful struggle seemed to ease his troubled feelings. The lines on his face softened. He thanked them for their response. After sharing his story, classmates responded to him differently. They made sure he didn't sit by himself in class and invited him to social functions. His demeanor was so polished, it was impossible for of us to have guessed the pain he was in had he not told us of his concerns.

Helping a Friend
Even in a less formal situation, writing the autobiography of a character in a traditional story provides opportunities for discovery. A group of people decided to use storymaking sessions as a way of distracting a friend facing a devastating illness. Each of them brought a story to share. Although most of the stories had clear resolutions, the following story from the San people in South Africa caught their imagination. They decided that the puzzling ending of **"The Basket,"** was so intriguing it could provide a good beginning for the first session.

There was once a farmer who worked diligently in his fields and took good care of his cows, milking them twice each day.

One evening, when he went to milk them, he discovered they had already been milked. He thought this strange and wondered who could have done it. The next night, the same thing happened. The third night, he decided to hide in the barn to see if he could catch the thief.

Before sunset, he settled into a hiding place, waiting to see what would occur. Just after the sun could no longer be seen, a ladder descended and a lovely young maiden, holding a basket in her hand, stepped off it and began milking the cows.

Amazed, the farmer could barely speak, especially because he didn't want to frighten her. Standing between the maiden and her ladder, he found his voice. "You are the most beautiful maiden I have ever seen. Will you marry me?"

The maiden looked at the handsome farmer and at the evidence of his hard work and care. "Yes," she said, "I will marry you, on one condition."

"What is that?" asked the young man.

"You must promise me that you will never look inside my basket."

"I love you. It shall be as you ask," said the farmer. "I promise." And so the two were married and lived happily together for some years.

One day, when they were both working in the fields, the farmer said, "I will bring us water to drink for the day is hot." He went back to the house to find a container for the water and stumbled on his wife's basket. He was so curious he forgot his promise and opened it. Looking inside, he saw nothing.

Just as he was about to put it back, his wife came in and saw him with the basket in his hands. "Oh," she said, "you have broken your promise. You have looked inside my basket."

"Yes, I have, but there is nothing in your basket. I don't

understand why you told me not to look inside it."

"You see nothing?" asked his wife.

"Nothing. Look for yourself." He turned the basket upside down. "See, there is nothing in it."

"Oh," she sighed, "if you see nothing I must leave."

Suddenly, the ladder descended and the man watched his wife leave, never to be seen again.

People made images of what they thought was inside the basket and then wrote words evoked by their images. Carol's image was a blob of yellow, red, green, black, and brown. She wrote: In my basket is what cannot be seen, only felt, such as courage and love and companionship. Jenny's image was a small yellow flower inside a brown circle. She wrote: Inside the basket is the magic of connection. Phil's image was a black ball. He wrote: I have hidden in my basket the fear that you will see who I am, rather than who I want you to think I am. David's image was a brown basket with a white space. He wrote: If you have to ask what is inside my basket you are not the man I need you to be. Nina's image was a small blue ball inside a brown basket. She wrote: What is inside cannot be seen with eyes, smelled by a nose, or felt with fingers. It must be taken on faith. What lives inside the basket is hope.

After sharing their images and words, David said, "Poor guy, how was he supposed to see what she had in the basket. They were using different systems. Couldn't she have explained hers to him if she loved him?"

Nina countered, "Sometimes, if you have to explain something, it loses its magic. Maybe all she wanted was to see if she could trust him to keep his promise. It's not as if they knew anything about each other before they married. He saw her descend from a ladder, milk his cows, and fell in love. Then she went back to wherever she came from."

"Yeah," grinned Phil, "but don't forget, she was beautiful."

"So she was beautiful," said Jenny, disgustedly. "So what? Are you saying that's all it takes to make a relationship? What about everyone who isn't handsome..."

"Whoa," protested Phil, "I was teasing."

"Then what do you think was going on?" asked Jenny.

"I think she came from people who could look into her basket and see whatever it was that filled it. He came from people who would look into her basket and see nothing. Does that make him a bad person?" Phil asked defensively.

"Why did he have to look in the first place?" asked Carol. "He promised he wouldn't look. He broke his promise."

"But what was so terrible about looking in her basket that he couldn't have a second chance?" asked David.

"We don't know anything about the world she came from. Maybe in her world breaking a promise is an inviolable act. We only know about his world," said Nina.

The next activity was a brief writing exercise. Each person chose to write from one perspective: What she says, what he says, or what the community says. Before writing, we sculpted an image of the narrator.

Carol's sculpture was the figure of a woman that she

broke into many pieces before reading what she wrote.

He said he would not look. He promised. I believed him. It was the basis for our marriage. When he broke his promise, he broke my heart. Just as he could not see the contents of my basket, so he could not see the contents of my heart. A man who cannot see, is a man who cannot love, for he does not know what love looks like. I ask that you take me back, not as I was, but as I am. Who am I? Can you tell me?

She looked at the four of us, challenging us to answer her question.

As if in response, David showed his sculpture, a figure bent over in grief.

I am a caring man. I work hard. I was good to her. Life with her was a dream. Now she is gone and my life is a nightmare. I was wrong to look inside her basket and I should have said so. I should have told her that I loved her. I go to my barn each night, hoping that a ladder will descend and I will climb to her community. I will admit my wrongdoing and ask for a second chance. I did not know what love was until I lost it. I did not know the meaning of pain until my loss. What will happen to me now?

After listening to their writing, Nina grew very quiet and withdrawn. "What's the matter?" asked Carol.

"I'm just thinking how difficult it is to be in a relationship where each person comes from a world that's unknown to the other. In a way, it's like when you deal with catastrophic illness. Your world changes but the world of your friends, maybe even your family, remains essentially the same. I know there's discombobulation from having to take over chores, or do extra driving, but that's outside stuff. Everyone can see it and deal with it. It's the inside stuff that no one can see or feel that makes the person with the illness feel so lonely."

No one asked Nina if she was lonely; they knew her well enough to know that she could be the loneliest person in the world and still say no, that she was fine, that she was managing. There was a long, uncomfortable silence.

Carol asked Nina, "Would you read what you wrote?"

"Sure," she said. "In case you can't guess, I wrote it from the perspective of a person who lived in his village."

We don't see him much. Never did. Don't think we ever saw her. Don't know why, but he always came to town by himself. Had a big smile on his face, I'll grant you that. Looked like a cat living on cream. And maybe he was, for a while. Now he comes in, sells his milk and cheese and leaves, quick as he can, looking like he died but had to keep on living. Never did talk much, but now he's so quiet and silent you wonder if he's breathing. I asked him once how he was, soon after he lost his smile, "Okay," he said, though it was clear as day he wasn't. He's a private man and I guess he's grieving something. Maybe she died... Don't guess we'll ever know what happened, at least not from him.

"Wow," exclaimed Phil, "that's different."

"Why?" asked Nina, ready to hold him to account.

"Well," he said, "I wrote from the same perspective only mine's totally different."

He says she was beautiful and she worked hard. It's too bad she died. A love like that doesn't come along very often. He says living with her was like a dream. He says even his cows gave better milk when she milked them. He says he doesn't know what to do with all the love that's left in his heart. It's such a pity when good people die young.

"But that's a lie," said Nina, shocked.

"So? The villagers don't know. And besides, what difference does it make? As far as the guy's concerned it's like a death," said Phil. "She's gone, that's what matters."

"But what if she came back? Would he tell them she'd been resurrected?" asked Nina.

"She'll never come back. She drew the line. He crossed it. She left. End of story."

"But, Phil, how's he going to heal if he has to keep lying?" persisted Nina.

"You're a fine one to talk," said Phil disgustedly. "Look at all the..." he stopped, aware of the warning looks the group was giving him.

"Look at all the what?" challenged Nina.

Phil smiled wryly and took a deep breath. "Okay, you asked, I'll tell you. Look at the story you wrote. The guy doesn't talk to his community. Doesn't bring his wife with him to town. Doesn't connect his life with the people who've probably known him since he was born. Your story is you. Here we are, offering to help, and you keep saying you don't need help when that's a bunch of crap. Did you ever stop to think that allowing us to help you would make us feel better? It's like you pride yourself on always being the one to give and that means we always have to take.

What kind of relationship is that? I offered to drive you to your doctor and you said you didn't need help and then you told Diana you had to pull over and wait till a dizzy spell passed. You're more macho than most guys I know."

Nina looked as if she'd been punched in the stomach. Jenny said she had to go to the bathroom. Carol rearranged the cake on the plate. David stared out the window. The silence stretched into an abyss. Embarrassed Phil stood up, mumbling an apology.

When Nina spoke, her voice was soft, almost a whisper. "Having a chronic illness means it's never going away. I'm afraid if I ask for help, you'll get tired of dealing with me and leave. I couldn't bear that. Sometimes I think my fear of being a burden is worse than the illness." She stood up, looking like she was ready to cry.

Phil said, "I shouldn't have come at you like I did."

"Maybe it's time for my story," said Jenny. "I wrote from the point of view of a person in her village after she returned.

We raised her to be clear. There is right and wrong, good and bad. Our children learn the difference at an early age. A promise is a promise. Once it is broken, there can be no trust. Our ways work well here but perhaps in other places there are different ways. We had no time to think of this. She left and stayed for many years. We saw that she was happy and our hearts filled with joy. Now she is home. She says nothing. She does her work and carries on. We watch and want to weep for she is merely a shadow of the woman who climbed down the ladder and milked the cows. We tried to warn her but she would not listen. Her heart overflowed with love. Then, when she saw him look into her basket she knew no other way. He broke his promise and her heart. There is no going back. Not for her. Not for him. Would that we could mend their hearts but we have no cure for intransigence. It is our way but it did not serve her well.

Nina nodded. "It's the same theme again. There's no one way that works for everyone."

"What amazes me," said Phil, "is how our stories reflect who we are even though, I, at least, didn't think about it when I was writing. There just wasn't time."

"I agree," said Carol. "Who would have thought a little story could have such power."

The group continued to meet for three more sessions. At the end of what was supposed to be their last session, Nina asked Phil if he could drive her to her doctor's appointment. He said yes. While driving, they decided to ask if the group was willing to meet once a month on a regular basis. They were.

Changes in Meaning over Time
The meaning of a story can change as we deal with new life experience, changing information about our lives, or challenges to our perception of self. To illustrate how this can happen, let us look at Nina's response over a period of three months to a Native American story, **"How People Came to the Land that was Home."**

The People were bumping around in the dark and the cold. Someone asked, "Is this all there is? Will there never be anything more?" No one could answer for it was the only world they had ever known.

They continued to live in their cold dark world until one day, a strange creature appeared. They asked it, "Is this the only world there is?"

The strange animal answered, "I do not know, but sometimes, I go to a place that feels different."

"How is it different?" someone asked.

"I cannot tell you for I am blind. All I can tell you is that it feels different."

One brave person asked, "Will you take us to the place that feels different?"

"Yes," answered the creature whose name was Mole. "I can, but you must know that when I travel, I dig out the earth in front of me and place it behind me. If you come with me you will never be able to return to where you came from."

The People talked and argued among themselves. Some were frightened to leave the only place they had ever known, but others were willing to try anything to live a better life. And so it was. The People followed behind Mole as he burrowed his way to the place that felt different, digging the earth in front of him, passing the earth back to the people who put it behind them.

It was a long difficult journey. People complained. They were tired and cold. It was still dark. Some longed to be where they had been for at least there they could stand up. Then, without warning, Mole said, "This is the place that feels different. This is where I must leave you. Goodbye," he said and left.

No one knew what to do. Although it was dark, it did feel different; it was not as cold. People began to walk around. A few ventured into a place that hurt their eyes so badly they retreated into the dark, crying and moaning in pain. Now there were many who wished they had never left the place they knew, where they had lived for so long.

DANCING WITH WONDER * 174

In the dark, nursing their eyes, the People heard a kind voice speak to them. "Hush my children, do not cry. Listen to me."

"Who are you?" they asked.

"I am your Grandmother Spider. I am here to help you. If you do as I tell you, all will be well. Your eyes hurt because they are not used to light. The sun is very bright. You must look slowly, to give your eyes time to learn to see light. When you walk outside, keep your fingers closed in front of your closed eyes. Slowly, open your fingers but keep your eyes closed. Take a few breaths before you open your eyes. Even then, do not look up at the sun for it will hurt your eyes. Do as I say. Your eyes will thank you."

People followed Grandmother Spider's advice and it was as she promised. Their eyes learned to see light. But, all too soon, the light began to disappear. Not knowing what else to do, the People huddled together in the dark, wondering what was going to happen, waiting, too frightened to leave.

Once again Grandmother Spider spoke to them. "Hush my children, do not cry. All shall be well if you listen to me. The light will return. When it does, you will see four mountains. To the north is White Mountain. Do not go there for you will find only ice and snow. You will freeze to death. To the east is Red Mountain. Do not go there for you will encounter fierce creatures who will attack you. You will bleed to death. To the west is Black Mountain. Do not go there for your crops will not grow. You will starve to death. To the south is Green Mountain. It is the furthest and the way is uncertain, but if you keep your eyes open you will know how to travel. And, when you see a creature who reminds you of Mole but is not Mole,, and a creature who reminds you of Grandmother Spider but is not Grandmother Spider, you will know you have arrived at the place that is home."

And so, just as Grandmother foretold, the light did return.

Some of the People looked at White Mountain and said, "We are not afraid of cold and White Mountain is not far. We can manage. Stay here. We will tell you what we find." But they never returned.

Soon, a few of the People became restless and said, "Black Mountain is quite close. We know how to live in darkness. Stay here. We will tell you what we find when we return." But they too did not come back.

"We are not afraid of fierce creatures," said all but two of the People who remained. "Why walk a long distance when there is Red Mountain, a place that we can clearly see. We will fight whoever attacks us and win. Stay here. We will tell you what we find when we return." None of them were ever seen again.

Only one man and one woman were left. They looked at each other. Even in the bright sun, they could barely see Green Mountain. The woman said, "I think Grandmother Spider spoke the truth. We must walk to Green Mountain if we wish to survive." The man agreed and they began walking toward the south, toward Green Mountain which they could barely see.

It was a long journey. Walking in the hot sun was not easy. Only the memory of those who had not returned kept them from giving up. The man and woman continued walking toward the mountain that seemed to keep its distance despite their fatigue and discouragement for it was all they knew to do.

One morning, when they stopped to rest, the woman saw a strange creature passing by her. Cautiously, she moved closer to it. The man said, "Be careful, it might be dangerous." The woman kept looking.

The man joined her and they crept near enough to see the markings on the creature's back. "Look, said the woman," it reminds me of Grandmother Spider."

When the creature heard the woman's words, it pulled in

its head. "Oh," said the man, "it cannot see where it is going. It reminds me of Mole."

The man and the woman looked at each other. They remembered the words of Grandmother Spider. They had arrived at Green Mountain. They had come to the place that was home.

The first time the group worked with the story was shortly after Nina started treatment. To begin the session, Phil told the story and then everyone made an image of a telling moment, a place in the story that sticks in our memory, a moment that can be funny, poignant, cruel, irritating, arouse anger--whatever the emotion--as long as it is memorable. For Nina, the moment occurred when the People ask, "Is this all there is? Will there never be anything more?" Her image was a circle of blackness with black spikes radiating outward into zigzag shapes. She titled her image: This is all there is. The task was to write the story of the title. She wrote:

In the blackness people could conceal their feelings. They could hide their tears. The dark was a comforting blanket, giving each person a sense of space and privacy where there was none. Nobody saw, and if you were quiet, nobody heard. This suited her. She didn't want to talk. She didn't want to explain the tears that sometimes dribbled down her face without permission. She wanted the others to think of her as solid and predictable and invisible.

When Nina shared her image and read what she had written she glared at her friends, as if to prevent any commentary. Even Jenny, the peacemaker in the group was momentarily stunned by the bleakness of Nina's expression.

Given her obvious unwillingness to explain or discuss her story, the group left it alone.

Two months later, the group decided to revisit the story. This time Nina chose the moment when Mole says: "I can take you to a place that *feels* different." Her image was similar, a black circle radiating black spikes but this time, the zigzags had tiny bits of brown and green 'smushed' into the black. Her words were: It can't be seen, only felt. Her writing reflected the shift in her image:

> *He said it was a place that felt different. They asked, "How is it different?"*
>
> *"It's just different, that's all I can say. When you can't see you can only feel. It's hard to explain a feeling. Maybe it can't be done. So, come or don't. It's up to you. I can only promise it's a place that feels different."*
>
> *"I'll come," she said. "Any place you go has to be better than this." Yet even as she spoke so bravely, she wondered what she would be giving up. If there was one thing she knew, it was that nothing was ever gained without some kind of loss.*

Nina was willing to compare the two stories, acknowledging that she chose a different place in the story without thinking. She decided it would be a good idea to "check in with the story" in a few months. About three months later, while waiting for a check up, she told herself the story as a way of passing the time. Although she had no paints or clay, she made a mental image of her current telling moment. This time it occurred when the people first saw the light and recoiled in pain. She wrote:

"We can't go back. We can't go forward. Where are we? What have we done?" People glared at her. "It's your fault. You were the one who said any place would be better than where we were. You were wrong. Now what?"

She had said this. She couldn't deny it. So, summoning up a belief she didn't really believe, she told them, "Mole said this place was different. We don't know exactly how it's different. Maybe there is something more and we just don't know what it is."

She could feel them pressing toward her, their anger and frustration like a wall, pushing her backwards into the darkness. She had no strength to move them but she pushed back anyway, hoping something would save her, would save them. It was better than lying down and letting them smother her.

Nina could definitely relate to the feeling of being caught between the past and an unknown future, not sure there would even be a future. The medicine kept her illness in check but she felt sick all the time. She often wondered if the trade-off was worth it. About a week later, feeling exhausted and depressed, she found herself thinking about the story. Once again, her telling moment had changed. A new story emerged. Grandmother Spider's words were soothing.

"Hush child. Be comforted. Listen to me and all shall be well. Your eyes hurt because you looked too soon, without proper preparation. Change cannot be rushed or controlled. It happens in its own way. Take your time. Do not move so quickly. You will crush your spirit. Be gentle with your curiosity and your fear. Know that I am here to help you in your hour of need. Always."

The story began to feel like an old friend, ready to help with what she needed most although she could never predict how it would resonate at any given moment. Only after her medical treatment was successful in stabilizing her illness, and the dosage considerably reduced, did the end of the story became her telling moment.

My inner and outer selves have walked to this place of new beginnings. Nothing is guaranteed, yet the mountain is green and the sun is shining. Grandmother Spider's words have proven to be a trustworthy guide. What she promised has come true. Perhaps if I am quiet and centered, she will keep speaking and I will keep hearing what she says. It is only her presence that keeps me from losing my way.

Making images and telling and writing stories over a period of time enables participants to explore and confront old views and assumptions. The process is gentle because the first forays into new ways of thinking and being take place through character interaction and change. It is not until people are ready to acknowledge an issue that they are able to become aware of new choices as characters. Even when Nina noticed that she repeatedly created characters who were unable to ask for help or talk openly and honestly about what was going on in their lives, change didn't happen immediately. Only after creating several characters who were able to ask for help was she able to make new life decisions and to begin changing longstanding behavior patterns.

The storymaking process requires spontaneous response to a specific task. Although people may ask questions that seem to be clarifying the direction, what they are usually asking is: "Is this right?" The tasks are designed to provide participants with a way into a story that is theirs. Too much specificity will color group members' responses and make it more difficult for them to be authentic. Participants need to respond however they respond, with no time to plan and therefore, no worry about being right or control over how they respond. This results in uncensored images and stories with characters, situations, and events that provide group members with nonjudgmental ways to look at what has been created over time as patterns emerge and clarify. Even then, when changes are integrated internally, the first evidence of a new point of view is the transformation in habitual character response. One of the interesting aspects of storymaking is that trying to address an issue directly is usually of no avail. It's as if the psyche has its own agenda and schedule. It decides what and when and how to deal with issues. Perhaps the idea of the wisdom of the psyche, that whatever is said or done in an unforced situation is appropriate, should also include the idea that whatever issue spontaneously emerges is appropriate for the person, group and circumstance.

The story journeys in this section have been included to show how storymaking affected a variety of participants. Although no one reacts in exactly the same way, most people found the storymaking process to be revealing in ways they could not have predicted. At the very least, people were astonished at the ease with which they wrote stories. Sometimes there was new knowledge that took a while to be felt, yet after the sessions had finished, when people reported back, most everyone attributed at least part of the changes to the imagemaking and storymaking, as well as sharing ideas and feelings about what the sessions had evoked.

Hearing and working with stories from around the world opens us up to cultural practices and ways of being that are both similar and different from our experience. They raise questions we might not think to ask. For example, in the San story, "The Basket," the woman tells the man he must promise not to look in her basket, yet when he breaks his vow and looks inside, he sees nothing. Is this because she is from another culture and there is no bridge between their differences? Are there ways to explore diversity without judgment? Without blame? Without the loss of love?

Many of the stories participants tell deal with sadness, unhappiness, disappointment, and loss. Perhaps these are the stories we need to tell, transforming the energy of despair and anger into something more hopeful. I have noticed that even when stories deal with painful experience, after writing and sharing their stories, people feel better. Perhaps storymaking affects the production of neuro-chemicals in the brain so that after making an image or story, we transform the stress-produced chemicals into those that create feelings of well-being.

The more we paint, sculpt, make and share stories, the easier it seems to be to access issues, ideas, feelings, and experiences that have been buried in time and memory. Equally important, the process is fun, often accompanied by laughter, occasionally tears. Groups that have worked together report feeling a sense of closeness and connection that has, at times, lasted for years. Foibles, folly, wisdom--

whatever it is that makes us human--all become evident as we continue to explore who we are and what makes us unique. Yet, as human beings, we have more in common than we do in what divides us. Focusing on issues we all face helps to create community, thus making it easier to resolve differences.

5

CREATING A STORY JOURNEY

We today are convinced that we know. We
are a generation of know-alls. But few of us
have the life-giving feeling of being known...
The supreme expression of the spirit of the
San people was in their stories. They were
wonderful storytellers. The story was their
most sacred possession. These people know
what we do not: that without a story you
have not got a nation, or a culture, or a
civilization. Without a story of your own to
live you haven't got a life of your own.
Patterns of Renewal by Laurens Van der Post

ENTERING INTO A story is like opening the door to a place
we've never been, no matter how familiar we may be with
the story. All that is required for this journey is the
willingness to explore with "beginner's mind," a mind open
to possibility, free of expectations, willing to go where the
story takes us.

The tasks designed to create the story journey are
simple—so simple that people often ask, "Do you mean
this? Or that?" But, if the task is to paint an image, anything
that anyone paints is what is called for. If the task is to
sculpt, whatever is sculpted is the meaningful response.
Sounds straightforward? It is exactly that. So, why the
questions? In school, too often, what the teacher or the test
demands is the "one right answer." We become used to the
idea that for every question or task there is one correct

response. People, wanting to do their best, naturally, want to have as much information as they think they need, clues as to what constitutes right or best or correct. Changing this almost knee-jerk reaction is not easy. We are beset by suspicion, worry, anxiety, distrust—all products of schooling that did/does not value our imagination and creativity. As adults, we may find it difficult to switch gears, but switch gears we must if we want to embark on an authentic journey into the story and the richness of our inner world of possibilities.

In storymaking activities, as long as the directions are followed, for example: paint an image of "crisis" on the right side of the paper, sculpt an image of "despair," or, write five words that come to mind, all responses are correct, right, best, desirable...in other words, perfect. Where we *are,* is where we *start,* and where we start is the level at which we choose to work. What we need is the confidence to trust ourselves, our responses, and the group with whom we are working.

Creating a Storymaking Community

Regaining access to our stories is one way of reclaiming our lives. Making and telling stories connects disparate pieces of our selves into a coherent whole that makes it possible for us to know not only more about who we are, but also our companions and community. Making and telling stories is our natural birthright, part of what makes us human, yet they are easily lost in a culture that tends to value product over process—that which can be sold over the ability to make. The urge to tell a story is fueled by our wanting to convey something we have noticed, felt, sensed or experienced. Even if the story is written rather than told, the impulse is the same although the sense of immediacy may be different. Telling requires a listener and this can make us feel uncomfortably vulnerable if we are worried about keeping our audience interested. Therefore, especially in the beginning, it is important to tell stories to caring listeners, people who want to hear what we have to say, who understand that telling stories, whether they are "real" or "created" opens us up to being known, perhaps in ways we cannot predict.

It is possible to create a story journey by one's self, with a partner, or in a group. Small groups facilitate the most growth but if you don't have a partner or friends with whom to work, it's helpful to choose a person with whom you can share your stories. Regardless of the situation, it is *imperative* that the stories be respected and told without fear of criticism or judgment. If we are to let our imaginations run free, we need to feel safe to express ideas, feelings, attitudes, or requests for help without denigration or mocking. Because it is easy to forget our initial efforts, I suggest that all images and stories be collected, dated, labeled and kept in a loose-leaf binder. This creates a record of progress and allows us to reread and reconsider possible meaning and symbolic value at various times, long after the storymaking session has ended.

Beginning
Beginnings are difficult. There are so many unknowns. Taking the first step is an act of faith, a step whereby we acknowledge that we have what we need to survive and succeed. To begin a storymaking session we can start with a

story, a feeling, an experience, a sense that something inside needs to come out, even an intuition that cannot be verbalized. What remains common to each choice is the speed with which imagemaking and storymaking is done (in a minute or less). This allows participants to reconnect with first thoughts and makes self-censorship more difficult. All stories, whether written from prompts or as popping-out stories are most revealing when written in one sitting. When sharing images or stories, people may say what they see, think, hear, or feel, but it must always be from the point of view of "I," or "From my perspective," or "From where I sit it looks like..." or "It reminds me of..." Using "I" creates a space for each person to talk about personal experience without having to judge, be judged, or comment on what others have said.

Creating a Structure

As with any journey, we might not know all the in between points, but where and how we depart determines in some measure where and how we arrive. The thread that holds the storymaking journey together is what we designate as our *focus*. This may be as general as creating a story within the story or discovering characters that could be in the story. When starting with a feeling or idea we wish to explore, the focus for the session might be: exploring fear, working with wonder, moving into courage, creating community... Each selected activity is then designed to help participants learn, achieve clarity, become more articulate—to enter into and safely return from the unknown. Designing a structure is complicated. Participants need to know what to do (description) but not how to do it (prescription). For example, the group might decide that the first activity will be to hear a story, the second to paint an image of *a* telling moment. If people are asked to paint an image of *the* telling moment, instead of *a* telling moment, participants are liable to worry about choosing the most important moment and then defending whose moment is most telling. Similarly, if people are asked to sculpt, they should not be told *which* character to sculpt or *what* the character is thinking, feeling, or saying. I usually ask people to sculpt a character that is or could be in the story. This provides the necessary starting point but is not prescriptive.

Since clay is a three-dimensional material, I find that one effective task is to ask people to sculpt two ideas/characters/situations in relationship at a critical point in the story. This adds urgency and encourages people to find the moment that is for them, the *essence* of the story

Beginning with at least one *imagemaking activity* in a session helps to concretize nonverbal reaction. Writing words that come to mind after making the image, whether in paint or clay, helps connect nonverbal knowing with verbal expression. Including all images and stories in a storymaking journal provides a potent record of one's inner life experience. Some participants photograph their clay sculptures so they have a record of these images as well their paintings

When people are *writing stories* they may not have enough time to complete the story in the session yet it is important to find a satisfactory place to stop, a place that allows the writer to feel that for the moment, all is well. Using the metaphor of a journey, there are three possibilities. The first, *resting place*, is analogous to stopping for water and a brief rest before continuing. The second, *stopping place*, is as if we stop for the night. The third, *ending place*, is the arrival, the end of this particular journey. Each choice implies a point while traveling; there may be many resting and stopping places before the sojourner arrives at the final destination. Those who have experience with music might use the idea of ending a phrase, a movement or the whole piece as their guide. In every instance, writers need to feel they have done what they can for the moment and are able to take a breath and rest before continuing.

Ending each session with a period of *reflection* allows participants time to put what has happened in perspective. Sometimes, people sit quietly, thinking, painting or writing about what has been done. Other times, participants share ideas and feelings about their experience. Even if little is said, allowing time to reflect enables people to center themselves before leaving the group. If you are working by yourself, take at least a minute to process your experience before doing something else. Whether you are working by yourself or with a group, keeping a *storymaking journal* enables you to reflect on what you have done, providing a record of where you have been and how you feel about your process at the moment.

Starting with a Story

Although any story can be used, traditional stories work best because they have no authorial voice or point of view. Myths, tales, and legends have been told and retold across cultures, generations, and time, from a communal rather than personal voice. Story collections can be found in bookstores and libraries. If you find multiple retellings, choose the most essential version, the tale told with the least amount of added material. Reading several versions of the same story makes clear what is essential and what has been added from the imagination of the person retelling the story. Examining a variety of collections of stories from around the world, retold by many people, helps develop an appreciation for the power of myth, fairy tale, and legend. Noticing the patterns or themes that most easily attract us gives us clues as to issues we might want to begin exploring.

In the beginning, it is useful to work with short stories that have few characters and clear and positively resolved endings. The story acts as the container for the session so it helps to use one that provides a compelling roadmap for personal discovery and enjoyment. The container is important because it acts as a kind of unconscious safety net. When the story ends well, we are comforted that no matter what troubles we experience in the course of a session, our story will also end well. Select stories for which you feel a resonance or affinity. Stories that end with loss, devastation, or are unresolved can also be used but these are more complex and are best used after reading and retelling many stories, by those who have experienced a variety of imagemaking and storymaking sessions, who understand how to structure sessions so that all participants can be safely guided toward a healthy outcome. Some good beginning choices in this book are: "Hummingbird and Panther," (p. 97) "Li Chi, the Serpent Slayer," (p. 49) "How People Came to the Land that was Home,"(p. 173) and "How Light Came to the People." (p. 62).

Starting with an Image, Feeling, or Intuition

Although it may be difficult to verbalize the image in our mind's eye, a feeling or an intuition, it is still important to structure the session. The focus can be general—exploring intuition, entering into the image in our mind's eye, or concretizing the feeling we are experiencing, naming it as best we can. Once we have selected our focus, the way of working is the same as beginning with a story.

Storymaking sessions that begin with an image, feeling or intuition are more complex because everyone shares a different stimulus, yet a common session is still possible by structuring the session more generally. For example, participants might paint an image of a feeling, title the image, and write down words that come to mind. Even though the beginning point of each participant's image may be different, the shared images and words can be explored with a partner or the group. Let us say that Jane paints an image of "courage," titles her image, "Can I?" and writes the words: fear, hope, determination. Joe paints an image of "fear", titles his image, "Too much," and writes the words: shame, anxiety, bad. In this example, Jane, Joe or other participants could quickly point out that fear is a factor in both images. As Jane and Joe share their images, each might decide both are dealing with elements of fear and courage. The subsequent activities might focus on what makes us afraid, what gives us courage, and how we move back and forth between the two.

Perhaps the next task would be to sculpt an image of the feeling in relationship to what gives it power. Jane might sculpt an image of a figure emerging from clump of clay. She might say that what gives her courage is the support she gets—from family, friends, her work or even the environment. Joe might sculpt an image of a figure hiding from a large object. What feeds his fear, he might say, is the feeling that he isn't strong enough or smart enough or safe enough to confront the large object.

One suggestion for the next task might be to write the story of the sculpture. Let us suppose that Jane's story ends on a positive note, with Jane feeling good about being courageous. Joe's story, however, ends with him trying to hide from the object, fearing that if he becomes visible he will be squashed, annihilated or in some way greatly incapacitated. This is not a good place to end a session because Joe, in all likelihood, will leave feeling worse than when he began. However, one cannot change feelings through force or command. It might be helpful to write a story or monologue from the point of view of the object. For example, suppose the object Joe is hiding from is a huge dog. Writing a story from the point of view of the dog might give Joe some ideas as to how to deal with his fears. Another possibility would be for Joe to write the dog a letter describing his fear, his need to stop being afraid, and his wish to have suggestions from the dog as to how this might happen. If he is working with a group, perhaps the others can respond to Joe's letter as the dog. When this happens, he is likely to get a variety of responses ranging from the earnest to the comic, yet each one, in its own way, will likely prove helpful. If, despite everything, Joe's issue is unresolved or he is still feeling bad, participants can paint a blessing on a small piece of paper (no larger than 4"x 4") and write a few words of encouragement. Joe receives the blessings and shares them with the group. Even though the situation remains unchanged, it's likely that Joe will feel better knowing he has the support of the group. When people experience the sense that a group of people care about you no matter what you are feeling, facing, or doing, it is a powerful source of healing and emotional support. If Joe is working by himself, he can still paint himself a blessing and tap into the often-unused inner resources that all of us possess.

Structuring a Session

Storymaking works best and is most effective for participants if the group works with a predetermined structure. For the first session, group members can bring stories they'd like to share, decide how they want to proceed, and end with a reflection. Thereafter, one member can be designated to design the next session but it is always possible for the group to do this in community.

Framing the Session

For those with little or no experience in storymaking, starting with a traditional story means that everyone has a common frame of reference, although each person hears it according to his/her history, experience, mood, and circumstance. The story may be the only thing the group shares in common and therefore creates a communal experience to which each member of the group can relate and return. People can take turns telling the story to begin each session. Telling is more immediate than reading and allows the teller to make the story his/her own. If you are working by yourself, you can still tell yourself the story out loud. Noticing what is added or left out as you tell the story can be an important source of information as to what's going on inside you. People with little or no storytelling experience often have fears about not being good enough storytellers. It helps to think of telling as simply one way to share a story you love with people you care about. Obviously, it's not a good idea to tell a story you don't like or even one you feel neutral about. Find a story that moves you and think of your storytelling as a gift to people who value what you have to give. If you make a mistake, don't worry. Just continue. I remember one of the first times I led a storymaking session. I was so nervous I could hardly breathe. As I was telling the story, from China, I realized I was telling it with a Yiddish accent. Afterward, I apologized. One of the participants, an old gnarled woman with an Irish accent said, "Don't worry darling, to us, a story is a story."

Designing Imagemaking-paints

I use finger-paints because they discourage precision and diminish feelings of inability but any water-based paint thick enough to spread with fingers will do. If people don't like to get their fingers dirty or find the texture of finger-paint disagreeable, the use of surgical gloves alleviates discomfort. Using fingers to smear paint on paper obviates the sense of making "a pretty picture" or "creating a work of art" that people tend to have when using more precise implements such as a brush, magic marker, or crayons which involve precise lines. Most people find these materials less encouraging of free expression than painting with fingers although using the non-dominant hand mitigates some of the precision. What matters is the imagemaking. People need to use what they find most comfortable or convenient. The two aspects of imagemaking that do not change are the speed with which it is done and the variety of colors available. There must be black and brown as well as bright colors to express the full range of human emotion..

Attitude matters. Marianne, a student in one of my classes complained, "We've finger-painted a bunch of times and it's getting boring."

"What do you bring to your painting," I asked her. She looked puzzled so I rephrased the question. "What do you want to learn from it?"

She didn't have an answer but one of her classmates, Joseph said, "The first few times we painted, all I could think was, 'cool,' but then I began to notice I hardly used color. The first pot of paint I used up was black while some people never touched theirs. I even thought about trading my yellow or red for someone's black. As I was riding my bike home from class last week, I kept thinking about all the black. 'I'm not depressed,' I told myself, so why all the black?" He sighed. "It took a while to figure it out, but the black paint was telling me something I didn't want to admit to myself. As soon as I did, I felt better even though nothing had changed. Well, something had, me."

Marianne challenged Joseph, "What do you bring to your painting?"

"I'm not sure I can put it into words. It has to do with trusting my fingers. I know that sounds weird, but when I think about what I want to paint before I do it, what comes out feels phony. I'm used to thinking about everything before I do it so this is hard for me, but I think it's good to do something quickly, in response to hearing or seeing or feeling something, without planning. It makes me feel like there's more to me than I can verbalize."

Joseph asked Marianne, "What makes it boring for you?"

She shrugged. "There's no surprise anymore." She shrugged again. "I don't really think we can learn anything about ourselves from smearing paint on paper. Mine just look like the messes of a two-year old."

"Have you taken another look at the images you've been making?" asked Carol. Marianne shook her head. "Well, I have to admit I also thought finger-painting was silly, but the other night I was trying to figure out what our next assignment was and I started to look through the images in my journal. Joseph used mostly black but all my images had red smeared over them. When I read the words I had written, I was shocked. All of them related to illness. I didn't know I was so worried about my kid sister. She's in the hospital with leukemia. I still don't understand how I could be so upset about something and not consciously realize it."

Marianne's complaint proved to be a catalyst. Students talked about their feelings, for and against finger-painting, without feeling pressured or defensive. Observing images and words over time provides an unexpected and powerful way of discovering what's going on in our inner lives.

Designing Imagemaking-clay

The best kind of clay to use is non-hardening because it doesn't need to be kept wet and stays soft at room temperature. Some brands of clay can be baked in the oven and this is important if people want to keep what they have sculpted.

The three-dimensional medium of clay is best used to explore relationships, change, and connection. For example, when working with "Li Chi the Serpent Slayer," (p. 49) I asked a group to sculpt an image of a character that is or could be in the story, in relationship to a character, place, or thing, at a particular point in the story. Two people in the group sculpted an image of Li Chi talking with the Magistrate. The first sculpture showed the Magistrate as much taller than Li Chi, taking up a lot of space, crowding out Li Chi who is in a subservient position, looking up in awe at him. Annie talked about her image. "I identify with Li Chi. She's a person with no power. By volunteering, she saves the Magistrate the difficult task of finding another young girl to be sacrificed to the serpent. She can only hope he will keep his promise that her parents will be taken care of in their old age. I think she feels she has so little choice that even this choice is better than nothing."

Jessica's sculpture of the same moment was strikingly different. Her Li Chi and Magistrate are the same size. Their eyes meet. Li Chi is standing very straight, leaning toward the Magistrate who is leaning away from her. "I think Li Chi has a lot of power and she' s using it to get what she wants--care for her parents in their old age. Unlike the nine girls who were previously sacrificed, she has a plan and she asks for and receives what she needs and wants. She feels pretty confident she will slay the serpent and return home alive."

Phil asked, "We all heard the story and yet the two of you see Li Chi so differently. How does this happen?"

Annie and Jessica shrugged. Neither of them wanted to explain what might lie behind their choices. Instead of pushing the issue, the group questioned each Li Chi, in role, switching roles as the need arose. Phil asked the first question. "As the Magistrate, I want to ask you (Annie) what made you volunteer? You have five sisters, two of whom are older than you. Isn't taking care of your parents the oldest child's responsibility?"

Annie sighed, entering into her role as Li Chi. "My sister is going to be married next week. She will leave our home and go to live with her husband who lives many hours from here. She cannot take care of them. My next oldest sister is fifteen, too old to volunteer. My younger sisters are too young. I am the only one who can do this."

Melissa spoke to Jessica, in role as Li Chi's mother, "I forbid you to take this dangerous journey. Your father and I have always managed. We will do so until the end of our days. What will our ancestors say to us when we meet them if we permit you to undertake this perilous journey? You must not go."

Jessica, as Li Chi, spoke softly. "I honor you in all ways, Mother, but you know that when we sisters marry, we must go to the homes of our husbands. We will not be able to help you when you are old or ill. I think the ancestors will honor my action, knowing there were no male children to take care of you when you grew old." She stood up. "Mother, I have made a good plan. I believe I will return safely. If I do, you will have riches enough to keep you in comfort until the end of your days for there is a reward for the one who slays the serpent. If I do not return, the Magistrate has promised to protect and care for you and father for as long as you live. Please, give me your blessing; it will give me strength and courage."

After each group member had a chance to speak and question the two as Li Chi, the group reflected on the issues that were raised and the observations they had made. Annie summed up the group's feelings. "Working in role gives me a chance to explore ideas and emotions without being defensive or feeling I have to attack to protect myself. I also like it that Jessica had such a different take on Li Chi. At first I was astonished but then it gave me a lot to think about."

Designing Activities

Each session tends to work best if there are a variety of nonverbal and verbal activities that flow outward (painting or sculpting an image) and inward (writing words that come to mind, a monologue or a story). Successful spontaneous story writing (ideas pour forth without being forced) needs to be nourished, especially for those just beginning the storymaking process.

Start with clear prompts and limit the scope of the task, creating a framework that makes it easier for beginners to respond spontaneously. For example, it may be hard for some to write a story from the prompt, "Write a story," but they may find it easier to respond to the prompt, "Li Chi tells her friend what happened after she returned to the village with the bones of the sacrificed maidens. Write the story Li Chi tells her friend."

Titling an image often acts as a beacon, pointing the storymaker in the direction of the story. Sometimes, the original title is too broad to be of use. In this case, participants can explore titles within a title until one strikes a chord with the writer. If the writer is stuck, asking the group for suggestions is often useful.

Writing a monologue at the moment of the sculpture provides clues as to what motivates the character's choice and, at times, clarifies internal issues or questions generated by the differences in sculptures of similar moments. However, when participants share their monologues it is best if they speak without reference to the written material. Speaking tends to be more emotional, immediate, and less reflective than writing, therefore, what emerges from speaking extemporaneously often differs significantly from the written version. However, both versions are valuable, providing information as to how participants view their character at a given moment at a time of crisis.

For example, when Sheila wrote her monologue in role as a prisoner in a concentration camp, she focused on her surroundings, the dirt, the smells, the cold, and her feelings about other prisoners, but when she spoke, all she could talk about was her thirst. When the class asked her to explain why the two versions were so different she said, "When I was writing the monologue I was thinking about where I was and what it was like but when I started to speak, all I could think about was my thirst. It was overpowering, even more terrible than my hunger."

Creating dialogue between two sculptures or characters or between one character and his/her alter ego deepens and enhances participants' understanding of what a character might be thinking and feeling at a given moment. Drama focuses on action and is therefore a useful counterpart to description and exposition.

Choosing a telling moment, making an image and then telling the story located in the telling moment, either in first or third person often explicates the power of the story in unexpected ways. When people write in third person and feel they have little to say, switching to first person and focusing on feelings, fears, hopes, and the five senses often helps the person discover the richness of the story.

Asking questions that cannot be answered with a yes or no, that must be answered quickly--who, what, when, where, why, helps to form the arc of the story.

Finding the story within the story helps develop imagination and gives people a place and information that makes starting easier. For example, develop an incident that happened to Little Red Riding Hood after she says goodbye to her mother and before she first meets the wolf.

Creating a story that leads to the story being worked with gives people a way to end their story, making it easier for some people to begin. For example, tell the story of the interaction between the Magistrate and the serpent before the beginning of "Li Chi the Serpent Slayer."

Creating a story that begins after the story ends enables people to know most or all of their characters thus making it easier to begin. For example, tell the story of what happens to Li Chi after she slays the serpent and returns to her village with the bones of the sacrificed maidens.

Sharing the Work

All sharing of work, ideas, and reflection needs to be voluntary. Sometimes shy or frightened participants have to learn they can trust the encouragement and support of their group and this can happen only if they have positive experiences. Asking for trust or telling people they can trust the group is usually ineffective. Joe was so anxious about having to show his image, he could barely speak. "This is my image of courage. My words are: action, risk, lonely." His face was bright red when he put down his image. People in the group began by asking him if it was all right if they asked him questions. He nodded but his expression was one of fear.

Charlie began. "I notice you use a lot of red and black but way out in the upper right hand corner is a bit of yellow. Could you tell us about that?"

Joe shrugged. "The red and black are fear, the yellow is courage." He looked at his image and seemed about to say something, then stopped and looked down at his shoes.

Jerry showed his image, surprisingly like Joe's. His blobs of red and black covered most of the paper except for a small circle of yellow in the lower left hand corner. His words were: powerful, silent, risk, bravery, lonely. Joe looked surprised and then replied defensively, "I didn't copy him." Sitting opposite one another in the circle made this obviously impossible and the group noticed his defensive response.

"Why would you think we would accuse you of copying?" asked Jerry. "What I find interesting is how similar our images and words are. I don't know what you were thinking but mine is from when I was in the army. I saw how hard it was to do the right thing sometimes. Were you in the service?" he asked Joe.

Joe nodded. "Yeah, I was but..."

Jerry asked, "Want to go out for a beer afterward?"

Joe nodded.

No more was said about their images. When people were asked to select a piece of their image and write the story that emerged, Joe wrote about how a soldier ran into a burning building to save an 'enemy' child in spite of his commanding officer's order to the contrary. He surprised himself by volunteering to read it.

Reflection

At the end of each session, it is important to leave time for participants to reflect on what has been said, done, thought, and/or felt. At times, there will be a period of silence before someone speaks. Occasionally, no one will speak, but providing time at the end for people to contemplate deepens the experience whether or not there is commentary. It is also helpful, especially when no one is speaking, if people write or paint their response to the session. Participants usually find it useful to create workshop journals in which they comment on what they have thought, felt and done, including their dated images and stories in the order in which they have been made and written.

One way to encourage people to talk about what the session has evoked in them is to ask if there is unfinished 'business.' This might happen if someone remembers an upsetting incident, recognizes an issue or experience that was previously denied, or has trouble with a task and feels bad about him/herself. Although there are many ways to deal with these situations, I recommend participants find ways to support the person without intruding, analyzing, interpreting, or pronouncing judgment. Some groups have developed ending rituals where they hold hands in a circle, standing silently for about a minute. Others go around the circle giving each person an opportunity to talk about how they feel. In this group, if someone is upset, he/she might say, "I feel unsettled." As a response, the group might paint or write on small pieces of paper, blessings, words of support, or helpful suggestions or advice from characters in the story used during that session. In another group, people decided to end their session with a breathing-meditation practice that helped to center the participants.

> NOTE: If you are working by yourself, read your writing or speak about what you are feeling out loud. Even though you are alone, speaking is a different experience than thinking. When I have written a play, I write and read what I have written silently. Then I read what I have written out loud and I hear the material, its nuances and rhythms in ways not possible when reading silently. Even if you work alone, try to find a friend with whom you can share your work.

6
SAMPLE STRUCTURES

There was once a poor tailor. Though he had made coats for many people, he had never made one for himself as much as he wanted one. One day he decided to save money so he could buy material for a coat. Little by little and bit by bit he saved until he had enough money to buy the material he needed to make himself a coat. He chose material and brought it back to his shop. Cutting it out very carefully so as not to waste any of the cloth, he worked all through the night and when morning came, he had a coat to put on. He was very pleased with himself and wore his coat until it wore out. One day he looked at it and thought if he was careful he could cut a jacket from the less worn bits of the coat. And so he did. He wore the jacket until it too wore out. One day he looked at it and thought if he was very careful he could cut a vest from the jacket. And so he did. From the vest came a cap, from the cap two pockets, from the pockets a few buttons. And from the buttons, there was just enough material to make a story. And he did. **"The Poor Tailor"** (Eastern Europe)

THE ABOVE STORY is an example of the journey a story may take as its focus changes. The following examples of ways to create story journeys are suggested to give readers a sense of how sessions might be structured around a chosen focus. There is no one right way or one possible focus. What does matter is that a specific focus be chosen for each session and that people respond spontaneously to the story and activities, leaving at the end with a sense of completion. This doesn't mean that if difficult issues are raised, each person has a sense of closure after the session. What it does mean is that each person has come to a place of rest and feels that for the moment, all is well. It is difficult to determine how long each activity will take—the larger the group, the more time it takes to share work. Therefore, each of the suggested structures includes activities with no time limit as well as questions that might be posed during the period of reflection, a highly recommended part of every session.

Each story has four different foci to provide ideas as to what might be evoked by the story. These are only suggestions, as are the activities, to help begin the storymaking process. Since the focus is the organizing principle, it has to be clearly stated. If people in the group want to change the focus, it is best to finish the current structure before working with a new one so that participants have a sense of a journey completed. Every focus offers possibility, there is no right, best or worst. As people acquire experience, more complex ideas can be explored, but even the simplest focus offers the prospect of new learning.

NOTE: The space between reflection and the next activity in the suggested structures is an indication of where a group might take a short break or stop if participants decide to do only part of a structure. Ending the session with the final reflection is *essential* because it provides time for group members to think about and respond to their experience, and if possible, to write or paint their reflection.

"Coyote Gets His Name" (Native American)

Great Spirit gathered all the Animal People together and told them the New People were coming. All the Animal People were going to have a name that would be theirs forever, a name they would hand down to their children and their children's children, a name for all time. The next morning, the Animal People were told to come to Great Spirit's lodge and each in turn would receive their name, first come, first served. The naming would start at dawn.

Coyote hated his name. He didn't want to be known as Trickster or Imitator. He wanted a great name, one that all the Animal People would respect and honor. He would ask to be Grizzly Bear, the strongest of the four-legged animals. If that name was taken, he would ask to be Eagle, the swiftest of the flying birds. And, as third choice, he would ask to be Salmon, the most powerful swimmer. Satisfied that he had a good plan, when evening came, he stuck small twigs between his eyelids to make sure he did not fall asleep. He intended to be the first animal to receive a forever name.

The next morning he grinned when he saw no one around. Surely he was the first to appear before Great Spirit. Joyfully he requested that he be called, Grizzly Bear. "Grizzly Bear was here already. He has taken his name," said Great Spirit.

"Oh," said Coyote. Pleased he had thought of this, he said, "In that case, I will be Eagle."

"I am sorry," said Great Spirit, "Eagle has already been here. He has taken his name."

"Well," said Coyote, a little sad, "in that case, I will be Salmon."

"That too is impossible," said Great Spirit," Salmon has come and gone. His name is already taken."

Coyote was upset. He tried to think of another name he could request but he was too miserable. "What name has not been taken?" he asked.

"All the Animal People have come and gone. You are the last to appear before me. No one wanted your name." Coyote looked so unhappy Great Spirit said, "It was I who made you sleep so long. I need you to be who you are, Coyote."

"But I don't want to be Coyote, the Trickster, the Imitator. I want a new name."

"I need you to keep your name. I have important work for you to do," said Great Spirit. Coyote looked up to see if he was making fun of him. "The New People who are coming do not know anything. You, alone among the Animal People, know how to laugh and cry. You are brave and cowardly, wise and foolish, hard-hearted and kind. I need you to teach the New People who are coming how to be fully human, for that is what they are, human beings."

Coyote asked, "But if I am foolish, they will laugh at me. And when I am cowardly, they will lose respect. How can I teach them?"

Great Spirit said, "When you are foolish and wise, when you are cowardly and brave, when you are mean-spirited and kind, they will understand that no one is always foolish, always brave, always mean. You will see them through bad and good times. And, to help you do your work, I will give you a special gift. You will be able to change yourself into any shape you choose. You will understand and talk to all who speak to you. If you die, you will be reborn. Shapechanger, go and do your work. You will do it well."

Coyote felt his heavy spirit lighten and his heart fill with joy as he went out into the world to meet the New People, to do the work of Great Spirit.

Structure #1

Story:	Coyote Gets His Name
Focus:	To be who we are

Tell:	Coyote Gets His Name.
Paint:	An image of a telling moment (a point in the story that sticks in your mind).
Write:	Words that come to mind.
Share:	Images and words.
Reflect:	On issues raised.

Sculpt:	An image of Coyote meeting a New Person.
Answer:	Quickly write answers to the following questions:
	Where are they meeting?
	How do they come to meet?
	Why does the New Person need help?
	How does Coyote help him/her?
	How do Coyote and the New Person feel after their interaction?
Share:	Highlights of the encounter with group.
Reflect:	On encounters.

Sculpt:	An image of the first New Person meeting a second New Person.
Tell:	As the first New Person, your version of your encounter with Coyote.
Reflect:	If something changed, what was it? How did it change? What might account for the changes?

Reflect:	On story and session. What do we mean when we say we want to be who we are? Is there such a thing as an authentic self? How do we know when or if we are being authentic? What does it take to be able to acknowledge the full dimension of what it means to be human?

Structure #2	
Story:	Coyote Gets His Name
Focus:	Developing resourcefulness
Paint:	An image of a talisman—something that keeps you safe in difficult times.
Share:	Images.
Reflect:	What makes an image a talisman image? How can an object help to keep us safe?
Tell:	Coyote Gets His Name.
In pairs:	Create a two-line chant that Coyote might say to himself in a time of trouble. (If there are only two, each person creates a chant to share. If you are working by yourself, create a chant that works for you.)
Share:	Chants.
Reflect:	On qualities chosen and how chanting feels.
Think:	Of a time when you were in trouble. What might have given you more wherewithal?

	What happens if you chant words to give yourself courage or a sense of possibility?
Reflect:	On the use of chanting to give us courage.
Sculpt:	An image of Coyote in relationship to a person, place or thing, at a moment of crisis.
Create:	A way for Coyote to resolve his situation successfully.
Share:	Situations and resolutions.
Reflect:	On strategies used.
Reflect:	On what helps to develop resourcefulness in a time of trouble.

Structure #3	
Story:	Coyote Gets His Name
Focus:	What's in a name?
Tell:	Coyote Gets His Name.
Paint:	On the left side of the paper, an image of Coyote and his name before the morning when Great Spirit gave permanent names to the Animal People.
Write:	Some words that come to mind.
Paint:	On the right side of the paper, an image of Coyote and his name after the morning when Great Spirit gave Coyote his permanent name.
Write:	Words that come to mind.
Share:	Images and words.

Reflect:	On Coyote's feelings before and after the naming ceremony. What's in a name?
Paint:	On the left side of the paper, an image of you and your name.
Write:	Words that come to mind.
Reflect:	On your name and how you feel about it. Do you have a nickname? If so, how did you get it? How do your feel about your nickname?
Imagine:	If you could have any name you like, what name would you give yourself?
Paint:	On the right side of the paper, an image of you and your new name.
Write:	Words that come to mind.
Share:	Images and words.
Reflect:	On how you feel about your name, some quality that a new name might evoke in you. If you have children, how did you name them? How do they feel about the names you gave them?
Write:	A letter Coyote writes in a time of crisis.
Collect:	Letters. Each person picks one.
Respond:	To letter either under your real name or the new name. If you are by yourself, answer the letter you wrote as Coyote and notice what you have to do to switch gears and answer the letter under your own name or the new name you have given yourself. How do

you sign the letter—cordially, sincerely, etc.
What affects your choice?

Share: Letters from and to Coyote.

Reflect: On issues raised, on letters written from different parts of our selves. What affects your choice of name in your response to Coyote?

Structure #4

Story: Coyote Gets His Name
Focus: On tricks and Tricksters

Paint: An image of Trickster.
Write: Words that come to mind.
Share: Images and words.
Reflect: On how you view Trickster. What is your relationship with your inner Trickster? What experience have you had with Tricksters?

Tell: Coyote Gets His Name.
Write: An episode in Coyote's life before he became Shapechanger.
Share: Episodes.
Write: An episode in Coyote's life after he became Shapechanger.
Share: Episodes.
Reflect: On the before and after episodes. What, if any, differences do you see in Coyote before and after? What does it mean to be a Shapechanger?
Reflect: On the story, the archetype of Trickster, and

the session.

"The Magic Brush" (China)

Ma Liang was a poor boy who took care of himself after his parents died by chopping wood and cutting weeds for his neighbors who were also poor. He found moments of pleasure by noticing the world around him--the soaring birds, the rippling grasses, the changing waves on the water. He entertained himself by drawing birds in the wet sand with broken twigs. The more he drew, the more lifelike his images became. Hawks waited for his newborn chicks. Chickens fled from his foxes.

One day he delivered firewood to a rich man who was having his portrait painted by a famous artist. Ma Liang begged the artist for a bit of paint and an old brush but the artist sent him away, refusing to give him anything.

That night, Ma Liang fell asleep on the beach and dreamed that the sea spewed forth a wave. An old man who rode the wave, glided to the shore, knelt next to Ma Liang and whispered to him, "Take this magic brush and use it well. Within it lives a mighty spirit. Honor it and you will live well." When Ma Liang woke, he found a brush in his hand.

Quickly, he saw a piece of driftwood and painted a seagull. As soon as Ma Liang finished the last stroke, the seagull came to life and flew away. Ma Liang looked at the brush with awe and promised, "I will use you to create only that which is good."

When a fisherman's net was torn, he painted a few lines and the net was as good as new. When a farmer told him that his well went dry, Ma Liang painted water and soon the well was full.

News of Ma Liang's skill spread. He realized that others would ask him for special favors so he made a decision. "I will draw only that which is unfinished; then I will be safe. Each day he went to the marketplace and painted, selling a painting for food, always taking care to leave one detail unfinished so the picture could not come to life.

Then, one day, as he was finishing a bird, someone jostled his arm and a dot of paint completed the unfinished eye. To the amazement of all, the bird flew away. News of the boy's gift spread. The Emperor sent his guards to find Ma Liang, threatening them with death if they failed. They captured Ma Liang and brought him to the palace.

The Emperor commanded Ma Liang to paint a dragon of scarlet and gold to bring him luck. Ma Liang painted an enormous snake and the Emperor commanded his guards to kill it. The Emperor was a clever man. He understood that he could not force Ma Liang to paint what he did not choose to paint so he pretended to be kind. "Paint me a phoenix, the bird of happiness." Ma Liang painted a crow that flew into the tapestries, soiled the carpets, and broke precious vases. The Emperor grabbed the brush and had his servants throw Ma Liang into the dungeon.

The Emperor painted a ruby and it came to life. He painted diamonds and emeralds, delighting in his creation. When his arm grew tired, he tried to stop, but the brush kept painting precious stones until there was a mountain of jewels that grew so high it collapsed on top of the emperor. He would have died had his servants not rescued him. The Emperor realized that Ma Liang controlled the brush so he told his servants to free the boy.

The Emperor pretended to be sorry, and apologized for treating Ma Liang so badly. Then he sighed. "Ah, if only I could have a tree of gold."

Ma Liang drew an island and said to the Emperor, "You shall have it." He drew a tree of gold on the island.

"But how will I get there?" asked the Emperor.

"I shall provide a boat for you," said Ma Liang, and painted a fine ship. The Emperor boarded the vessel with his servants and soon they were sailing. But the Emperor was still not satisfied.

"It moves too slowly," he complained. "At this rate I shall never arrive." Ma Liang painted a wind. "Faster," cried the Emperor. Ma Liang painted until the wind became a gale and the gale became a typhoon. "Stop," screamed the Emperor. Ma Liang wiped out the entire picture by painting white over everything. Nothing remained except for the faint blur of a forgotten image.

Structure #1

Story: The Magic Brush
Focus: Curses and blessings

Paint: On the left side of the paper, an image of "curse."
Write: Words that come to mind.
Paint: On the right side of the paper, an image of "blessing."
Write: Words that come to mind.
Write: In the middle of the paper, words or phrases that might transform a blessing into a curse or a curse into a blessing.
Share: Images and words.
Reflect: On idea evoked by words and image.

Tell: The Magic Brush.
Create: A powerful curse and a powerful blessing.
Imagine: The circumstances under which you would

	use each.
Share:	Curses and blessings and how and when you might use each.
Reflect:	On curses and blessings.

Sculpt:	An image of a character who experiences a blessing transformed into a curse or a curse into a blessing.
Write:	The story of what happened.
Share:	Stories.
Reflect:	On issues raised by stories, on the story of The Magic Brush, and the idea of curses and blessings.

Structure #2

Story:	The Magic Brush
Focus:	On being given a gift.

Tell:	The Magic Brush.
Paint:	A telling moment.
Write:	Briefly what this moment means to you.
Share:	Images and writing.
Reflect:	On issues raised.

Recall:	A time when you were given a gift. What, if any were the expectations? How did you feel about being given the gift? What did the gift mean to you?
Reflect:	On the difference(s) between being given and choosing a gift.

Sculpt:	An image of Ma Liang at a particular moment in his life, in relation to a person place or thing.
Write:	A monologue that Ma Liang would speak at this moment.
Share:	Monologue without reading or referring to what you have written.
Read:	Written monologue.
Reflect:	On spoken and read monologues. What, if any, are the differences in content, tone, and feeling? How do you account for this?
Write:	A letter to Ma Liang about a gift you have received. Ask for a particular kind of response from him.
Collect:	Letters and put them into a box.
Choose:	A letter and respond to the writer as if you are Ma Liang. It doesn't matter if you chose the letter you wrote.
Share:	Original letters and responses.
Reflect:	On letters. Return them to original writers.
Reflect:	On story, on session, and on receiving gifts.

◎

Structure #3	
Story:	The Magic Brush
Focus:	The power of creation
Tell:	The Magic Brush.
Paint:	An image of creation.

Write:	Some words that come to mind.
Share:	Images and words.
Reflect:	On what it means to create.
Recall:	A time when you felt creative.
Reflect:	What were the circumstances? What did you create? How did you feel about your creation? What nourishes your creativity? What drains your creativity?
Share:	An aspect of your experience.
Reflect:	On what it takes to create and your process of creation.
Sculpt:	An image of the spirit in the dream where Ma Liang is told, "Take this magic brush and use it well. Within it lives a mighty spirit. Honor it and you will live well."
Write:	A brief story about how the spirit acquired her/his power.
Share:	Sculptures and stories.
Reflect:	On ideas and stories.
Imagine:	You are given a gift of creativity with the same words the spirit spoke to Ma Liang.
Create:	A story in which you use your gift.
Share:	Stories.
Reflect:	On story, session, and the power of creation.

Structure #4

Story:	The Magic Brush
Focus:	Staying true to one's principles.
Paint:	An image on the left side of the paper of "unethical."
Write:	Words that come to mind.
Paint:	An image on the right side of the paper of "ethical."
Write:	Words that come to mind.
Share:	Images and words.
Reflect:	On what works against and for staying true to one's principles.
Sculpt:	An image of Ma Liang and the Emperor, in relationship, at a critical moment for either Ma Liang or the Emperor.
Share:	Sculptures.
Reflect:	What makes the moment critical? What helps you to make a decision at a time when who-you-are is being tested?
Create:	The next episode in Ma Liang's life after he paints the image with white paint.
Share:	Stories.
Reflect:	On story, session, and what it takes to act ethically

"The Coming of Fog" (Canadian Indian)
As a young child, Sila was rescued from the sea after the boat in which she was traveling with her family, capsized, drowning her parents. Her five older brothers took care of her, even after some of them married and had children of their own.

Sila loved the sea and swam far and better than anyone else in the village. At first her brothers were proud of her ability, but when the villagers complained they were not teaching her properly, the brothers told her it was time to stop swimming and learn the ways of village girls. Sila loved her brothers and did as she was told, but away from the sea she grew thin and pale. Her brothers were so worried about her they asked Raven for help. Raven told them, "Your sister is not like other young girls. She must be allowed to be who she is if you want her to be healthy and happy." Reluctantly the brothers agreed for they loved their sister.

As she grew up the villagers ridiculed Sila and her brothers. The brothers grew ashamed and forced Sila to do the tasks of young village women. Sila tried but she became quiet and sad. Once again her brothers called on Raven. He reminded them, "Your sister is not like other young women. She must be allowed to be who she is if you want her to be healthy and happy." Fearing for her life, the brothers allowed Sila to return to the sea.

This time, their fears were larger than their love. They followed Sila and noticed that she swam with a strange creature. The brothers were afraid the creature would harm their sister so they tried to kill it but the creature escaped. The brothers made new, sharper arrows. Sila pleaded with her brothers, "Let the creature be. He is no danger to anyone." But her brothers refused to listen. In time, an arrow found its mark and the creature died.

Sila's grief upset her brothers. They assured her they had killed the creature for her sake but Sila was not comforted and refused to speak. The brothers kept her under their guard in a tepee and when she gave birth to a child they were horrified to notice the child did not look like other children. They were afraid and asked Raven for advice. Raven said, "Your sister is not like other young mothers. She must be allowed to be who she is if you want her to be healthy and happy." The brothers listened reluctantly, watching Sila and the child closely.

Although Sila swam with her child, she feared for his life. She knew she could not keep him safe. One day, she swam with her son to a place he had never been. She told him what he needed to know and bid him leave her.

For a second time Sila was consumed with grief. Her brothers tried to keep her busy helping their wives and children but she yearned for her child. She knew her brothers would kill him if they saw him so she called on Raven: "Help me safely see my son. I cannot live this way."

Raven took pity on her and created a thick white cloud that separated Sila from her brothers. They could not see her as she swam in the sea, greeting her son. When Sila did not return, the brothers called on Raven to help them find her but Raven refused. "You will not let her be who she is, therefore you do not deserve to live with her. She has gone to live with those who love her as she is. There will always be a thick cloud of fog between you."

This time it was the brothers who grieved.

Structure #1

Story:	The Coming of Fog
Focus:	Creating an authentic life
Paint:	An image on the left side of the paper of "inauthentic."
Write:	Words that come to mind.
Paint:	An image on the right side of the paper of "authentic."
Write:	Words that come to mind.

Share:	Images and words.
Reflect:	On what constitutes in-authenticity and authenticity. How do we know if or when we are being inauthentic or authentic? What forces/issues/events affect our choices? Are we always able to choose? If so, what helps and hinders our choice?
Tell:	The Coming of Fog.
Sculpt:	An image of Sila at a critical time in her life in relationship to a person, place or thing.
Create:	A short dialogue between Sila and this person, place or thing. If you chose a place or a thing, animate your choice so that it has a voice. Create a critical situation in which the dialogue takes place.
Share:	Dialogues.
Reflect:	On issues raised and mechanisms used to cope with the situation.
Sculpt:	An image of a character faced with a dilemma that challenges the core of who this person is.
Write:	Brief answers to the following questions:

* Who is she/he?
* What is the dilemma?
* What are the person's choices?
* What are the consequences of a decision?
* What choice does the person make?
* What effect does the choice have on a critical aspect (choose one) of the person's life?

	★ How does this make the person feel?
Create:	And title the story based on your answers.
	If other possibilities come to mind as you write, feel free to explore these ideas.
Share:	Stories.
Reflect:	On stories and choices, on "The Coming of Fog" session, and ideas about authenticity.

◎

Structure #2

Story:	The Coming of Fog
Focus:	And that is how…

Choose:	An aspect of nature that interests you.
Paint:	An image of the world without this aspect.
Write:	Words that come to mind.
Share:	What the world is like without this aspect.
Think:	About what might have called this aspect of nature into being.
Write:	A story about how this aspect of nature came to be, ending with the words: and that is how … came into being.
Share:	Stories.
Reflect:	On stories and what encourages or stimulates something new being created.

Tell:	The Coming of Fog.
Consider:	A world without fog. What might this mean? To people? To creatures? To plants?
Paint:	An image of you and fog.

Write:	A brief memory of a time when you experienced fog. How does your experience compare with Sila's?
Share:	An aspect of your experience.
Reflect:	On the nature of fog.
Sculpt:	An image of you and Raven in relationship to each other.
Ask:	Raven how fog might have come into being had Sila's brothers acknowledged and supported her need to swim in the sea.
Write:	A brief dialogue between you and Raven.
Share:	Dialogue.
Reflect:	On dialogues. For what reason might you have or have not created fog?
Reflect:	On story, session, and the nature of being.

◉

Structure #3

Story:	The Coming of Fog
Focus:	For your own good
Tell:	The Coming of Fog
Paint:	A telling image.
Write:	Briefly about why this moment of the story resonates within you.
Share:	Images and writing.
Reflect:	On issues raised.
Sculpt:	An image of "for your own good."

Create:	A short story where one character says to another character, "This is for your own good. "
Share:	Stories.
Reflect:	On an experience where you have been told, "This is for your own good."
Consider:	Sila's brothers love their sister Sila. They accept responsibility for her and try to do what is best for her. They ask Raven for advice and hear his warning, yet eventually the brothers are unable to put her happiness and needs ahead of their worries and fears.
Write:	A letter as Sila or one of the brothers at a critical time, raising a burning question or issue.
Collect:	Letters and redistribute them.
Write:	A response to or from Sila suggesting a different possibility than what was chosen. Feel free to respond with a poem or a story.
Share:	Letters and return to original writer.
Reflect:	On letters and responses, on "The Coming of Fog," the session, and what "for you own good," means/ has meant in your life.

Structure #4

Story:	The Coming of Fog
Focus:	Personal power

Paint:	An image of "un-empowered" on the left side of the paper.
Write:	Words that come to mind.
Paint:	An image of "empowered" on the right side of the paper
Write:	Words that come to mind.
Share:	Images and words.
Reflect:	On a definition of personal power and what it takes to lose and gain personal power.
Tell:	The Coming of Fog.
Sculpt:	An image of you and Sila in relationship at a critical moment.
What:	Moment have you chosen?
How:	Does this moment relate to your life?
Write:	A dialogue between you and Sila.
Share:	Dialogues.
Reflect:	On issues raised and strategies discussed.
Paint:	An image of you in relationship to personal power in the center of the paper.
Write	What connects you to your personal power close to the painted image.
Write:	What disconnects you from your personal power further away from the painted image.
Write:	What strengthens your ability to connect and use your personal power, placing it where you think it best fits in relation to the painted image.
Recall:	A time when you lost or gained personal power.

Write:	The story of this time using imagined characters.
Share:	Story.
Reflect:	On stories
Reflect:	On story and issues of personal power.

"Anniko" (Africa)

Anniko leaned her tired body against the tree. She knew her village was too far away to find her way back before nightfall. She looked up at the bird whose lovely song made her forget to look where she was going and where she had come from. She shivered; watching the sun leave, knowing night would soon come.

The return of the sun's warmth woke her, welcoming her to the new day. When she looked around, Anniko knew she was utterly lost. Afraid of walking in circles, she decided to follow the path of the sun and just before dusk, she came to a village.

Anniko and the villagers stared at each other, amazed. She had never seen people with such long necks. They had never seen a person with such a short neck. They might have stared at each other until the sun went down, but Anniko was hungry and thirsty and tired. "Please," she asked, "Could I have something to eat and drink?" Overcoming their astonishment, the villagers gave her food, water, and a mat on which to sleep.

The next morning, Anniko rose with the sun, and as she had done every morning in her village, sang a song to welcome the day. Once again the People of the Long Necks were filled with wonder. They had never heard such beautiful sounds. Anniko was happy they liked her music and offered to help with the day's chores. As she worked, she sang, her music easing the burden of their work.

Although the villagers and Anniko grew to be fond of each other, there was one man, a mean-spirited man, who did not like Anniko. He especially did not like to hear Anniko sing and waited for an opportunity to get rid of her. One day, when Anniko was alone, sitting in the sun, combing her hair, he quietly crept up behind her. After looking around to make sure no one else was near by, he confronted her. "You are ruining our village. If you stay here we can no longer be known as the People of the Long Necks for you have a short neck and you will never have a long neck. Leave our village, now!"

Anniko was too upset to say anything. Perhaps the others think as he does but are too kind to tell me, she thought. With the mean-spirited man's words stinging in her ears, Anniko quickly left the village.

That evening, the villagers heard no song to greet the evening. "Where is Anniko?" they asked. No one knew. The mean-spirited man said nothing, pleased with the unusual quiet. When the villagers left to return to their houses, there was one who said, "I think I know the person we should ask. Follow me." So the villagers went to the place where the mean-spirited man lived and asked, "Where is Anniko? We think you know where she is. Tell us!"

At first he denied knowing what they meant, but the villagers kept asking. "All right," he said, "I will tell you. Anniko does not belong in our village. We are the People of the Long Necks. She has a short neck. If she lives with us we will no longer be able to say we are the People of the Long Neck. Listen to me, I am right. We are better off without her. Let her go wherever she has gone. We don't need her to spoil our ways and we don't need her songs. We did well enough before she came."

But the villagers missed Anniko. They had grown fond of

her singing and liked her helpful ways. They decided to go into the forest to look for her even though they had no idea where she was, or in which direction she had gone. After they had been walking and looking for a time, one of the villagers suggested, "Perhaps we could sing to her as she sang to us. Perhaps she will hear our singing and we will find each other." Although everyone thought this was a good idea, they looked at each other, puzzled. No one knew how to sing. But, they wanted to find Anniko so badly they decided to try.

Their first sounds were noises, more like screeches and squawks than song. They put their hands over their ears and kept trying. Finally, they decided it was too hard to learn to sing and to sing a song so they simply sang, "Anniko. Anniko. We are here. Anniko." Although there was no response, they kept singing. "Anniko. Anniko. We are here. Anniko." Then, in the distance, they thought they heard a sound. A song. Listening intently, they followed the sound as it got louder and sweeter until the villagers and Anniko were face to face.

They greeted her joyfully, but she remembered the words that had made her flee into the forest and remained quiet. The villagers understood. "Never mind what that mean-spirited man said. "We want you to live in our village. We are the People of the Long Necks and we will always be so. Your presence does not change this. Your songs lift our spirits and make our hearts joyful. Please, come back with us. Please, stay with us."

Anniko looked at the villagers and saw they spoke truthfully. Holding her head high, she sang to them as they left the forest and made their way home.

Structure #1

Story:	Anniko
Focus:	Lost and Found

Paint:	Paint an image of "lost" on the left side of the paper.
Write:	Words that come to mind.
Paint:	An image of "found" on the right side of the paper.
Write:	Words that come to mind.
Write:	In the middle of the paper, what helps you lose your way and then what helps you find your way.
Share:	Images and writing.
Reflect:	On the process of losing and finding one's way.

Sculpt:	An image of "lost" and "found" in relationship to one another.
Create:	A dialogue they might have.
Share:	Highlights of dialogue.
Reflect:	On dialogues and what each might have to offer the other.

Tell:	Anniko.
Write:	The story of how and why Anniko left her village to go into the forest.
Share:	Stories.
Reflect:	On choices.
Reflect:	On story, session, and issues around lost and found.

Structure #2
Story: Anniko
Focus: A joyful noise

Tell: Anniko
Consider: In the village where Anniko lives, people
            learn to sing as very young children. There
            are songs for every occasion and experience.
            How do you feel about singing? How did
            you come to feel this way?
Write: About an experience you have had with
            singing. How did you feel? How did it affect
            your decision to stop or continue singing?
Share: Writing.
Reflect: On the role singing/song plays/played in
            your life.

Choose: A melody that you feel comfortable singing.
            Think of something you would like to ex-
            press in a song. Create your own words to
            the melody you have selected.
Sing: Your song.
Reflect: On what it means for you to sing in public.

Paint: An image of "speaking" on the left side of
            the paper.
Write: Words that come to mind.
Paint: An image of "singing" on the right side of
            the paper.
Write: Words that come to mind.

Share:	Images.
Reflect:	On issues evoked by images and words.
Reflect:	On story, session, and singing.

Structure #3

Story:	Anniko
Focus:	Leaving what is known

Paint:	An image of "known" on the left side of the paper.
Write:	Words that come to mind.
Paint:	An image of "unknown" on the right side of the paper.
Share:	Images and words.
Reflect:	On ideas and feelings about known and unknown

Sculpt:	An image of "known" and "unknown" in relationship to each other.
Create:	A short dialogue between the two.
Share:	Highlights of the dialogue.
Reflect:	On which, if any, seems or feels more powerful, comfortable, interesting.

Tell:	Anniko.
Paint:	An image of departure.
Create:	A character who is leaving.
Answer:	Questions briefly and quickly.
	Who is leaving?
	Why?

	Where is she/he going?
	Why does the destination matter?
	What, if any, are her/his expectations of the trip?
	Does she/he expect to return to the place of departure?
	What will help us have a safe journey?
Write:	A letter saying goodbye. The person to whom you write can be real or made up. Use your answers to the questions as the basis for your letter.
Share:	Letters.
Reflect:	On issues, ideas, and feelings evoked by letters.
Reflect:	On the idea of leaving what we know, on the story, session, and what it means to leave what is familiar.

◎

Structure #4	
Story:	Anniko
Focus:	Coming to a place that is home.
Paint:	An image of "journey" on the left side of the paper.
Write:	Words that come to mind.
Paint:	An image of "home" on the right side of the paper.
Write:	Words that come to mind.
Share:	Images and words.
Reflect:	On what it means to arrive at a place that

	feels like home after a journey.
Tell:	Anniko.
Consider:	The journey that Anniko makes from the time she leaves her village until she decides to stay with the People of the Long Neck.
Write:	An adventure she has during this journey.
Share:	Journey stories.
Reflect:	On what it means to travel by one's self in the unknown.

Sculpt:	An image of home.
Share:	Ideas about and meaning of home.
Reflect:	On ideas and meanings about home.

Imagine:	Anniko has been in the Village of the Long Necks for a period of time. What might her life be like? Do you think she ever finds a way to return to her village?
Create:	A picture in words or images or both, of Anniko at home.
Share:	Concepts of home.
Reflect:	On story, session, and what it means to be home.

"The Tug of War" (West Africa)

It was a glorious summer morning. Birds were chirping, the sky was blue, a soft breeze gently played with leaves in the trees, and Mother Sparrow was sitting in the nest on her eggs. Everything was perfect except that Father Sparrow was grumpy. Very grumpy.

"I went down to the river to bathe in our favorite place,"

he told Mother Sparrow, "and there was Old Crocodile. He took up all the room and when I politely asked him to make a little space for me, do you know what he said? 'Find your own place to swim, I was here first.'"

As if that wasn't bad enough, at that very moment, there was a tremendous jolt against the tree, nearly toppling the nest. Father Sparrow flew to see what caused it was and there was Brother Elephant, taking his morning stroll. "Hey, Brother, you nearly pushed my wife off of the nest. She's sitting on our eggs you know."

Brother Elephant shrugged. "Didn't fall, did she? No harm done." He kept on walking without the tiniest apology.

"No harm? She almost fell. The eggs nearly spilled out of the nest. You gave us all a fright." When Father Sparrow saw that Brother Elephant was not in the least bit sorry, he said, "If you ever do it again, I'll fix you. I'll tie you up and you'll never get out."

Brother Elephant laughed. "Tie me up if you like. There aren't nearly enough sparrows in the world to keep me tied up." He laughed again and kept on walking.

Father Sparrow was so mad he shouted, "We'll see about that." Elephant swished his trunk and laughed even harder. Father Sparrow flew up to the nest. For a long time, he and Mother Sparrow talked and talked and talked. Then, Father Sparrow flew to the river.

His anger grew when he found Crocodile still splashing and bathing in Father Sparrow's much loved pool of calm water. "If you are still in this pool when I come by tomorrow morning, I am going to tie you up."

Crocodile grinned, showing his pointed teeth. "Tie me up if you like. With my sharp teeth, there isn't a rope strong enough to keep me tied even if you and every sparrow in the world tightened the knot." Crocodile grinned a particularly irritating grin.

Father Sparrow flew back to the nest, ready to discuss plans with Mother Sparrow. After singing for friends and relatives to join them, hundreds of sparrows appeared. They approved the plan and began to gather green creeper vines that they twisted and plaited and wove until they had a length that was as strong as any rope.

They didn't have long to wait. Brother Elephant soon came crashing through the forest, banging into the tree where Mother Sparrow sat in her nest on her eggs. Brother Elephant sneered, "Ready to tie me up?"

Father Sparrow smiled at Mother Sparrow and said, "Yes, we are." With a nod to his friends and family, sparrows of every size and age, holding the long green rope in their mouths, flew up and down, in and out, around Brother Elephant's body until he was bound as tightly as the sparrows could manage. Brother Elephant laughed, ready to burst out.

"We would greatly appreciate it if you would lie here, just for a few minutes," said Father Sparrow politely. "If you don't mind that is."

"As you like," snickered Brother Elephant.

The sparrows flew away, holding the other end of the green rope, twisting and turning it among and around the bushes and trees, choosing the strongest plants with the deepest roots. When they came to the river where Crocodile lay, he opened one eye and giggled, "Have you come to tie me up, Father Sparrow?"

"Yes, if you don't mind."

Crocodile chuckled. "Have fun." The sparrows began, twisting and pushing and pulling, in and out, up and down, around and around, until the green rope was taut and tight against Crocodile's body.

"Now, when I say pull, pull as hard as you can and don't

stop until you are free," ordered Father Sparrow.

Crocodile nodded, closed his eyes and sank into the mud. The sparrows flew to the top of a tree where they could see Brother Elephant and Crocodile though neither of them could see the other.

As loud as he could, Father Sparrow chirped, "Pull!"

All of a sudden Crocodile was jerked out of the water, up on to the riverbank, slithering against nettles and thorns. Crocodile tried to use his teeth to shred the green rope but it got tighter and tighter. Brother Elephant found himself being dragged toward the river, crashing into sharp-edged bushes and against sturdy trees. The harder Crocodile and Brother Elephant pulled, the more tangled they became.

The green rope cut into their hides causing each to grit their teeth in pain and embarrassment. As sunset approached, neither animal was any closer to freeing himself than he had been hours before. Both had too much pride to let any of the other animals see them tied up when they came to drink and bathe in the river. Crocodile was the first to speak. "Very well, Father Sparrow, you are stronger than I imagined. If you untie me I promise not to take your bathing place again."

Brother Elephant whispered to Father Sparrow, "If you stop pulling and untie me, I promise I will never bump into your tree again."

Father Sparrow talked it over with Mother Sparrow, and soon, all the sparrows hopped and pulled and poked and pecked until Crocodile was free. He slid into the river, too mortified to do anything but mutter, "Thank you."

Then the sparrows set to work on Brother Elephant who still couldn't believe such a tiny bird could be so strong. As soon as he was free, he sneaked away, too humiliated to speak.

From that day on, Father Sparrow enjoyed his daily bath

and Mother Sparrow sat on her eggs in the nest with no fear of falling out of the tree.

Structure #1

Story:	The Tug of War
Focus:	Using one's imagination
Tell:	The Tug of War.

Paint:	A telling image.
Write:	Words that come to mind.
Title:	Your image.
Share:	Image, words, and title.
Reflect:	On issues evoked by images, words, titles.

Write:	The story of your title without retelling The Tug of War.
Share:	Stories.
Reflect:	On the stories.

Consider:	A time in your life when you felt the odds were against you. How did you deal with the situation?
Briefly:	Write down what happened.
Consider:	How might Father and Mother Sparrow have dealt with it?
Share:	Your experience, telling it as if you are a character in the story.
Reflect:	On shared experiences. Does telling it as a character affect the telling? If so, how?
Reflect:	On story, on the use of imagination to deal

with difficult situations.

Structure #2
Story: The Tug of War
Focus: Point of view

Tell: The Tug of War
Consider: The narrator's point of view.
Paint: An image on the left side of the paper, of the narrator's idea of the relationships among the four main characters.
Title: Image.
Choose: A new narrator with a different point of view.
Paint: An image on the right side of the paper of this narrator's idea of the relationships among the four main characters.
Title: Image.
Share   Images and explore what affects point of view.
Reflect: On point of view and how it affects what we see, hear, decide.

Write: A new version of the story from another point of view.
Share: New versions.
Reflect: On how point of view affects the telling of a story.

In Two's: Tell partner something that happened to

	you.
Partner:	Retells your story from his/her own point of view without changing specific details.
Repeat:	Process with partner sharing something that happened to her/him.
Reflect:	On what happens when the point of view is changed.
Reflect:	On story, session, and how point of view can affect what is told and heard.

Structure #3

| Story: | The Tug of War |
| Focus: | The power of the small |

Tell:	The Tug of War
Paint:	An image of "large" on the left side of the paper.
Write:	Words that come to mind.
Paint:	An image of "small" on the right side of the paper.
Write:	Words that come to mind.
Share:	Images and words.
Reflect:	On what lies behind "large" and "small."

Sculpt:	An image of "large" and "small" in relationship.
Create:	A short dialogue between "large" and "small."
Share:	Dialogues.

Reflect: On choices made.

Consider: A time in your life when being small was
                a source of power.
Share: Experiences.
Reflect: On story, and issues around the power of the
                small.

◎

Structure #4
Story: The Tug of War
Focus: The power of community

Paint: An image of "community."
Write: Words that come to mind.
Share: Images and words.
Reflect: On ideas about community.

Tell: The Tug of War.
Briefly: Write about what helps to create commu-
                nity? What works to destroy community?
Share: Writing and an experience you have had
                with a community.
Reflect: On ideas and feelings about/around com-
                munity.

Paint: An image of your ideal community and
                place yourself in relationship to it.
Write: Briefly what it is that makes it ideal. What
                prevents it from being real?
Reflect: On story and on ideas, attitudes and feelings

about community.

"Catherine's Fate" (Sicily)

There was once a young girl who was smart, beautiful, and rich, with parents who loved her. One day while sitting in her garden, a strange woman approached her. Catherine was astonished and asked, "Who are you? How did you get past my guards?"

The woman smiled and turned to smell a yellow rose.

"What do you want?" asked Catherine.

The woman remained silent. Catherine was tempted to call for help but something about the woman intrigued her so she too remained silent, waiting for the woman to speak.

In time the woman said, "I am Fate. I have come to offer you a choice."

"A choice?" asked Catherine. "What kind of choice?"

"It is your time of choosing. You must decide if you want to be happy while you are young and unhappy when you are old, or unhappy when you are young and happy when you are old. Choose one or the other. Your preference will be honored."

"These are not choices I wish to make," said Catherine.

"Choose now or lose your opportunity."

The woman's intensity frightened Catherine. She called for her guards but none came. She tried to leave the garden but could not move. The woman smiled. "You cannot escape Fate, my dear. I ask you for the last time, do you want to be happy when you are young and unhappy when you are old, or do you prefer to be unhappy while you are young and happy when you are old?"

"Wrinkles and misery make poor companions, I choose to be unhappy when I am young and happy when I am old," Catherine said reluctantly.

"So be it," said the woman who then disappeared.

Soon after, one of Catherine's serving women brought her a cool drink. "You look pale my lady, is something wrong?"

Looking around, Catherine saw that nothing had changed. "Perhaps I have just had a bad dream. Thank you for your kindness." She sipped the refreshing liquid and tried to pretend that all was well.

For a few days, all was as it had always been, yet Catherine felt uneasy. She sensed something was amiss. Her fears proved true. Her father's ships with all his wealth were lost at sea. Thieves attacked those defending the mansion, taking what was valuable, setting fire to the house as they left. Only Catherine survived, escaping with only the clothes on her back.

"Oh Fate, could you not have spared my parents? Surely they deserved better. They have done no harm..." Catherine begged and pleaded, but there was no response.

A servant who saw what had happened gave Catherine a few of her clothes and a basket of food. "Take these, Miss. You were good to me and my children and we have not forgotten your kindness." As the woman was about to leave, she warned, "Remember, the world is not as you have known it. Be careful." Catherine nodded, too grief-stricken to speak.

For many days she walked, wondering what to do and where to go. When she arrived in a large town Catherine decided to seek out a kind looking woman and ask for work. Up and down the streets she trudged, not seeing anyone she dared to ask. Just then, a well-dressed woman appeared in an open window. "Please good woman, I am the daughter of a wealthy man who lost his fortune. I seek work as a ladies maid. Although I have few skills save embroidery, I am willing to learn."

"You have come at the right time. My serving woman left this morning. I will teach you what you need to know."

And so for a time, Catherine was content. Her mistress was kind and patient. Perhaps, thought Catherine, I was merely meant to learn to serve. Perhaps all is now well. A few more days passed without incident.

One morning, her mistress said, "I leave this morning to visit with my sister. I will return tomorrow. Take good care of everything while I am gone." No sooner had the woman left than Fate appeared.

"So my sweet Catherine, did you think to hide from me? Did you think that I forgot your choice?"

Catherine watched in horror as Fate smashed glasses, tore curtains, broke furniture, and slashed paintings. Sobbing, Catherine ran out of the house, too afraid and upset to stay. After she disappeared, Fate restored the house to its former condition. When the woman returned, she looked for Catherine. Not finding her she checked the whole house but nothing was missing. All she could do was wonder what had happened.

For seven years Fate followed Catherine, disrupting her life wherever she went, however she fled. Catherine learned to be observant and prepared for she could not predict when or how Fate would strike. She wondered what age she had to be before she was old enough to be happy.

On her travels in a remote village at the foot of a mountain, Catherine once again found employment and asked what her duties would be. She was surprised to hear her mistress say, "Every morning, I will need you to take a special plate of bread and cheese up the path which winds around and ends at the top of the mountain."

Catherine could not hide her astonishment. "May I ask why?"

"Certainly. It is well that you know. You are bringing an

offering to my Fate. I shudder to think what my life would be like were she not to receive this every morning. It was easier when I was younger. Now, each day the climb becomes more difficult. I have been worrying what would happen when I could no longer walk the steep path. I am happy for your service."

"Your Fate?" asked Catherine.

"Yes," said the woman. "Fate and I have had many encounters. My care of her takes care of me. Listen well. Tomorrow morning, when you approach the top of the mountain, you will smell a sweet scent. Follow your nose and it will lead you to the home of Fate. Knock three times. A door will open and a tall woman will stretch out her hand. Give her the plate and wait. She will soon return it to you. Bring it home and wash it carefully. Place it where you found it."

"Oh," said Catherine, looking unhappy and frightened.

The old woman asked, "What is wrong?

After telling her what had happened since Fate first appeared in her garden, Catherine asked, "Do you think it is possible that your Fate might help me find a way to please my Fate? I will do anything to appease her."

"Be careful what you promise. Fate is a hard taskmaster. Still, when you have fed my Fate, and you feel the time is right, ask for her help. Do not beg. Be pleasant. Accept what happens without complaint."

For seven days, Catherine fed the woman's Fate. On the eighth day, she decided the time was right to ask for help. The tall woman who took the food answered, "Now is not the time to ask. When you return tomorrow, I will take you to her." Catherine thanked her and gathered a bouquet of flowers which she laid in front of her door.

The next morning, after receiving the plate of bread and

cheese, the tall woman took Catherine to meet her Fate. "Sister, here is one who begs an end to your torment. She looks deserving of a rest."

Fate stared deep into Catherine's eyes for a long time. It was all Catherine could do to meet her gaze, politely, without flinching. "Very well, my dear Catherine, here is a skein of silken thread. If you continue to take good care of it and me, we will treat you well." Before Catherine could thank her, Fate disappeared. This time Catherine gathered two bouquets of flowers, laying them in front of each door.

All the way down the mountain Catherine tried to make sense of what had happened. Even her mistress was puzzled. "The thread looks ordinary to me but I advise you to follow Fate's advice. Take good care of it and in time, we shall know its use."

The next morning, after Catherine returned from the mountain, her mistress told her what she had heard. A proclamation had been issued. The King was to be married and there was no more silk thread of the right color. Without it the King's wedding robes could not be finished. Anyone with silk thread the color of the royal robes was to bring it to the court. "Go, Catherine. I am sure your thread is the right color. Give it to him and you will be rewarded."

When Catherine appeared before the King she noticed how handsome he was and thought it a pity he was soon to be married. "Your majesty, is this thread suitable for your purpose?"

The thread matched perfectly. "Bring the scales. You shall have gold equal to the weight of the skein." The scales were brought in and the skein put on one side, gold on the other. But no matter how much gold was put on the scale, the skein weighed more. Exasperated, the King put his crown on the scale and immediately there was balance.

"Where did you get this thread?" asked the King.

Catherine told him all that had happened. The King listened, noticing her intelligence and beauty, the grace with which she spoke. "I have changed my mind. I want to marry you."

And so it happened as Fate promised. Catherine lived to be a very old woman and each year was happier than the one before.

Structure #1
Story: Catherine's Fate
Focus: Bargains

Paint: An image of "bargain."
Write: Words that come to mind.
Share: Words and images.
Reflect: On what is involved when we make a bargain.

Tell: Catherine's Fate.
Sculpt: An image of Catherine and Fate at a telling moment in the story.
Create: A dialogue that amplifies an aspect of their relationship.
Share: Dialogues.
Reflect: On issues raised.

Consider: A time when you made a bargain. What were the circumstances? What was the outcome? Would you make the same bargain now? If not, why not?
Share: Experiences of bargains and bargaining.

Reflect:	On the nature of bargains and bargaining.
Imagine:	A bargain Catherine might have made in her life after she has made peace with her Fate.
Write:	The story of this bargain.
Share:	Stories.
Reflect:	On stories and issues raised.
Think:	About your own life. What bargain would you like to make? For what? With whom? To what end?
Reflect:	On story, session, and the nature of bargains.

◎

Structure #2

Story:	Catherine's Fate
Focus:	Unforeseen consequences
Paint:	An image of "unforeseen consequences"
Write:	Words that come to mind.
Share:	Images and words.
Reflect:	On choices. Notice if expectation plays a role in our reaction to what is unforeseen.
Tell:	Catherine's Fate
Sculpt:	An image of Catherine at a moment that could be in the story, when Catherine is dealing with a crisis.
Share:	Sculptures.
Discuss:	Ways that Catherine dealt with the crisis.

Reflect:	On the variety of the crises.
Consider:	After a time, Catherine realizes that no matter where she goes, Fate will find her and destroy the security of her employment. For seven years, Catherine suffers, yet not all of life remains the same, not even when it comes to suffering.
Create:	An episode where Catherine encounters a time of unexpected pleasure or joy.
Share:	Episodes.
Reflect:	On what Catherine learns from this experience.
Paint:	An image of a time when you experienced unforeseen consequences.
Write:	Briefly what happened, how you felt about it, and the effect or impact it might have had on you.
Share:	Experiences.
Reflect:	On story, session, and unforeseen consequences.

◎

Structure #3

Story:	Catherine's Fate
Focus:	Deriving meaning from what happens
Paint:	An image of "meaningless" on the left side of the paper.
Write:	Words that come to mind.

Paint:	An image of "meaningful" on the right side of the paper.
Write:	Words that come to mind.
Share:	Words and images.
Reflect:	On how we differentiate "meaningless and meaningful." What factors affect our differentiation?

Tell:	Catherine's Fate
Sculpt:	An image of Fate when she first became Fate.
Imagine:	Her first encounter with a human.
Create:	A short monologue, as Fate, where she has to decide what is meaningless and what is meaningful for her and for those she chooses to encounter.
Share:	Sculptures and monologues.
Reflect:	On issues raised.

Consider:	A powerful and important moment in your life. What made it meaningless or meaningful? When you think about it now, are your feelings the same as when the moment originally occurred? If not, what happened to change your feelings?
Imagine:	Catherine meeting Fate some years after the story ends.
Create:	A conversation they might have about what was most meaningful in the seven years that Fate intervened in Catherine's life.
Share:	Highlights of the conversations.

Reflect:	On the story, session, and what gives meaning to our lives.

Structure #4	
Story:	Catherine's Fate
Focus:	Developing inner resources

Paint:	An image of "inner resources."
Write:	Words that hinder and help the development of these resources.
Share:	Images and words.
Reflect:	On images and words, what hinders and helps the development of our inner resources.

Tell:	Catherine's Fate
Consider:	Catherine is the beloved daughter of wealthy parents. It is likely there were servants at her beck and call, doing whatever she required or asked them to do. Yet with no preparation, she is forced to live by her wits, pursued by a relentless Fate.
Imagine:	An encounter that Catherine has before meeting the woman who first employs her.
Sculpt:	An image of this encounter.
Share:	Encounters and ways in which Catherine deals with the situation.
Reflect:	On how Catherine develops the wherewithal to survive in a radically different situation from which she was brought up and so re-

cently lived.

Imagine: You have the opportunity to meet with Fate. What would you ask for, if anything? How would you deal with her?

Write: A brief story of your encounter with Fate.

Share: Stories.

Reflect: On stories and issues raised.

Remember: A situation where your inner resources were tested. What enabled you to deal with this situation? Were you to deal with it now, what might you do differently? What accounts for this change?

Share: Highlights of experience.

Reflect: On story, session, and developing inner resources.

"Stan and the Dragon" (Rumania)

Once upon a time there was a husband and wife who lived in a comfortable house, owned a herd of healthy cows, and had a fine garden with many fruit trees. Still, the wife was unhappy because they had no children. Unable to see her miserable for one more moment, her husband, Stan, left early one morning to consult a magician. After making sure that Stan really wanted children the magician told him, "Go home, your wish is granted."

Imagine Stan's surprise when he opened the front door and there were oodles and heaps of children of every size, shape, personality and color. "How will we feed all these children?" asked Stan. "There must be more than a hundred."

"No matter," said his wife cheerfully. "They are all wel-

come."

The next morning Stan left to find a way to feed and clothe his children. After walking all day, asking for work at every farm and receiving only no, no, and another no, he felt more than a little discouraged. When he saw a shepherd herding his sheep, Stan was ashamed to realize all he could think about was what a fine dinner his children could have if he stole a few of the sheep. He decided to hide in a thick bush and hoped he wouldn't fall asleep.   Just before midnight, when his eyes were so heavy he could barely stay awake, he heard a horrible noise, so loud the ground shook. A dragon, swooped down, picked up a lamb in each claw and flew away.

Stan took pity on the shepherd and helped him gather the frightened sheep. In return, the man offered him half of his dinner. He told him how the dragon came each night and stole two sheep. "If this keeps up I'll soon have no more sheep to herd."

"Hmm," said Stan. "If I rid you of the dragon, how will you reward me?"

"It's not likely you can, but if you do, I'll give you sheep enough to start your own flock." The two men agreed and the shepherd soon fell fast asleep. Stan was wide-awake, trying with no success, to think of a way to make the dragon stop stealing the shepherd's sheep.

The next day, while helping the shepherd tend his sheep, he wanted to think of a plan, but horrendous memories of the hideous sound drowned out his thoughts. As midnight approached Stan's fear intensified until he was so frightened he could hardly stand up.

When the dragon appeared, rushing down toward the sheep, the noise was even worse than the night before. Terrified, Stan screamed, "Stop your atrocious noise or I will…"

The dragon was so startled it stopped mid-flight, landed, and said, "Who are you?"

Stan's fear spoke for him. "I am Stan, the mighty man. I eat dragons for breakfast. These sheep are mine. Leave now or I will eat you."

"Go ahead. Eat me," bluffed the dragon.

Stan moved toward the dragon, knife and fork in hand, looking as ferocious as he knew how.

The dragon stepped away from Stan and said, "Well, if these sheep are yours I better look elsewhere." He flapped his wings, preparing to leave.

"Just a moment," snarled Stan. "We have a score to settle. You've already eaten too many. You have to pay me for my losses. That man over there, he's my shepherd and he knows the exact amount that is due. Pay up or else."

"I don't have any money but my mother does. If you come with me and help with our chores, she'll take a liking to you and give you more gold than you can carry."

Stan's terror turned to amazement. He felt himself grow bold and strong. "Lead me to her," he growled, as best he could.

The dragon's mother was bigger and more fearsome than her son. Sam was terrified but thinking about his hungry children gave him courage. "You say you're stronger than my son, do you? Well, we'll soon see," said the dragon's mother. She gave her son an enormous iron barrel and said, "Throw it as far as you can."

It fell so far from where Stan was standing he could barely hear it crash. "Your turn," said the dragon.

"Oh, it's such a pity that I might have to kill you with this barrel," said Stan, sounding mournfully sad.

"What?" yelped the dragon.

"A long time ago I did a favor for a magician and now,

any time I throw something, it comes back. Since it's your barrel it will probably smash right into you and kill you before you know what's happened."

"Well, in that case, there's no hurry. My mother will think of another way to see which of us is stronger."

The next morning the dragon's mother gave them each a huge pail and said, "The one who is stronger will carry the most water." The dragon lifted the pail as if it weighed nothing, ran to the well, filled it up, and was back in an instant. "Your turn," he said.

Stan bent down and with his pocketknife, began to dig up the earth. "No sense carrying a pail all that way when I can dig a well close by."

"Stop," screamed the dragon. "The well was dug by my grandfather's great-grandfather. It mustn't be disturbed. "I'll carry the pail for you." Stan kept digging.

"I'll give you twice the gold I promised if you'll stop digging," cried the dragon. Before Stan could reply, the dragon filled and emptied the pail twice. When the dragon mother saw how much water she thought Stan had carried, she devised another plan.

The next morning she said, "Let us see who can collect the most wood in the next hour." The dragon had no trouble lifting huge oaks out of the ground but Stan climbed to the top of the highest tree and noticed a vine creeping up toward him. He tied it to a strong branch and then, holding it, climbed to the top of a second tree. When he noticed the dragon watching him he said, "It's too much work pulling out one tree at a time, I'm going to tie all of the tallest trees with this vine and then I'll pull them up, all together."

Terrified the dragon yelled, "No! Stop! My great-grandfather's great-grandfather planted this forest. You mustn't *ruin the forest. I'll give you three times the amount of gold I promised if you'll leave the trees alone."*

"Very well, but this is the last time I'm going to promise to stop. Once I start something, I finish."

The dragon and his mother decided it didn't matter who was stronger, they just wanted Stan to leave. "Very well," said Stan, who was enjoying himself, "but if you want me to go, you'll have to carry me and the gold back to my house."

Quicker than an eye can blink, the dragon loaded up the gold and bent down so Stan could get on his back.

As they approached Stan's house, they could hear the laughs and shouts of his children. "Hmm," said Stan. "Maybe you better stop here. I have hundreds of children and they're all stronger than..." Before he could say another word, the dragon dumped the gold, shoved Stan off his back, and disappeared into the sky.

Stan grinned. Hmm, he thought, there's enough gold here to feed and clothe my children for the rest of their lives. Not bad for three days work.

Structure #1

Story:	Stan and the Dragon
Focus:	Facing fear
Paint:	An image of "fear" on the left side of the paper.
Write:	Words that come to mind.
Paint:	An image of "courage" on the right side of the paper.
Write:	Words that come to mind.
Write:	In the middle of the paper, words, phrases or objects that help you move from fear to

	courage.
Share:	Images, words, and objects that help you move from fear to courage.
Reflect:	On ideas and feelings about fear and courage.

Tell:	Stan and the Dragon.
Paint:	An image of a telling moment.
Title:	The image.
Write:	The story of the title creating events that could be in the story but were not in the story as it was told.
Share:	Stories.
Reflect:	On stories and issues raised.

Consider:	The dragon meets a friend who thinks the dragon's a coward. The friend tells the dragon that he's heard stories about how a man got the better of him (the dragon).
Create:	The story the dragon tells his friend.
Share:	Highlights of the story.
Reflect:	On stories we tell to ourselves and to others and what affects how we tell our story.

Think:	About a time when you were afraid. How did you deal with your fears? How might you deal with them now? What might make the difference?
Share:	Coping mechanisms for dealing with fear.
Reflect:	On story, session, and ways to deal with fear.

Structure #2
Story: Stan and the Dragon
Focus: Reframing a challenge

Tell: Stan and the Dragon.
Sculpt: An image of Stan at a critical moment in his
            life, in relationship to a person, place or
            thing.
Create: An episode that Stan might remember that
            helps him in his dealings with the dragon.
Share: Sculptures and episodes.
Reflect: On the impact prior experience can have on
            our present lives and choices.

Consider: That the dragon and his mother are having a
            fight. She wants him to do what he thinks is
            impossible. Think about what's at stake for
            each of them.
Write: A letter from the dragon to Stan. He tells
            Stan what his mother wants him to do and
            asks Stan for his advice.
Collect: And select letters. It doesn't matter if you
            get your own.
Write: A letter to the dragon, as Stan responding to
            the dragon's plea for help.
Share: Letters and return to original writer.
Reflect: On letters and issues raised in the
            writing.

Think:	About something someone asked you to do in the past that you could not, would not or did not do.
Reframe:	The way you dealt with the situation so that you are able to succeed on your terms.
Share:	Reframing.
Reflect:	On what it took for you to transform failure into success.
Retell:	The story using humor.
Share:	Highlights of your retelling.
Reflect:	On story, session, and what it means to reframe a challenge.

Structure #3

Story:	Stan and the Dragon
Focus:	Overcoming great odds
Paint:	An image of "great odds" on the left side of the paper.
Write:	Words that come to mind.
Paint:	An image of "resourcefulness" on the right side of the paper.
Write:	Words that come to mind.
Share:	Images and words.
Reflect:	On ideas as to what might help you to overcome great odds.
Tell:	Stan and the Dragon.
Sculpt:	An image of the feelings of the shepherd and

	the dragon before Stan arrives.
Write:	A brief dialogue of an encounter between the shepherd and the dragon.
Share:	Dialogues.
Reflect:	On the strategies the shepherd and Stan use to deal with the dragon.

Sculpt:	An image of "overcoming great odds."
Think:	Of a time when you overcame great odds. What enabled you to meet the challenge? What allies, if any did you have? What resources came into play? How did this affect you? Does it still have impact?
Write:	The story of how you overcame great odds creating a fictional character to tell your story. Feel free to "elaborate" or "exaggerate."
Share:	Stories.
Reflect:	On story, on strategies used to overcome great odds, the differences between what "really" happened and what you created, and what it might take to overcome great odds.

Structure #4	
Story:	Stan and the Dragon
Focus:	Confronting power
Sculpt:	An image of "powerless and an image of "powerful" and place them in relationship.

Write:	Words or phrases that might help you move from feeling powerless to powerful.
Share:	Images, words and ideas about moving from powerless to powerful. Talk about the relationship of the two sculptures. After sharing words, feel free to change the relationship of the two sculptures.
Reflect:	On ideas evoked by images and words.
Tell:	Stan and the Dragon
Paint:	An image of Stan and the dragon meeting at some time after the story ends.
List:	Some questions Stan might ask the dragon and questions the dragon might ask Stan.
Create:	A short dialogue that is fueled by questions each has for the other.
Share:	Dialogues.
Reflect:	On issues raised by each character.
Remember:	A time when you felt powerless.
Briefly:	Write a brief description of the situation.
Remember:	A time when you felt powerful.
Briefly:	Write a brief description of the situation.
Share:	Highlights of each situation and what made the difference between feeling powerless and powerful.
Reflect:	On what makes us feel powerless and what makes each of us feel powerful. Are there ways in which we can change feelings of being powerless into feelings of being power-

ful? If so, what are they? Are there extenuating conditions?

Sculpt: An image of a character who feels powerless.
Create: A story in which the character proves to be powerful.
Share: Stories.
Reflect: On story, session, and ideas about feeling powerful and powerless.

7

PROBLEMATICAL AND UNRESOLVED STORIES FOR EXPERIENCED STORYMAKERS

The old man in Budapest had given my father's story to Paula, who had given me the story too; Sola had offered hers to Diego, and to me as well. We needed the stories to tether us to the world; sharing them among ourselves could keep us connected to the dead and to one another.

Voices were filaments in the ether.

We could live in two places at once—carry the past inside the present. We could travel faster than the speed of light.

The Speed of Light by Elizabeth Rosner

ALTHOUGH EVERYONE CAN benefit by exploring the stories and exercises from the preceding chapter, the following stories have problematical endings—in that they either don't end happily ever after or have unresolved issues. I suggest these stories NOT be attempted by people who have little or no prior participatory experieince in storymaking sessions. However, these advanced stories do offer interesting and creative possibilities if people are able to take what is offered and make choices that shift the negative, or seemingly unfinished ending, into a story that is healing, whole, and resolved. It is important to choose a focus that enables participants the opportunity to each work through difficult aspects of the story. The following foci and structures provide suggestions as to how to explore the presented issues.

"The Journeys of Little Duck" (Australia)

Little Duck lived in a pond with her family and lots of other young ducks. They were constantly warned, "Never, ever leave our pond. Downstream lives a monster just waiting to eat you. Or worse…"

"What does a monster look like?" asked Little Duck who was very curious. No one answered her question. No one knew for certain, but they all had ideas. None of their answers satisfied Little Duck. One day, when no one was looking, she swam downstream. All she wanted was to have just a bit of a look, but the monster caught her and refused to let her go.

"You will be my wife," he told her. Little Duck refused and tried to escape but the monster watched her closely and she was unable to find a way to go back to her home. Even though she became pregnant, he continued to watch her day and night.

One night, when the monster could no longer keep his eyes open and fell into a deep sleep, Little Duck escaped and swam back upstream to the pond. Everyone was overjoyed to see her, welcoming her home with great happiness. Once again, Little Duck swam and splashed, delighted to be living among friends and family.

But, when she gave birth, her children did not look like the other duck children. They did not look like their mother. The other ducks were afraid of Little Duck's children and told her, "Take your children and leave." Little Duck tried to convince the ducks that her babies could do no harm but they would not listen. "Babies grow up. They are the children of the monster and they will hurt us when they can."

So, Little Duck gathered her children and left the pond, swimming upstream until she came to a big lake. Here her children grew and flourished. In time they mated and had children of their own. Their children looked like their parents. None looked like Little Duck. The children were ashamed of Little Duck. They told her, "You must leave our lake. We do not want to see you. You do not look like us. We do not know you."

Little Duck took one last look at her children and grandchildren and then, with an aching heart, she swam away, into unknown waters.

Structure #1
Story: The Journeys of Little Duck
Focus: Reconnection across generations

Paint: An image of "past," "present," and "future" on one paper.
Write: Words for each image that come to mind.
Share: Words and images.
Reflect: On how each aspect of life affects the others.

Tell: The Journeys of Little Duck.
Sculpt: An image of two characters who are or could be in the story, at a telling moment.
Create: A dialogue that reveals a critical issue that each is struggling with.
Share: Sculptures and dialogue. Talk about why you have chosen to sculpt this moment.
Reflect: On what has been revealed, why specific moments were chosen, and feelings and thoughts evoked by choices.

Imagine:	It is some time after Little Duck has swum away. Some of her grandchildren ask questions about their ancestors. When they are told about Little Duck some think about her and wonder how she is. One grandchild writes a letter to her grandmother.
Write:	A letter the grandchild might write to her grandmother. In it, the grandchild asks Little Duck a question of great importance to her/him. Decide how you want to open and close the letter.
Collect:	Letters and redistribute them.
Imagine:	Little Dick receives the letter. Answer it as if you are Little Duck. Address the question asked. Decide how you want to begin and end the letter.
Share:	Letters and return them to the original writer.
Reflect:	On letters, questions and answers, story, session, and issues arising from work.

◎

Structure #2

Story:	The Journeys of Little Duck
Focus:	Reframing the story
Tell:	The Journeys of Little Duck.
Paint:	An image of three "people" who are close to Little Duck before she meets the monster.
Briefly:	Describe who these people are, their rela-

	tionship to Little Duck, and how they feel about her before she meets the monster.
Share:	Images and descriptions and how you came to choose these three.
Reflect:	On choices and possible ramifications of choices.

Paint:	An image of these three people after Little Duck returns from the monster.
Briefly:	Describe their actions toward her and how each person feels about her.
Share:	Images and writing.
Reflect:	On how these people felt and acted toward Little Duck before and after she meets the monster. What occasions the change, if any?

Sculpt:	An image of Little Duck and the parent with whom she is closest at a particular point in the story.
Create:	A dialogue that takes place before and after she meets monster. If you chose her parents as part of the three people, choose another person who plays a significant role in Little Duck's life.
Share:	Highlights of dialogue and feelings before and after her meeting with the monster.
Reflect:	On story, session, and issues arising from changes in relationships.

Structure #3

Story:	The Journeys of Little Duck
Focus:	Being/feeling different
Paint:	On the left side of the paper, an image of "apart from."
Write:	Words that come to mind.
Paint:	On the right side of the paper, an image of "a part of."
Share:	Images and words.
Reflect:	On issues arising from these concepts.
Tell:	The Journeys of Little Duck.
Paint:	An image of a telling moment.
Write:	A memory evoked by this moment.
Share:	Images and memories.
Reflect:	On how stories live inside us.
Imagine:	Yourself as Little Duck at a specific point in the story.
Write:	A brief monologue describing what you are experiencing and feeling. Pose a question that you keep thinking about.
Share:	Questions. Speak the monologues first without reference to what was written, then read what was written.
Reflect:	On the questions asked and the difference in expression between oral and written monologues.
Select:	One question that interests you, as if you are a character in or who could be in the story of Little Duck.

Write:	The question on a piece of paper.
Collect:	Papers.
Choose:	A paper and write a short story as if you are a character in or who could be in the story. Address the question as part of your story.
Share:	Questions and stories. Return to the person who asked the question.
Reflect:	On story, on session, on being apart from or part of community.

◎

Structure #4

Story:	The Journeys of Little Duck
Focus:	New ways from old

Paint:	An image of "old" on the left side of the paper.
Write	Words that come to mind.
Paint:	An image of "new" on the right side of the paper.
Write:	Words that come to mind.
Reflect:	On images and words, on personal meanings of old and new.

Tell:	The Journeys of Little Duck
Sculpt:	An image of Little Duck, an image of one of her children, and an image of one of her grandchildren in relationship to each other.
Share:	Images.
Reflect:	On what they have in common, differences, and new potential for relationship or interac-

tion.

Imagine:	The grandchildren and great-grandchildren decide to write the history or their family.
Select:	One of the offspring and create a charac ter.
Write:	The history from this character's point of view.
Share:	Histories.
Reflect:	On point of view, issues raised, and what emerges from the stories.

Paint:	An image of a time when you made a choice that was an abrupt change from previous choices.
Write:	Words that come to mind.
Briefly:	Write what happened.
Consider:	The consequence(s) of your choice and your feelings about this time.
Share:	Highlights of your experience.
Reflect:	On story, how new ways emerge from old, the consequences and what we learn from breaking with the past.

"The Old Man and the Villagers" (Africa)

There was once a village where the people enjoyed many years of prosperity. The rains came regularly and their crops flourished. In time, their grain bins were so full, one of them collapsed and the grain scattered. However, the people had so much stored they left the grain where it was.

In a short time, birds found the grain and decided the vil-

lage was a good place to live. When the people finished working in the fields, the birds flew down and began eating. The next morning, when the people saw how much grain the birds had eaten, they began to worry that the birds would find a way to eat the stored grain. So, when the birds flew down to eat, the people tried to chase them away with noise. When this didn't work, they shot arrows into their air but this too failed to deter the birds.

The villagers called a meeting to discuss how to get rid of the birds. Although no one wanted to be the first to mention the Old Man, he was on everyone's mind. They looked at the Headman who said, "We shall soon starve if we do not rid our village of the birds. We have tried but nothing worked. Perhaps the Old Man will once again help us." Everyone was silent. "It is true we chased him away because we were afraid of his magic but he is our only hope. I will go to him. Perhaps he will take pity on us and agree to return to help us."

The next morning the Headman went in search of the Old Man. Although he was dressed in worn clothes and had little in the way of goods, the Old Man was not at all pleased to see the Headman, nor did he want to return to the village. But, when the Headman told him the children would starve if he didn't help them, the Old Man agreed to return.

Before returning to the village, the Old Man collected roots and plants to make a powder. That evening, after the villagers thanked him for coming, he showed them how to dip their arrows into the powder and how best to use them..

The leader of the birds saw the people with their bows and arrows but he was not afraid and continued to eat. When the Old Man quietly said, "Now!" the villagers shot their arrows into the leader of the birds and killed him. Seeing this, the other birds flew away in fear.

The villagers held a great feast to honor the Old Man and for a time, all was well. Then, whispers began. People said, "If he has magic to kill the birds, he can kill us. We must tell him to go." The whispers grew into a loud chorus and soon, the villagers forced the Old Man to leave.

In time, the birds returned. The villagers watched helplessly as their grain disappeared. Once again, they tried, but could not get rid of the birds. The villagers decided there was nothing to do but to ask the Old Man to come back to help them.

The Headman told the Old Man of the village's troubles and how sorry they were that they had asked him to leave. The Old Man listened carefully. Then he said, "No!"

Structure #1

Story: The Old Man and the Villagers
Focus: Action and reaction

Paint: An image of "action" on the left side of the paper.
Write: Words that come to mind.
Paint: An image of "reaction" on the right side of the paper.
Write: Words that come to mind.
Create: One title for both images and write it somewhere on the paper.
Share: Images, placement of titles, and titles.
Reflect: On images, words and titles.

Tell: The story of the Old Man and the Villagers.
Sculpt: An image of action and an image of reaction

	in relationship to one another.
Create:	A situation for the sculptures.
Share:	The situation and move the sculptures to reflect the situation.
Reflect:	On the situation and the beginning and ending positions of the sculptures.

Consider:	A time when your action provoked an unexpected reaction. How did the reaction affect you? What, if any, action did you take in return? What were the consequences?
Write:	The story of the action and reaction using fictional characters, writing in third person.
Share:	Stories.
Reflect:	On the story and the nature of action and reaction. Is there any difference between writing in third or first person? If so, what?

◎

Structure #2

Story:	The Old Man and the Villagers
Focus:	Speaking one's truth

Paint:	An image of "truth."
Write:	Something that you know is true.
Write:	Something you believe is true.
Write:	Something you hope is true.
Share:	Images and writings.
Reflect:	On the nature of truth.

Tell:	The Old Man and the Villagers

Consider:	One of the villagers keeps a secret diary. He or she writes about what happens in the village in his or her diary.
Sculpt:	An image of the diary writer.
Describe:	The person.
Create:	Significant diary entries.
Share:	Sculptures, descriptions, and diary entries.
Reflect:	On what constitutes one's truth.

Create:	A monologue that the Old Man speaks at a critical point in his life.
Share:	Monologues.
Reflect:	On the story, the chosen points, and issues raised in the monologues.

Structure #3

Story:	The Old Man and the Villagers
Focus:	A part of, apart from

Tell:	The Old Man and the Villagers
Write:	An incident in the life of the Old Man when he was growing up in the village.
Share:	Incidents
Reflect:	On incidents and what might have contributed to his becoming the Old Man.

Write:	An incident in the life of the Old Man when he lived in the village before the villagers asked him to leave the first time.
Share:	Incidents

Reflect:	On incidents and his relationship with the villagers.
Paint:	An image on the left side of the paper of "a part of."
Write:	Words that come to mind.
Paint:	An image on the right side of the paper of "apart from."
Write:	Words that come to mind.
Share:	Images and words. Talk about the role "a part of" and "apart from" have played in your life.
Reflect:	On the story and the power and impact of "a part of" and "apart from."

◎

Structure #4

Story:	The Old Man and the Villagers
Focus:	The consequences of knowing

Tell:	The Old Man and the Villagers.
Paint:	An image of a telling moment from a particular person's point of view.
Write:	Words that come to mind from this person's point of view.
Share:	Images, words and points of view.
Reflect:	On moments chosen, characters chosen and their points of view.
Consider:	The Old Man's relationship with the people in his village. Think about how he got to be

the person with more knowing that any one else. Is this knowing knowledge or wisdom?

Write:	An episode in his life that foreshadowed his being exiled from his village the first time.
Share:	Episodes.
Reflect:	On episodes and what it means to be the one who knows, and on the difference(s) between knowledge and wisdom.

Consider:	The scene in which the Headman comes to the Old Man for the second time and tries to persuade him to return, promising him the villagers will never ask him to leave again.
Paint:	An image on the left side of the paper of the Old Man before the Headman comes the second time.
Write:	What the Headman is thinking.
Paint:	An image on the right side of the paper of the Old Man after the Headman comes the second time.
Write:	What the Headman is thinking.
Share:	Images and words.
Reflect:	On the responsibility the Headman has, trying to get the Old Man to help people who have treated him badly and on the Old Man's reaction.

Sculpt:	An image of the Old Man after the Headman leaves the second time.
Consider:	The Old Man keeps a journal.
Write:	His journal entry for that day.

Reflect: On the story and the consequences of being the person who knows.

"The Whippoorwill's Song" (Native American)

A boy heard the song of the whippoorwills one night and it was so beautiful, he decided to find the place where the whippoorwills sang. He began to walk, following their song, thinking the place where the birds lived was close by. Although he walked for hours, he still could not find the place. After struggling to climb over rocks and cross over streams, he found himself on a well-worn trail and stayed on it until he came to a clearing where Coyote sat on a tree stump, singing. Coyote stopped singing and asked the boy, "Why are you following me?"

Frightened, the boy replied politely, "I was following the beautiful song of the whippoorwills. I wish to find the place where the whippoorwills sing."

Coyote grinned, "Is my song not beautiful?"

"Oh yes," said the boy, even more politely. "Your song is nice. But I love the whippoorwills' song."

Furious, Coyote said, "Listen to my night song, you might like it." Coyote opened his mouth wide and sang. The boy covered his ears; the noise was terrible.

"Thank you for your song but I must leave if I want to find the place where the whippoorwills sing."

"Well," said Coyote, "if you like, I will show you a short cut. Follow me." He pointed to a bend in the woods, a smile curling up at the side of his mouth. The boy hesitated.

"I thought you wanted to find the place where the Whippoorwills sing," snickered Coyote.

"Yes, I do" said the boy, feeling uncomfortable.

"Then stop dillydallying and follow me."

The boy decided to do so and kept up as best he could but Coyote moved quickly, leaping over gopher holes into which the boy plunged, jumping over streams into which the boy fell, scampering over boulders the boy struggled to climb. Soon Coyote was nowhere to be seen. As the sun rose, the whippoorwills stopped singing.

The boy, covered with burrs, mosquito bites, bruises and scratches, realized there was nothing to be done but to find his way home.

Structure #1
Story: The Whippoorwill's Song
Focus: Listening to one's self

Paint: An image of "listening to one's self."
Write: Words that come to mind.
Share: Words and images.
Reflect: On what it takes to listen to one's self. What
                hinders? What helps?

Tell: The Whippoorwill's Song
Sculpt: An image of a telling moment.
Share: Sculptures.
Reflect: On sculptures, telling moments, and the im-
                portance of the chosen telling moments.

Paint: An image of a time when you gave yourself
                an important message.
Write: The message someplace on your image.
Share: Images and messages.
Reflect: On whether you listened to the message you

gave yourself and what made you decide as
you did.

Write: A letter as if you are the boy, telling what
           happened to an important person in his life.
           Decide who this person is, the relationship
           to the boy, and why the boy decides to write
           to this person at this time.

Share: Letters.

Reflect: On story, on how we learn to listen and/or
           ignore what we think and feel, and the con-
           sequences of listening and ignoring our
           thoughts and feelings.

Structure #2

Story: The Whippoorwill's Song

Focus: Listening to others

Paint: An image of "listening to others."

Write: Words that come to mind.

Share: Images and words.

Reflect: On when, why and how we listen
           to others.

Sculpt: An image of you in relationship to someone
           to whom you listened.

Write: The story of what happened as if you are a
           character in the story.

Share   Sculptures and stories.

Reflect: On your experience of listening to someone

else.

Tell:	The Whippoorwill's Song
Paint:	A telling moment.
Write:	Words that come to mind.
Reflect:	On images and words and what it can mean to listen to someone else, especially if you feel you are going against what you are telling yourself.

Sculpt:	An image of you and the boy in relationship.
Write:	Down a question the boy asks you.
Answer:	The question.
Share:	Questions and answers.
Reflect:	On the story and issues around listening or not listening to others.

◎

Structure #3

Story:	The Whippoorwill's Song
Focus:	Developing resilience

Paint:	An image of "resilience."
Write:	Words that come to mind.
Share:	Images and words.
Reflect:	On images and words.

Tell:	The Whippoorwill's Song
Imagine:	It is the next morning.
Write:	A diary entry as if you are the boy.
Share:	Diary entries.

Reflect:	On issues and feelings raised.
Imagine:	It is some time after the boy returns home.
Write:	One sentence beginning with the words: The next morning... Place the papers around the room. Each person writes one sentence on each person's paper. No one can deny what was written. For example, if someone writes there was a terrible storm, the next person cannot write there was no storm. Each sentence needs to incorporate what has been previously written and further the story. Continue until there are at least ten entries. The number of people participating will determine how many entries each person writes. Return stories to first writer.
Read:	Your story. If necessary, create an ending.
Share:	Stories.
Reflect:	On responses to the boy's encounter with Coyote.
Sculpt:	An image of the boy and Coyote some time after the story takes place.
Create:	A dialogue between them.
Share:	The sense of the dialogues.
Reflect:	On story and issues around developing resilience,

Structure #4
Story: The Whippoorwill's Song

Focus:	Finding one's way
Paint:	An image on the left side of the paper of "a path that goes nowhere."
Write:	Words that come to mind.
Paint:	An image on the right side of the paper of "a path that goes somewhere."
Write:	Words that come to mind.
Share:	Images and words.
Reflect:	On what it takes to find one's way.

Tell:	The Whippoorwill's Song
Sculpt:	A telling moment.
Share:	Moments. Talk about the importance of this moment to you.
Reflect:	On moments chosen and what is evoked by them.

Imagine:	The boy wakes up the next morning and makes a decision. What does he decide and what are the consequences?
Write:	A brief account of the boy's day.
Share:	Accounts.
Reflect:	On choices and stories.

Imagine:	A character who is finding her/his way.
Sculpt:	An image of the character in relationship to a person, place or thing.
Paint:	An image of the journey and how the character finds his/her way.
Share:	Sculptures and images and ways in which

characters find their way.

Reflect: On story and on what is involved in finding one's way.

"The Golden Fish" (Burma)

There were once two sisters who had two different mothers. The older sister was jealous of her younger sister. One day, when they were away from the village, in a fit of jealous rage, the older sister killed her younger sister. The gods took pity on the dead girl and transformed her into a golden fish.

Some time later, when the prince was out fishing, he looked into the water and saw the golden fish. He was so struck by its beauty he decided to catch it and marry the lovely fish.

Imagine his surprise when he caught the fish and it turned back into the younger sister. Naturally, he asked how she had been transformed into a golden fish. When the prince heard her story he wanted to find the older sister and punish her but the younger sister stopped him. She told the prince, "My sister is still suffering. Her evil deed has not brought her happiness."

Structure #1

Story: The Golden Fish
Focus: Sibling relationships

Paint: An image of "sibling relationship."
Write: Words that come to mind.
Share: Images and words
Reflect: On what hinders or helps relationships between/among sibling(s).

Tell:	The Golden Fish
Paint:	A telling moment.
Write:	As if you are a character who is or could be in the story, in the form of a diary entry, and include why this moment is important to your character.
Share:	Aspects of your character and the diary entry.
Reflect:	On images and diary entries.
Imagine:	An incident when the two sisters are relatively young.
Create:	The incident.
Share:	Incidents and talk about possible consequences to their later lives.
Reflect:	On choices made and possible consequence, both short and long term.
Sculpt:	An image of you in relationship to your sibling(s). If you have none, sculpt yourself in relationship to an important peer who was, or who you wished was in your life at a critical point in your life.
Share	Sculptures and important moments.
Reflect:	On the story and on sibling relationships.

◎

Structure #2

Story:	The Golden Fish
Focus:	The energy of feelings

Divide:	The paper into four spaces.
Paint:	The energy of four different feelings.
Write:	Words that come to mind.
Share:	Images and words.
Reflect:	On images, words, and the qualities of the different energies.

Tell:	The Golden Fish
Sculpt:	An image of the feelings of the older sister toward her younger sister at a critical moment in the older sister's life.
Write:	And title the story of the moment.
Share:	Images and stories.
Reflect:	On how the older sister was feeling and what, if anything, she chose to do about her feelings.

Consider:	A time in your life when you felt strongly about something or someone. What was the nature of the energy of your feeling?
Write:	A brief story about how you dealt with the energy of your feelings. If you wished you had dealt with them differently, write a second version as if you had a chance to choose a different response.
Share:	Stories.
Reflect:	On story and on ways to deal with different kinds of energy created by feelings.

Structure #3

Story:	The Golden Fish
Focus:	Transformation

Sculpt:	An image of "transformation."
Share:	Sculptures.
Reflect:	On transformation—what it is, how it happens, what it means.

Tell:	The Golden Fish
Imagine:	The scene where the gods learn of the girl's murder.
Create:	The story of how they come to know about the girl's murder and how they decide to transform her into a golden fish.
Share:	Stories of transformation.
Reflect:	On how transformation may occur.

Paint:	An image of "me" in relationship to "transformation."
Write:	Words that come to mind.
Share:	Images and words.
Reflect:	On images, words, and your relationship to transformation.

Consider:	Your life. Have you experienced transformation? If so, under what circumstances? What effect, if any, does it continue to have on your life? If not, what transformation might you envision for yourself?
Write:	A fictional story about your experience of transformation inventing characters. If you

have never experienced transformation, create the story of what you think a fictional character might have experienced.

Share: Stories.
Reflect: On the story and issues and ideas of transformation.

Structure #4
Story: The Golden Fish
Focus: The power of love

Paint: An image of "love."
Write: Words that come to mind.
Share: Images and words.
Reflect: On love, what it means to love, and the power of love.

Tell: The Golden Fish
Consider: The younger sister is murdered by her older sister, yet the younger sister refuses to allow her husband, the prince, to punish the older sister. How do you suppose she has come to this decision?
Create: A brief monologue where the younger sister talks about her feelings about what happened and why she doesn't want her older sister to be punished by the prince.
Share: Monologues.
Reflect: On ways in which the younger sister might have come to feel and act as she does.

Sculpt:	An image of the two sisters in relationship at a pivotal point in their lives.
Create:	A dialogue between them that might have far reaching consequences.
Share:	Sculptures and dialogues.
Reflect:	On sculptures and dialogues.
Imagine:	The older sister's life after her younger sister is transformed into her mortal self, marries the prince, and intervenes so she, the older sister, is not punished for her act.
Create:	A brief scenario that reveals something of the older sister's life and choices she might make in regard to one or more important relationships.
Share:	Scenarios.
Reflect:	On the story and the power of love.

8

SUGGESTIONS FOR STORYMAKING ACTIVITIES: PROMPTS, PROPS, AND IDEAS FOR CREATING STRUCTURES

"I'm lonely. I want to make a world," cries
Bhagavan, one creator god... Hence creation myths. Because to tell how the world
began, how we came by fire—and food—
and death—even to hazard guesses at how it
might all end--is in a sense to recreate it for
ourselves...

Creation Myths of the World

NOTE: The productive use of any storymaking activity depends upon the specific focus of the particular session. Without it, activities remain generic and it becomes more difficult for a group to have a satisfying experience. For example, Trickster masks can be used to explore a variety of possibilities including: one's inner Trickster, creativity, or the creation of a community of Tricksters. To make Trickster masks without an explicit focus is generally unproductive and can be frustrating due to the lack of shape to the exploration.

Group activities such as poems, stories, chants, and paint-ings can serve to create community, develop interpersonal relationships, create deeper possibility, and enhance indi-viduality within community—depending on the focus of the session.

Trickster Masks:

Masks can be made out of any material that appeals to the maker but all masks MUST have mouth and nose holes large enough to permit talking and breathing, and be secured in such ways as to allow free use of hands and body movement with ease. Concentrate on liberating your inner Trickster rather than on making a "perfect mask." What you make needs to be purposeful. Work metaphorically, not literally. Focus on creating a fully developed fictional character. Remember that Trickster is the embodiment of paradox, a creature who does not reflect and acts out of the moment, who wants what he/she wants when he/she wants it. While wearing your mask, invent the autobiography of your Trickster. Create the occasion, song, dance, and/or a ritual he/she might make.

Making a Character Mask:

1. Wrap layers of newspaper around a sphere of crushed newspaper to form the basic size and shape. Use masking tape to hold the layers together.

2. Wrap a plastic bag around the paper sphere. Twist it tightly and tie it with masking tape opposite the side where the face will be. Cut off the excess plastic.

3. Cut a two-inch plaster bandage to a length that will encircle the sphere midway between front and back. This frames the mask and allows removal of the newspaper ball later. Hold the long piece of plaster in warm water until it is soft. Squeeze out excess water and apply it to the sphere. Attach shorter pieces of bandage across the front of the

mask in all directions until a smooth shell several layers thick has been built up.

4. Construct the features of the mask with molded wet tissue paper. Then cover the tissue with small pieces of plaster, reworking the features as necessary while the plaster is wet. Use string, yarn, plaster strips or other material to form hair. Set the mask to dry for about an hour.

5. Paint the mask with water-based acrylic paint. When the paint is dry, remove the plastic bag covering the newspaper. Use masking tape to smooth off rough edges. Wear the mask to make sure you are able to breathe, talk and move comfortably while wearing your mask. Make necessary adjustments to ensure ease of use.

Making a Life Mask:
1. Grease your face with any non-toxic, non-irritating product that will allow the mask to be pulled off without hurting your face. Cover your hair with a plastic bag greased on the outside.

2. Wet strips of plaster as you use them.

3. If possible, work with a partner who wraps strips of wet plaster around your face, allowing for nose and mouth holes. If you have no partner, look in a mirror as you wrap the strips to make sure you have covered the desired area and left holes for breathing and talking.

4. When strips feel solid, remove from face.

5. When plaster is dry, paint and decorate the surface.

Trickster Chants:

Trickster figures such as Anansi the Spider, Hare, Tortoise, Coyote, and Raven have the reputation for being smart and stupid, wise and foolish, brave and cowardly, afraid and fearful, kind and cruel, creators and destroyers, helpful and mean-spirited. They embrace all human possibility. Before working with Trickster stories, many groups have found it helpful and comforting to create a simple two-line chant to honor our paradoxical human qualities.

Depending on the size of the group, work singly or in pairs. If, for example, there are four participants, write two qualities and their opposites on four pieces of paper. The group might choose to work with brave and cowardly, helpful and mean-spirited. Each person chooses a piece of paper with a quality on it and then writes two lines the Trickster might chant at a time when he/she is feeling this quality. For example, one group wrote the following chant when Hare was feeling foolish: *I am silly; I am foolish. Help me learn to overcome this.* Another group wrote these two lines when Tortoise was afraid: *I'm afraid; I'm full of fear. Help me safely out of here.*

When the chants have been written, each person or group teaches their chant to all participants so that everyone knows each chant to use when necessary.

Group Poem:

After hearing a story, each participant writes one sentence that reflects, comments, arises from, or responds to the story. Sentences are then put in a chosen order negotiated by all group members. This process can also be done with an incident, film, theatre piece, or any activity/event experienced by the entire group.

Group Story:
After hearing a story, the group is given a beginning sentence that provides a starting place but no specific direction, such as: "The next morning, when he or she awoke, she/he sat on a stone and decided to ..." Each person legibly writes the beginning phrase on a piece of paper, adds one sentence to begin the story, and places the paper on the floor anywhere in the room. In turn, everyone reads what has been written and then writes one new sentence on each person's paper, furthering and shaping the story. The one rule is that no one can deny what has just been written. For example, if the preceding writer has written, "the boy gave the girl two shiny red apples," the next writer can't write that they were peaches or worms or that he didn't give the girl anything. What can be written is that soon after he gave them to her he took them back, or grabbed one and ate one, or traded them for something else.

When everyone has written one sentence on each person's paper, participants read what has been written on their paper. If there are only three or four in the group, and the stories seem incomplete, people may choose to repeat the process until the stories are finished. Before the stories are shared, each writer reads what has been written and may add one or two sentences to complete the story if this seems necessary or desirable.

Group Painting:

After hearing a story, participants might choose to express their feelings, thoughts, or ideas as a group. It helps to have a large piece of paper but even ordinary copy paper can be used. People can take turns or paint as they choose, sensitively selecting what, where and how to paint. The group decides when the painting is finished.

Need/Want/Wish:

How we start a session can reveal what each person is bringing to it. Painting an image of "myself at this moment," writing words that come to mind, and sharing what has been painted and written is one way to begin. Another useful way to start a session is to divide a piece of paper into three parts and to title each section at the top of each third of the paper. The first title is "need," the second title is "want," and the third title is "wish." Under each image write words that come to mind. This can be done in role, as a character who is or could be in the story, or as one's self. It is important to understand that these activities are of the moment and can easily change in the next.

Journey to Get/Receive/Find/What You Want:

Paint:	On a piece of paper, an image of a person or creature about to take a journey.
Give:	Person or creature a name and write it on the paper.
Write:	On the same piece of paper, what person or creature wants to find/receive/understand at the end of the journey.
Write:	On the same piece of paper, two qualities

the person or creature takes with her/him on the journey. (Possible qualities include: tenacity, willingness to try something new, courage, anxiety, fear, timidity, ability to go without food for a long time, intelligence.)

Paint: An image of "departure" on the left side of a new (second) piece of paper. The right side will be used later on.

Write: On the left side of this paper, words to describe what the person or creature is thinking and feeling as she/he departs.

Give: Participants four small pieces of paper.

Write: On the first two papers, the word, "helper" and then write one helper on each piece of paper the person or creature will find on her/his journey. (This could be real, like a wind or a hot meal, or imagined like the voice in a dream.)

Write: On the second two pieces of paper "obstacle" and then write one obstacle on each paper that the person or creature will encounter on her/his journey. (This could be something like money, time, an ill-wind or a raging river.) Sometimes a person will get the same word, such as "time," for both obstacle and helper. In this case, the participant has to use time both in a helpful way and as an obstacle.

Collect: Helpers and obstacles and put them in two separate piles. Participants select two helpers and two obstacles from each pile.

Write:	The story of the journey, of getting what is wanted, using "I." Incorporate the qualities, helpers and obstacles selected, creating an episode for each, rather than simply naming their effect.
Paint:	An image of "arrival" on the right side of the same paper on which you painted "departure."
Write:	On the "arrival" side of the paper, words that describe what the person or creature is thinking and feeling as she/he arrives and gets what she/he wants.
Share:	Journey stories.
Reflect:	On stories and the journeys.
Paint/Write:	For a few minutes while reflecting on your experiences during this session.
Reflect:	On what it means to ask for, and receive, what you want.

NOTE: Sometimes it is difficult for people to ask for what they want, and then to allow themselves to receive what they have asked for. In this activity, if people don't get what they say they want, it is possible that they will feel bad. It often helps to remind group members that this activity requires them to get what they want. Encourage them to do so before beginning the activity. If all else fails, the group might paint images of support and encouragement to give to the person, perhaps sharing ways to get what he or she wants or suggesting strategies that participants have used successfully.

Sending/Receiving a Letter:
As One Character and Answering as Another

Write a letter as a character who is, or could be, in the story, at a moment of crisis. As this character, ask for help or advice to solve a pressing and important problem. It is crucial that the crisis be urgent and immediate. The way the letter is addressed and signed needs to be considered because it has an influence on how the letter is received and answered. The letters are collected and participants choose one from a pile. It doesn't matter if a participant gets the letter he/she wrote. Participants answer the letter, in role, as if they are the person to whom the letter is addressed. As part of the answer, the writer suggests strategies to solve the problem and offers whatever help he/she is able to offer. How the letter is signed also needs to be well thought-out because it reveals the relationship between the responder of this letter to the original writer. The responder reads both the original letter and the response to the group before the letters are returned to the original writer. Participants reflect on questions or problems evoked by the story and suggested solutions, aids or advice that are offered by responders.

Creating a Story from a Person's Question

A character that is, or could be in the story writes a letter that includes a "burning" question, one of great importance to the character. In your letter, as the character, write a bit about your background, explaining why the question matters so much at this particular time. The character signs the letter in a way that reveals something about the character. The letters are put in a pile and participants choose one. It doesn't matter if participants get the letter they wrote. The responder chooses whether to know the original writer. In response to the "burning" question, the responder creates a story that addresses or answers the question. Responders read the letter and their story to the group before returning letters to the original writers. This activity is based on a practice common to a variety of traditional societies. People who are troubled by an event or experience go to a priest, shaman, elder or person known to be wise. They tell their troubles to this person who meditates while waiting for a response. After a period of time, the troubled person receives a story upon which to reflect and returns home, knowing the story contains the necessary wisdom to help ameliorate the problem. Participants reflect on the questions asked and the stories given in response.

One-Minute Monologue

Participants choose a character who interests, puzzles, annoys, irritates, angers, or otherwise intrigues them. They create a one-minute monologue, posing a question or dilemma at a moment of crisis where a choice has to be made immediately. Urgency is of the utmost importance. Participants write out the monologue but when they present it to the group, the monologue needs to be spoken, with no reference to what has been written, although after it has been given, participants may read what they wrote to compare oral and written dialogues. Group members, responding in role, may question, argue, support or take issue with the person giving the monologue. Group members may change role at any time as long as they identify the role in which they are speaking.

If the monologue is emotional and the discussion is

heated, it may be necessary to "debrief" the person giving the monologue. This can be done in many ways: sharing reasons why the character was chosen; talking about what it was like to give the monologue; sharing feelings before and after the monologue; asking for help from the group if the person feels stuck in the role. Sometimes it helps to paint an image of "being in role" on the left side of the paper and writing words that come to mind. On the right side of the paper, paint an image of "being myself" and writing words that come to mind. Writing words or a phrase that help participants move from being in role to being one's self helps differentiate being in and out of role. Sharing what has been painted and written is an important part of the process. Sticking to the one-minute limit helps people concentrate on the essence without undue exposition.

Alter-Ego Dialogue
Most of us have experienced the feeling of being at war with ourselves. After hearing a story, participants create alter-ego dialogues in pairs, in role, after which, partners reverse roles. The dialogues can be written or outlined and then spoken. Partners decide who they are, the occasion for the "meeting," the crisis that generates the urgency, and a question, issue, or event around which the dialogue is focused. The reflection focuses on the divergent points of view and any negotiation that might prove necessary or useful. Participants identify and reflect in role.

9
STORIES TO STIMULATE
STORYMAKING SESSIONS

"Stories are to society what dreams are to individuals. Without them we go mad."

Isabel Allende

THE STORIES IN this chapter have been used in diverse storymaking sessions with a variety of people in many different settings. They are offered as a kind of "smorgasbord," hoping that some of them will stimulate your creativity and imagination. I have chosen not to categorize the stories because categories depend on who makes the choices and can sometimes be misleading. Instead, I have selected stories from around the world that not only appealed to me, but also intrigued and interested most of the participants with whom I have worked.

"Suho and the White Horse" (Mongolia)
Long ago a poor shepherd boy named Suho lived with his grandmother in a yurt (a felt tent), in the middle of the Mongolian steppes. Each day Suho rose early to help his grandmother prepare breakfast before going out to take care of their small flock of sheep. As he kept watch he sang, and his rich voice rose over the grassy plains, breaking the stillness of the day.

One night, when Suho did not return home at his usual time, his grandmother and the other shepherds worried that something terrible had happened. Yet before the next rising of the sun, Suho appeared, carrying a newborn foal in his arms. Beaming with happiness, he told them how he had found the little one too weak to stand, with no mother or master around to feed him. "I was afraid the wolves would eat him so I brought him home."

Days went by and the colt grew strong and healthy under Suho's devoted care. The horse helped Suho look after the sheep, even staving off a bunch of wolves. Suho caressed the horse, rubbing him down, speaking to it as if it were his brother. "White horse, you fought well and bravely. The sheep are safe because of you. I will never forget you." As the years passed, Suho and the horse were inseparable. If his grandmother wanted Suho, she called to his horse.

One day, news spread that the governor declared he would give the hand of his daughter to the man who won the big race. The shepherds of Suho's village urged him to enter, knowing Suho's horse was the finest and fastest of all the horses. The day of the race, noblemen from all over the country came, riding fine horses, wearing silk clothing, but Suho paid them no mind. When the signal to begin was given, Suho and his white horse took off like the wind, easily winning the race.

Yet when the governor saw that the winner was only a poor shepherd boy, he gave him three pieces of silver and told him to be on his way, without the white horse—for the governor had decided to keep him. Suho retorted, "I came to win a race, not to lose my horse."

"Insolent beggar," shouted the governor. "You dare to answer me back? Guards, take him to the outskirts of the city and make sure he does not return." The guards rushed to obey their master's commands, leaving Suho beaten and bleeding at the edge of the city. He might have died there had not some shepherds nursed his wounds. Suho grieved the loss of his horse, his friend, his companion, but there was nothing he could do to get him back.

Meanwhile, the governor decided to hold a great feast to show off his fine horse. When the time came, the horse, richly bridled and saddled, was brought in for the governor to ride. As his guests admired the impressive horse, the governor heaved himself into the saddle and lightly flicked his whip. The great horse bucked and reared, throwing the governor onto the ground. He neighed once and then galloped off on the steppes, swift as the wind.

The governor shouted to his guards, "Go after him. Catch him if you can, but if you miss, shoot him with your arrows. Do not let him get away alive." The guards did as they were told but they could not catch him for the white horse ran too fast. Although they shot their arrows into his flanks, he kept galloping, leaving the guards in the dust.

Late that evening, when Suho was intoning his nightly lament, mourning the loss of his horse, he heard a noise outside the yurt and went to look. There, panting, with blood gushing out of his wounds, Suho saw his friend. Gently, he removed the arrows and bathed the wounds but the horse grew weaker. Just before the sun rose, his beloved horse died.

Shattered by grief, Suho lay sleepless night after night. He grew listless, forgetting to eat for days at a time. Then, one night, the white horse appeared to him in a dream, nuzzling Suho fondly. "Suho," said the horse in a soft voice, "you must not continue to mourn for me. Take my bones, hide, hair, and sinews and make them into an instrument to play upon when you sing. If you do this, I will remain with you forever."

Suho woke and followed the instructions he had heard in his dream, fashioning an instrument from the bones, hide, hair, and sinews of his beloved horse, ornamented by the figure of the horse's head which he lovingly carved.

Suho drew the bow across the strings as he sang about the

joys of riding his beloved horse, his grief at losing him, his sorrow when the horse died. Always, he sensed the presence of his white horse.

Others made horse-headed fiddles like the one Suho created. Even today, if you travel to the vast steppes of Mongolia, you will hear the songs created by Suho to honor the memory of his beloved friend, the white horse.

"The Vases of Harmony" (Gypsy)

The chief of the tribe gives two vases, one red and one blue, to a newly married couple but if no vases are available, two tins are used. One is for the husband, the other for the wife. They are also given a bag of mixed grains and broad beans. Daily the husband and wife each choose a single grain to put into his or her vase according to what kind of day each has spent with the other. For example, a red bean signifies a quarrel or anger; corn means a good day with some joy. A broad bean shows an exceptional day, really perfect (this is rare); and a lentil means a day of peace with no obvious discord. The husband and wife continue putting a grain into the vase every day without showing each other which one they put in. After a certain time, when they empty the vases in front of each other, they see the grains, put them back in the bag, and the couple begins again. When both vases are shown to contain only broad beans and lentils--the sign of harmony between the husband and wife--the couple plants these beans and lentils. They create images of a man and a woman out of the earth in which they have planted the beans and lentils to bless the newly planted seeds.

"The Little Parrot" (Tibet)

Little Parrot loved the jungle more than he loved life itself. Every morning, he flew over the greenery, looked at what lay below, and counted himself fortunate to live in such a beautiful place. Only when he was sure that all was well did he fly back to earth to eat his breakfast.

But one morning, when he flew overhead, he saw nothing but thick, dark smoke. The jungle was on fire! Little Parrot flew to the river as fast as his short wings permitted, took as much water in his mouth as he could, flew back to the fire, and spit out the water, trying to quench the huge flames. Back and forth he went, from the river to the fire, from the fire to the river, trying his best to put out the fire though he was not a big bird and could only take small gulps each time. He soon became exhausted but kept on going. His beloved jungle was at risk.

As he was flying to the river for the umpteenth time, worried that the jungle would burn before he could put out the fire, he heard a loud shrill laugh. Then a cackling voice squawked, "You are a silly parrot. Don't you know you are too small to put out such a big fire?"

Little Parrot looked up and saw Eagle, the largest bird in the jungle. "I don't need advice, I need help," he said quietly, continuing to fly to the river. The next thing Little Parrot knew, a huge stream of water poured from the skies dousing part of the fire. Little Parrot did not stop to see who was helping. He just kept flying to the river and back to the jungle, hoping that with this new help, the fire would soon be put out.

When there were no more flames, Little Parrot looked around to see if he could find the source of the help for which he was so grateful. He saw Eagle. Though utterly depleted, he flew up to Eagle and said, "Thank you from the bottom of my heart. Were it not for your help, the fire would still be burning. The jungle would be lost."

"No," said Eagle. "It is I who must thank you."

"The Location of Wisdom" (Laos)

In former times, the Akha had letters that contained all the wisdom of the tribe, but one year, the letters were swallowed by the water buffalo. The Akha moved every year and when it came to move this time, the water buffalo's skin was too big and too heavy to carry. The people were perplexed. Although they did not want to leave their letters and their wisdom, they could not move the skin.

The people went to the Headman. He thought about the problem and then spoke. "If we cannot move the water buffalo's skin, we must eat the water buffalo's skin. This way, we will keep the letters and our wisdom inside us, forever."

And so the water buffalo's skin was cut up into the number of people who lived in the community. Each person swallowed a piece. Thus was wisdom kept within the tribe forever.

"Why the Akha Wear Black Dresses" (Laos)

A long time ago, there lived an Akha man who saw a beautiful woman and wanted her to be his wife. However, she was not Akha and he knew her parents would not approve. Still, he loved her very much and spoke to her. "Will you be my wife?"

The woman loved the man and said, "Yes. But what shall we do about my parents? They will not agree to this marriage."

The man said, "Let us try. Perhaps they will not come to the wedding ceremony."

But the parents did come and when they saw their daughter in her brightly colored clothes they took her home.

Still, the woman and man were determined. They sat and thought. The woman looked at the man and said, "I have an idea. In my village, women wear clothes of many colors. Please ask the women in your village to wear black to our wedding. I will also wear black. If my parents come they will not know who I am."

Once again the parents came to the village to take their daughter home with them, but this time they could not find her. There was no woman wearing brightly colored clothes. All the women looked alike in their black clothes. The couple was happily married. But, to this day all Akha women wear black, just to be safe.

"Speaking Truth" (Thailand)

A long time ago people discovered that the lorikeet, a small, intelligent bird, could speak with little teaching. Not only was it able to repeat what it heard, it could also give voice to its own thoughts.

One day, a farmer was working in his rice fields and saw his neighbor's buffalo. The hungry farmer killed the buffalo, cut up the animal, made a fine meal for himself, and hid what he could not eat out of sight of his neighbor.

His neighbor came by and asked, "Have you seen my buffalo?"

The farmer said, "No."

The lorikeet flew to the neighbor and said, "He killed and ate part of your buffalo. He has hidden the rest in his fields and rice house." The neighbor looked and saw the meat, just as the bird foretold. He asked the farmer whose meat it was.

The farmer said, "This is not your buffalo meat. This is my meat."

The lorikeet repeated his words. "He killed and ate part of your buffalo. He has hidden the rest in his fields and rice house." The neighbor was puzzled and wondered who was speaking the truth. He asked the magistrate to hear the case the following day.

The farmer was clever. He covered the lorikeet's cage with a huge pot. All night he beat on the pot to make the sounds of thunder. He poured water over the pot to create rain and shook the pot to make it feel windy.

In the morning, the farmer took the bird and appeared in court. The bird told its story. The magistrate was impressed by the bird's intelligence and clarity.

The farmer spoke. "The bird speaks well, but it speaks nonsense. Ask it to describe last night's weather." The magistrate agreed.

The lorikeet replied. "Last night we had a ferocious storm with much thunder, heavy rains and a strong wind."

"You see," said the farmer. "It speaks well, but what it says is nonsense."

The magistrate spoke. "It is true. Last night was calm and clear. Case dismissed."

The lorikeet was exiled to the forest where it lived as it had before it knew man. One day in the forest, the lorikeet saw a new bird, covered with brilliantly colored feathers. It questioned the bird. "Who are you? Why are you here?"

The bird preened and spoke. "I have come from another country but I will live here. I speak the language of men."

The lorikeet said bitterly, "I welcome you with some advice. If you would speak to men, let him teach you what to say. Man is not interested in truth or wisdom. He wishes to hear only his own words."

And so it is. Parrots repeat what they are taught. Men are content.

"The Night of the Wolves" (Poland)
It was the coldest winter anyone anywhere could remember. So much frigid wind blew through the village and across the farms that people were afraid the land itself would freeze and blow away.

During the night of the Full Wolf Moon, the children were kept in the house for fear of the roaming packs of wolves. Their wails, long and jagged, started just as the last supper dish was cleared off the table. The howls wrapped the village in the darkest darkness. Again and again mothers counted their children sitting around the fire. As the moon rose brighter, the shrieks moved closer, and finally, it was the men who couldn't bear sitting still. They flung the doors wide open to see for themselves the fierce wildness approaching their families. The women stood near their men, looking out into the night, watching, waiting for the wolves.

There was nothing to see except for the moon, rounder and brighter than anyone could remember, and the glittering snow that stretched as far as anyone had been to and come back from. Children asked questions and were shushed by their mothers.

Then the wolves arrived. Hundreds, trotting through the snow, their yellow eyes sharp in the moonlight, the biggest wolves anyone remembered seeing anywhere. Not thin and knobby from the hard winter like the people in the village—these wolves were sleek as butter, their wide paws barely touching the snow as they expertly glided under the moon.

Passing the open doors, the tracks the wolves left filled with gold coins, so many you couldn't take your eyes away. Gold coins lay on the snow, heaped inside those big footprints, enough for everyone in the village, enough for every debt anyone anywhere had ever owed.

There was silence. Wives clutched their husbands' sleeves and didn't let go. The women closed the doors and silently gathered their families around the fire. No one picked up the gold coins.

In the morning, when the sun rose, there were no gold coins. There were no wolf tracks.

"Why People Are Different" (Brazil)

In the beginning, there were only two people in the world, a father and his son. The father spent much of his time tending cotton trees, waiting for the time when he could pick the bolls and spin thread. One day, when he went to water the trees, he stared in astonishment. Every tree had been uprooted. The dying trees made him weep with anger and frustration. Much to his sorrow, he knew there was only one person who could have committed such a terrible act--his son.

He found an armadillo and asked if he might put glue on its tail and then go into his hole but leave his tail sticking out. The armadillo agreed and when the son came by and saw the tail, he grabbed it and started pulling.

The armadillo was so strong, instead of the son pulling it out, he was pulled deep into the earth where he struggled to release himself. As the son wandered around, he met many animals and different kinds of men and women. A group of people took pity on him and helped him find his way home.

While the son was gone, the father's cotton trees flourished. Soon he was spinning balls of cotton thread. When his son returned, his father showed him what he had accomplished and the son pretended to be pleased.

He told his father, "While I was under the ground I met many kind and attractive people. Why don't we bring some of them to live with us?"

"Very well," said his father, who then spun a thick thread for his son to use.

The son went down deep into the earth and his father let down the thick thread. When he felt the thread moving, he pulled it up and saw a handsome man and a beautiful woman. He smiled at them and said, "Welcome."

He dropped the line once again and when he felt it move,

he pulled it up. *This time there were four people, neither handsome nor ugly. The father shrugged and said, "Welcome."*

For a third time, at his son's request, he dropped the thread and when he felt it move, he pulled. He had to use all his strength for this time, there were six people waiting to be pulled up and all of them were ugly and mean-spirited.

As he pulled up the thread, determined not to drop it again, his son emerged, laughing. "Now you'll never be able to cover the earth with only caring and handsome people. There will always be all kinds."

The father sat on a stone and thought about what happened.

"Getting a Ride" (West Sahara)

Once upon a time, Hedgehog and Fox were traveling across the desert. It was very hot and Hedgehog was tired. Noticing the skeleton of a camel, he said to Fox, "I think we need to take a rest. What do you think?"

"I think you are right. There is a tree over there, let us stop in the shade."

When Hedgehog saw that Fox was fast asleep, he chewed pieces of camel skin and made a kind of saddle complete with little reins. Moving as fast as he could, he placed the saddle on a rock, and then settled down beside Fox, falling fast asleep.

When Fox awoke he said to Hedgehog, "It is getting late, I think we best be on our way."

Hedgehog nodded and said, "I had a most peculiar dream, I dreamt that while we are walking, we will find a saddle on a rock."

Fox laughed.

"What if my dream comes true?" asked Hedgehog.

Fox laughed again.

"If my dream is true, and we do find a saddle, let us agree that the one it fits will carry the other for the rest of the journey."

Fox laughed even harder, knowing no such thing was possible. "If you like," he said, shaking his head at the foolishness of Hedgehog.

It was a very tiring journey for Fox.

"How Some Wild Animals Became Tame" (India)
In the beginning, all the animals lived in the wild. Although people hunted and fished for food and clothing, there was no milk and they had to carry their own loads. Perhaps this would have continued had there not been an old woman who lived with her daughter.

As the old woman was coming back home from the fields one evening she felt a pair of hands cover her eyes. When she could not free herself, the spirit said, "I will let you go if you promise to allow me to marry your daughter." And so it was.

After she had been married a year, the daughter came to visit her mother. When it was time for the daughter to leave her mother and return to her husband, she said to her mother, "It is very hard being so far from you, please come home with me, just for a few days."

Since the mother was not sure she could find her way back home, she marked her path. Her daughter noticed and smiled. When they were almost home, the daughter said to her mother, "When you leave, my husband will offer you a gift. Remember to ask for the basket that hangs in the center of our house. Do not forget."

When a few days had passed, and the mother said it was time to leave, the spirit offered a gift. The mother remembered her daughter's words and asked for the basket. Although the spirit tried to convince her to choose something else, the mother refused to change her mind. *"If this is the only gift you want, this is what you shall have,"* said the spirit. *"But, there are three conditions. You must not open the basket until you are in your own home. Before you open it you must build a strong fence. And, for five days you must take excellent care of that which leaves the basket."*

The mother agreed, but on her way home, while she was resting, her curiosity grew too strong to ignore. She had barely lifted the lid when she heard strange sounds: growling, squeaking, twittering, chirping and roaring. She tried to close the lid, but despite her efforts, out poured bears and tigers and monkeys and many other animals.

She was very upset and used all her strength and determination to close the lid. Hoping there were still a few animals left inside, she hurried home and built a strong fence. Out came cows and dogs and cats and buffalo and pigs and chickens: screaming and squawking and mooing and meowing and barking, running as fast as they could. The fence was strong and kept them contained. For five days the woman took care to feed and water them well. In time, they learned to like their new home. A year later, when the woman's daughter came to visit, her mother's house was filled with animals.

Some say that if the mother had not opened the lid before building the fence, all animals would be tame. On the other hand, had she not closed the lid as quickly as she did, all animals would be wild.

"The Gift of the Pointing Stick" (Inuit)

Everyone respected the chief of the village, a kind man who had great skill as a hunter. He and his wife had no children but they were very fond of a little girl who lived nearby with her grand-

mother. They often sent gifts of food to the two who were poor because they had no one to hunt for them. In return, the little girl fetched water for the chief and his wife, filling a skin by dipping it in a hole in the ice that covered the lake near where they lived.

One day, as usual, the chief went out to hunt and harpooned a fine, fat seal. He was pleased because he knew how happy this catch would make his wife. Much to his surprise, as he walked toward his house he saw no smoke. When he went inside, his wife was nowhere to be seen. He walked around the house in the freshly fallen snow but saw no tracks except his own.

Trying not to worry, he asked all the villagers if they had seen his wife but each person answered, "No." He went back to his house, too miserable to eat or sleep. When neighbors came by to offer help he would not talk to them. He sat outside his house surrounded by his weapons, looking so angry people grew fearful and avoided him.

The grandmother saw his misery and sent her granddaughter to bring him back to their house. "Don't be frightened. He and his wife love you. Take his hand and tell him I am cooking a meal for him. Ask him if he will do us the honor of eating with us."

The little girl did as she was told. Much to her surprise, the chief smiled when he saw her. He put his weapons away and followed her to the house she shared with her grandmother.

For the first time since his wife's disappearance he ate a hearty meal. He ate so much the little girl had to go to the chief's house to get more food. While she was gone, the grandmother said, "You and your wife have been kind to us. It is time to for me to help you. Find a piece of driftwood that will make a strong staff. When you find one that will not bend in the strongest of winds, tie these charms to it. In the evening, plant the staff in front of your house. In the morning, go where the staff points. If you use it as a guide, you will find your wife."

Filled with hope, the chief went home and planted the staff with the charms so securely the strongest of winds could not budge it. In the morning, after sleeping and eating, he felt prepared, ready to do what he could to find his wife. He saw that the staff pointed north so he pulled it up and journeyed north climbing up steep mountains, swimming in a river clogged with ice, traveling for two days and nights. Too tired to continue, he slept for a few hours and then planted the staff that continued to point north.

He walked across plains of snow and over the frozen sea, stopping to rest after three days and nights. In the morning, he noticed the staff did not point. Instead it lay almost on the ground and the chief knew his wife must be very close.

He continued north, through a blizzard, crossing an ice field with deep crevices. At noon the next day, the sun rose briefly, a dark red, reminding him of the color of blood. Shivering, the chief continued to walk until he came to the largest icehouse he had ever seen with a huge bird skin hung on four sturdy posts just in front of the house.

He hid behind a log lying flat on the snow, waiting to see what would happen. In time, a tall man emerged, put on the skin and flew away. When the Manbird could no longer be seen, the chief rushed inside the house. There, seated by a fire was his wife.

After much hugging, his wife said, "I knew you would find me."

Her husband asked, "How did you come to be in this place?"

"I was carried here by a horrible bird that turns into a man when he enters this house."

"Oh," said her husband. "That is why I saw no footprints. Let us leave here at once."

"No," said his wife, "that is not a good idea. He has not flown far and will soon be back. But, while I was waiting for you I made a plan. Go outside and cover yourself with snow so he will not see you. Do not move until I come for you."

The chief had barely covered himself when the huge bird returned, carrying a walrus in one claw and a seal in another. The wife pretended to be very upset. "I am so tired of eating walrus and seal, why did you not bring back a whale as I asked." The man looked displeased but decided to do as she asked. Soon he was in his bird skin, flying high into the sky.

As soon as she could no longer see him, the wife ran to her husband. "We must hurry. I do not know when he will return." They traveled over the fearsome ice field as quickly as they could, sleeping in a shelter made of snow. The next morning, while they were walking over the frozen sea, they saw the bird, holding a whale in two of his claws.

"Hurry," said the chief, "let us go into this cave. It is too small for the bird." But the bird was so huge that when he put his wing in the water, the sea began to rise. The husband and wife heard the bird cackle and saw the cave begin to fill with water.

His wife said, "Your father was a magician. Do as he would have done. Use the power he has given you." Although the chief had never thought to use what his father had taught him, he found himself repeating words to be said in a time of trouble. Seeing the doubt on her husband's face, his wife said, "Do not question the worth of what you are saying. Speak your truth knowing this is what must be done. This is what will save us."

The chief repeated the words with all the authority he had within him. Soon, it grew cold. So cold, the water in the cave turned to ice. Through a crack in the stone, the husband and wife saw the bird struggle to get its wing out of the frozen water. Seeing that the bird was caught, the chief noticed a huge icicle hanging from the roof of the cave and broke it off. Carefully avoiding its flapping wing, he stabbed the bird in the neck with the sharp point and killed it.

When they returned home safely, they invited the grandmother and her granddaughter to live with them. They held a great feast for the whole village. To thank the grandmother, the husband and wife gave her a huge feather to add to her cache of charms.

"Who Gave You Permission?" (Maori)

Ratu needed a tree to make a new canoe so he went into the forest and picked out the tallest and straightest tree he could find. With his newly sharpened axe, he chopped down the tree and went home to take a nap before cutting it into smaller pieces.

When he returned, the tree was standing as tall and straight as it was before he cut it down. Astonished, he cut the tree down once more and this time, he chopped off all the branches.

The next morning, when he went to cut the trunk into pieces for his canoe, once again the tree was standing straight and tall. He was so determined to use this tree to make his canoe he cut it down for the third time. This time, he not only chopped off all the branches, he cut the trunk to begin making his canoe. Too tired to continue, he decided to return at sunrise the next day.

Just before dawn, as he approached the tree, he heard flittering and buzzing and chirping and droning. He hid behind thick bushes and watched. All the birds and animals and insects that lived in the tree were putting it back together-branch by branch, leaf by leaf, fitting the bark together as if it were a puzzle.

Ratu's anger grew as he watched the spirits of the forest pull the tree upright. He rushed toward them and yelled. "Stop! This is my tree. I need it to make my canoe."

The creatures gathered behind the spirits and with one voice they asked, "Who gave you permission to murder one of our trees?"

"Sweet Music" (Brazil)

Jaboti the tortoise was sitting in the sun, playing his flute, enjoying the warmth and his music when a man quietly approached. Before Jaboti knew what happened, the man had put him in a basket and was carrying him home to make tortoise soup.

The man left the basket next to his hut, told his two children to pound roots, and went off to hunt. When they stopped to take a drink of water, the little girl said to her brother, "Listen! Do you hear the beautiful music I hear?"

The boy nodded, walking toward the source of the sound. "It's coming from this basket," he said. They opened the lid carefully and saw Jaboti.

"Your music is lovely," said the little girl.

"Well," said Jaboti, "if you think this music is good, let me out and I'll play even more beautifully." The children carefully took him out of the basket and sat down to listen. He was right. This music was even more wonderful than the sounds he had made in the basket.

When he stopped, Jaboti said, "I have to pee. Would you mind if I just go over to those bushes? I won't be long." The children nodded. Jaboti slowly made his way to the bushes. The children waited, wanting to hear more of his music.

After a time, when he didn't return, the children realized he had disappeared. The boy said, "Father will be angry at us for letting the tortoise escape."

"Don't worry," said his sister, "I have a plan. While I am gone, make us some paint."

She returned with a stone the size of the tortoise's shell.
They painted it and put the stone into the pot. When their father
came home and saw that the basket was empty, he questioned his
children. His daughter said, "Oh father, we got it ready for you to
cook and it's in the pot."

After the water had boiled for enough time, the father emp-
tied the pot and out rolled the stone. "Oh," he said, "I am so sorry.
We can't have tortoise soup for supper because I cooked it too long
and it has turned to stone."

In the distance, the children heard the sweet sound of
Jaboti's flute and smiled.

"The Education of Finn McCoul" (Ireland)

When Finn McCoul was young, grannies, aunties, and druidesses
watched over small boys, observing which among them was swift,
smart, obedient, daring, and kind. Those who showed the most
promise were given further instruction, and of these, Finn McCoul
stood out from even the bravest and most skillful. He could outrun
all the others without catching a strand of his braided hair on the
branch of a tree, an unacceptable event. His granny, aunties and
the druidesses taught him to fish and stalk game, to set traps that
did not maim animals, to always return with a full basket, and to
share what he had caught with those in need.

On his fifteenth birthday, Finn said to his granny and
aunties, "You have been good teachers. I have tried to learn the les-
sons that you taught. Now it is time for me to compete with other
boys to see how well I can do."

Each of his aunties gave him their blessings and bits of ad-
vice for which he thanked them. His granny, standing last in line,
gave him a cap and said, "I too give you my blessings but I have
one thing to ask of you. Show them any part of your body if you

must, but keep your hair concealed under this cap. If the old king sees you, he'll try to kill you as he did when you were a babe. He knows it has been foretold that you will prove to be the better man when you come of age."

Finn tucked his hair under his cap and went to his grandfather's castle where he entered and won every race and contest. As he was hoisted up on the shoulders of those he had bested, a strong breeze knocked his cap off. Down tumbled his long white hair. Seeing the hair, the old king ordered his soldiers to arrest him.

Finn ran as fast as he could. Although none of the runners, and most of the horsemen could not catch him, in time he grew tired and began to slow down. His grandmother appeared, picked him up, put young Finn on her back and took off.

"Granny, I didn't know you could run so fast," he said, full of admiration and relief.

"Didn't I always tell you, save your best for when you need it most?" As she was running she said, "Turn around and tell me who is chasing us."

"I see a man on a brown horse."

"Good," said his granny, "I can outrun him."

In time she heard the sound of the hoof beats change. "Look behind and see who is chasing us now."

"It's a man on a white horse," replied her grandson.

"Good." she said, "he is no match for me."

Once again she heard a different sound and asked her grandson to look.

"There's a man on a black horse," he answered.

"Too bad," sighed his granny. "It is prophesized that I can never outrun a man on a black horse, so listen closely. When I yell, 'leap,' jump off my back and run as fast as you can, keeping left at the crossroads as you head for the Boyne river. There you will find a wise old poet who will teach you what you need to know. It is said that no man should hurl a spear who cannot first hurl a poem."

"But what will happen to you, Granny? Who will keep you safe from the man on the black horse? Surely I should stay and fight."

"Do as I say and all will be well. Now, leap!" Finn leapt though his heart was heavy and even as he ran as fast as he could, thoughts of turning back filled his head and heart. Only his promise to obey kept him from looking to see what happened to her.

When Finn was out of sight his grandmother stopped running and waited for the man on the black horse. "Where is Finn McCoul?" he demanded to know.

"That I will not tell. Why should I help you slay the bravest man in Ireland?" Looking more closely she said, "You're only a lad, like him. Why not do the world a favor? Cut off my white hair and tell the old king you killed Finn McCoul, chopped him into a hundred pieces, and fed him to the fish. One day Finn McCoul will rule Ireland and he will thank you for your kindness." After hesitating for a moment, the young warrior whipped out his sword and cut off the old woman's hair, tied it to his waist, and rode off.

Following the instructions of his grandmother, Finn soon came to the Boyne River where he saw the old poet, also called Finn, sitting by the water's edge. To be polite, the young man refrained from telling him that he too was named Finn. "What brings you here young man?" asked the sage.

"I have come in search of wisdom," replied Finn.

"You have come to the right place," said the old man. "I have been sitting here for many years, waiting. It has been foretold that a young man named Finn will catch and eat the Salmon of Wisdom. Remain here and serve me for I am in need of rest."

Young Finn walked along the river and much to his amazement, saw a fish that could only be the Salmon of Wisdom. He stepped on a rock to get a better look at the fish and slipped into the freezing water. As best he could, he swam to shore weighed down by his clothing and shoes. Safely on shore, he felt a weight pulling on his hair and when he went to grab it, he discovered he had caught the Salmon of Wisdom.

The old man was delighted and amazed to see what Finn had caught yet he wasted no time giving him instructions. "You must cook it so that Wisdom can be brought into the world. Grill it to a turn and don't let it blister. Whatever you do, make sure you don't taste it, not even to make sure it is done."

Finn made a fire and carefully grilled the salmon, turning it so that both sides would cook evenly. A hot spit of juice burned his thumb and without thinking, he put it into his mouth to soothe the injury. As he sucked his thumb to ease the pain, his heart filled with pity and compassion for all living beings. His brain understood the ways of the world and what constituted wisdom and knowledge. Absorbed in the wonder of it all, he barely heard the old man ask, "Did you do as you were told?"

Finn explained how he had come to taste a drop of the Salmon of Wisdom and tried to explain what he had experienced, but he had no words. The old bard asked, "Tell me, how it is you have caught the Salmon of Wisdom? Who are you?"

"With all due respect, my name is also Finn, Finn McCoul."

"What was foretold has come to pass. Sit down and eat every bit of the Salmon of Wisdom and then we shall begin your learning."

After many years, the old man said, "Young Finn McCoul, you are ready. Go into the world and prove yourself through compassionate action and deeds."

Young Finn protested. "I do not think I am ready to face the evil that is in this world. How shall I know what is right and just?"

"There is a time for learning and there is a time for doing. You have learned all I know to teach you. Now is the time to put what you have learned into action. When you have doubts and fears, bite your thumb and savor the taste of the Salmon of Wisdom. You will know what to do." And so it was.

"Coyote and The Mouse Maids" (Native American)

It was almost deer season and the hunters were in the woods, looking for straight sticks with which to make their arrows, all except Coyote, who was more interested in sleeping. At the last minute, he picked up a few sticks, not bothering to check whether they would make good arrows that would shoot straight.

Unlike her husband, Coyote's wife, Mole, a skillful trapper, knew how to make good traps and to place them so that she always caught small game.

When it was time to hunt, Coyote arose long after the sun had begun to set, long after the other hunters had gone home. Spying a big buck, he shot his arrow but it was so crooked it almost hit Coyote. No matter how he tried, he couldn't make his arrows hit their mark so he returned home with nothing to show for his effort. When he arrived, Mole was cooking a delicious smelling stew from meat she had caught.

"How did you do today?" she asked.

"Not very well. Someone stepped on my arrows and bent them," lied Coyote.

"Hah! Your arrows were bent because you were too lazy to look for straight branches. Well, never mind. Sit down and eat, you

must be hungry."

"I'm not going to eat food cooked by a woman who insults me. I'm leaving. I may never ever return. See how you feel then."

"Suit yourself," said his wife, fixing herself a steaming hot delicious bowl of stew.

Coyote stomped off with his bent arrows, in such a hurry he forgot to pack. He spent a cold, wet night, too miserable to sleep until the sun shone, drying his coat and soothing his ruffled spirits. He woke to the sound of women singing and hid behind a tree to watch mouse maids bathing in the river.

Coyote got an idea and immediately felt better as he put his plan into action. He crept close to where they were and then started howling as if he were in great pain. The young girls wrapped themselves up and ran to him. One of them recognized him and said, "Uncle Coyote, what are you doing here? This is our bath; the men's bath is down the river by the big pine tree."

Coyote paid no attention and howled again, "I think there is something in my eye. Oh, help. I am in great agony."

As they bent down to help him, Coyote pretended to be blind and groped the girls, feeling them in places he had no right to be."

They stood up and yelled, "Stop it!"

Coyote acted as if he didn't understand why they yelled and said, pretending to be in great pain, "Help me to sit up." The youngest girl knelt down to put her arms around him, to help him up, and he grabbed her between her legs, pressing hard.

Furious, she pushed his head down and rubbed sand in his eyes. With the help of her sisters and friends, she dragged him into a prickle bush and dumped prickles all over him. "Don't think you can get away with your nasty tricks. We may be young but we're not foolish," she said, her voice full of scorn.

The more he thrashed about, the more the burrs and prickles cut him. By the time he was able to free himself he was a sorry looking, bloody, hungry, wretched, mess.

He decided to return home. Mole was just bringing in a rabbit she had caught. "Oh, wife, someone told me you were dead and I was so upset I cut my hair. My eyes are sore from crying."

Mole shook her head. "Someone told you wrong. What are you doing here? I thought you said you were never coming back."

Coyote was so mad he went out to find some straight branches.

"The Past is Prologue" (Hindu)

The battle was over. The King who was victorious captured the defeated king and queen and ordered their execution. Their son, the prince, escaped and found safe refuge until he was grown. Then he returned to the country of the King who had murdered his parents and offered him his services. Eventually he became the King's personal attendant and trusted advisor. Each day, the prince watched the King, waiting for the moment when he thought the time was right for him to revenge the murder of his parents.

One day, when the King was asleep, the prince ordered the other servants to leave the room. Drawing his sword, he was about to kill him when he remembered the last words of his dying father. "Hatred is not ended by new hatred. Hatred only ends when there is peace in the heart and calm in the mind."

As the prince held the sword above the King's head, the King awoke and saw the sword above his head. "What are you doing?" he asked the prince.

"I am the son of the king and queen you murdered. I have been planning to kill you to revenge their deaths but I suddenly

remembered my dying father's last words. They stopped my hand."

"Do not kill me," pleaded the King.

The prince, knowing the King would order his guards to kill him as soon as he relinquished his sword said, "Very well, I agree to spare your life if you will give me your word that you will spare mine."

The King readily consented and then, when the prince repeated his dying father's words, the King asked, "What did your father mean when he said hatred is not ended by new hatred?"

"It is like this," explained the prince. "If I kill you, one of your men would, in all likelihood, kill me. My children in turn might feel obligated to kill him. There would be no end to the killing. But, because you have spared my life and I have spared yours, there is no more hatred. Thus, hatred only ends when the mind is calm enough to think and there is peace in the heart."

"The Power of Song" (Russia)

There was once a king and queen who lived happily until the day the king decided to try his skill in battle. Although he was a fearless knight, commanding brave troops, his small band of soldiers was defeated. The king and his men were taken prisoners and treated cruelly.

After three years, the king found a way to send his wife a message and commanded her to raise a large army to pay his ransom and secure his release. The queen thought the plan was not sensible. Too many months would pass before she could raise the huge sum required so she decided to make her own plan.

Without telling her advisors, she changed her clothes and transformed from queen into troubadour. Taking only her lute with her, she started to walk and after a short time, met up with a band of pilgrims who invited her to join them. When her path diverged from theirs, she joined a group of merchants, leaving them to climb the steep mountains that surrounded the country where her husband was held captive.

She approached the castle playing her lute. Singing in a fine, sweet voice, she soon attracted the attention of the guards. In a short time, she was standing in front of the king who held her husband captive.

At his command, she sang songs of love and loss. The king was much taken with her and asked, "Sweet troubadour, from where do you come?"

The queen answered in a man's voice. "From far away. I wander as I will, earning my way by singing and playing for those who would listen to me."

The king was so touched by her performance he said, "Play for me for seven days and when you must leave, ask what you will of me. I will grant your request."

When the seven days had passed, the queen said, "The mountains are steep and the way is often dangerous. Perhaps you would allow me to take one of your prisoners to keep me safe company." And so, when the queen was ready to leave, she was taken to the dungeons where she found her husband. Because she was disguised as a man, he did not recognize her.

Safely home, the queen changed into her womanly garments and welcomed her husband home. He was displeased. "You have done nothing to secure my release. I asked you to raise an army and a king's ransom, but you ignored my command. Had it not been for a brave troubadour, I would still be languishing in a cold, dark prison."

The queen excused herself and changed into her troubadour's clothing. Once more she approached the king who greeted her with grateful ceremony. Then the queen stood before the king, removed her disguise and revealed her true identity.

The king did not understand.

The queen sang a song about the time and effort the king's plan required. She sang of missing him too much to wait so long. She sang of wanting a kingdom with full coffers and healthy people to greet him on his return. She sang of the plan she devised to rescue him with no loss of men, time, or money.

The king bowed his head in shame and begged her forgiveness.

The king understood.

"The Gift of Fire" (Mexico)

In the time of darkness, the gods gathered to decide how to make a sacrifice that would bring the blessings of light to the people. One by one, each god offered excuses until it came the turn of the littlest god, so covered with sores and scabs, the others would have nothing to do with him. "I offer myself. I will do what is needed."

The largest, most handsome god did not want to see the scabby god receive all the praise so he said, "Such a sacrifice requires the presence of two gods."

Each god made preparations. The scabby god was poor and did the best he could, decorating the altar using earth, branches and flowers. The handsome god was very rich and adorned the altar with jewels and rare treasures.

When the time for sacrifice arrived, a huge fire was built. Each of the gods sat around the fire waiting for the two to throw themselves into the fire. The handsome god stood. "I will be first." He walked to the far corner and ran to throw himself into the fire but when he felt the heat, his legs refused to carry him further. Three times he tried. Three times he failed.

The scabby god stood up and with a ceremonious bow,

threw himself into the fire. The handsome god was so ashamed he hurled himself into the flames. Thus did the blessings of light come to the people.

"The Necklace" (South Africa)

There was once a group of young women who were jealous of one of the village girls, wearing a necklace which they coveted. The young women waited until she came to the river and then pretended to watch the water. "Why do you stare at the water?" asked the girl.

"We have thrown our necklaces into the water as an offering to River God," said one of the young women.

Without hesitating, the girl threw her necklace into the water. The young women then dug up their necklaces and ran away, laughing at her pain.

The girl walked along the riverbank, wishing she knew how to recover her necklace, when she heard a voice that commanded her to jump into the river. Without wavering, she threw herself into the water and sank down to the deepest depths. There she found herself facing an old woman who was waiting for her.

"Lick my sores," commanded the old woman. With no concern for herself, the girl did as she was told. "For your good deed, I will save you from the demon that thrives on the flesh of young women," said the old woman.

When the demon came roaring, looking for the maiden, the old woman kept her promise and the demon stalked away, hungry. Then she returned the girl's necklace, with beads of beauty greater than before. "Leave now," she said. "Return to your village, but when you leave the river, and have taken a few steps, you will see a stone on your path. Pick it up and throw it into the river. Do not look back. Return to your life in the village."

The girl did as she was told. When the young women in the village noticed her beautiful necklace they asked where she found it. She replied truthfully, telling them all that had happened to her. Immediately, the young women rushed to the river, jumped in, and came face to face with the old woman.

"Lick my sores," she commanded. The young women laughed, demanding that they too be given beautiful necklaces. As they spoke, the demon appeared and appeased his hunger by eating them up.

"Truth is Truth" (Iran)

A long time ago, a king complained to Nasrudin, "My people do not always tell me the truth. This bothers me greatly. I will not have it."

Nasrudin answered, "It does not matter whether something is absolutely true or not. What does matter is that something is true in relation to other things."

The king was not pleased. "This is just one of your tricks. A thing is true or it is not true. It cannot be both."

The king thought of a plan to make sure his people told him the truth. He had a gallows built just inside the city gates and told his heralds to announce, "If persons want to enter the city they must first answer a question asked by the Captain of the King's Guards. If the answer is not the truth, the person shall be hanged."

Nasrudin came forward. "I want to enter the city."

"Why do you come?" asked the Captain.

"I come to be hanged," answered Nasrudin.

"This is not true," said the Captain.

"If I am not telling the truth you must hang me," replied Nasrudin.

"But this would make it the truth," complained the

Captain. "I cannot hang you if you tell the truth."

"You must decide, which truth is the real truth," said Nasrudin.

"The Way of Things" (Canadian Indian)

There was a time when the ocean had no tides and the shores were unpredictable. One morning people could easily wade in and catch fish, but the next morning, the water might be so deep people drowned trying to set out their nets. The People cried out to Raven for help but he told them, "I do not know the secrets of the ocean, I cannot help you."

One of the elders said, "We have seen someone as we gaze out over the water. We do not know his name but perhaps he could help you. He lives in the ocean. Surely he knows some of the ocean's secrets."

Raven flew into the wind and the mist, searching for the strange man described by the People as Fog Man. Just as he thought he caught sight of someone, the fog rolled in so thick he saw nothing, not even the tip of his wing. "Stop," cried Raven. The People are dying and I have come to do what I can to help."

After hearing Raven's tale, Fog Man shrugged. "I am not responsible for their troubles. I am sure that there is nothing I can do to help."

"Surely there is something to be done. Don't you know anyone I could ask?" Fog Man was silent for so long, Raven wondered if he had even heard the question. "Yes," said Fog Man, after a time, "I think I remember hearing that there is a giant who sits on the tide. Perhaps he is the one who knows."

Raven asked, "What is a tide?" Fog Man shrugged and disappeared into the mist. There was nothing to be done except to fly over the ocean, to try to find the giant. The winds were strong and Raven grew tired, but remembering the starving people gave him the strength to keep going until, in the distance, he thought he saw a mountain. Grateful, Raven flew toward it, imagining a place to rest and recover, but before he could alight, the top of the mountain opened.

Startled, Raven yelled. A huge mouth spoke, "Don't shout, it hurts my ears." The words came with such force Raven was hurled so far from the giant it took a whole day to fly back. This time he avoided the mouth and alit on what looked like a shoulder. He spoke as loudly and as forcefully as he dared.

"If you are the giant who sits on the tide, please tell me the secrets of the ocean."

The giant said sadly, "I have many secrets. I just don't remember them."

"Perhaps if you had someone to tell them to, your memory would improve."

"It might," agreed the giant. "But I don't remember them so I can't tell them."

Raven's frustration grew stronger. "If you don't remember your secrets, at least explain what the tide is and why Fog Man called you the Man Who Sits on the Tide."

"I cannot. It is just something I have always done."

Raven was ready to scream. "Well then, why do you sit on the tide? Why not stand on the tide, or dance on the tide, or jump on the tide?"

"Stop bothering me," complained the giant. "I sit on the tide because I have always sat on the tide. It is the way of things."

Raven was so furious he screeched, "Stand up this minute. I want to see what happens when you stand on the tide." When the giant wouldn't move, Raven flew with all his strength and poked his beak into the giant's backside.

"Ouch," cried the giant, suddenly standing up. As he did so, the force of his movement made Raven feel as if all the earth beneath the ocean was being sucked up.

Raven thought the ocean would disappear so he shouted, "Sit down."

The giant sat down and the water reappeared so slowly Raven could see fish and sea creatures he had never seen before, but before he could enjoy the sight, the waters rose and Raven took to the air just in time to avoid drowning. When he flew to the giant's shoulder, and recovered his wits, he understood one of the giant's secrets. "I will tell you what makes a tide. When you stand up, the waters begin to disappear and when you sit, they return. If you stand up and sit down too quickly, the people drown, but if you sit and stand slowly, the People will learn the rhythms of your movement and they will learn when it is safe to catch their fish."

"I don't want to stand up and sit down, quickly or slowly," whined the giant. "I am the Man Who Sits on the Tide, not the Man Who Stands Up and Sits Down on the Tide. Go away and leave me to do what I have always done."

Raven said, "If you do not stand up and sit down slowly, I will keep poking you." He jabbed his beak into the giant's backside even harder than he had the first time.

"I have done nothing to you," wailed the giant, "why do you hurt me?"

"Because you will not do as I have asked, to stand up and sit down slowly."

"But I am the Man Who Sits on the Tide. This is who I am. This is what I have always done," wept the giant.

Raven was unmoved by the giant's misery. "If you do not want me to hurt you, stand up and sit down slowly. You can do it, I am sure of this."

As Raven flew to poke him once again, the giant slowly stood up but only up to his knees, then he gently sat down again. Raven smiled. "Good. Keep doing this. I am going to fly to the People to see if this is what is needed."

But the giant was angry and as soon as Raven was out of sight he stood up and sat down with all his strength, creating a storm that threatened to destroy all of life. Raven knew he must find a way to calm the giant if the earth was to survive.

Once again Raven flew to the giant and sat on his shoulder. "I am your friend and I have come to help you change your ways," he said.

The giant looked puzzled. "What is change? I do not remember who you are. Go away!"

Raven explained but to no avail. "Perhaps I can improve your memory."

When the giant felt the first poke he screamed, "You are the one who hurt me. I will kill you." And as he stretched his huge arm, Raven flew up, out of reach.

"You say that change is bad, but when you stood up so violently, you almost destroyed all life on earth. Is that keeping things as they have always been? No. You stood up many times Do you not remember this? How can you continue to say you are the Man Who Sits on the Tide?"

The giant stared at the water all around him for so long Raven began wondering what else he could do. Then, so smoothly Raven thought it might be his imagination, he felt a slight up and down movement. Raven was pleased and flew off to see if this was what the People needed. He found them fishing with great contentment.

When Raven flew back to thank the giant he said, "Thank you for sitting and standing so gently. The People are grateful."

"There is no need to thank me," spoke the giant solemnly, *"This is what I have always done. It is the way of the world."*

"The Story Bag" (Korea)

"Tell me a story," said the little boy to his servants, parents, aunts, uncles, and cousins. No matter how short or long the story, he listened attentively and when it was over, he asked for another story, from someone else. Even after his parents died, and he grew from a child to a boy, every night before he went to sleep, he made sure that someone, usually his faithful old servant, told him a story. Yet when anyone asked him to tell a story, he refused.

Time passed and the boy grew into a fine young man. His uncle arranged for him to marry a young woman from a neighboring village. The night before the procession to the bride's home, the old servant heard angry voices coming from the young man's room.

"This is our last chance!"

"He deserves to die for what he's done to us."

"We have no choice."

"It's his fault."

The servant looked all around the room but found no one. Just as he was about to leave, he noticed an old bag hanging from the ceiling. Whatever was inside was tied tightly, bumping around, trying with no success to escape. He curled up, making himself as small as he could, and listened carefully. *"Tomorrow, when the young man passes the strawberry field he will feel hungry and ask for a strawberry. I will be inside it and when he eats the strawberry, he will die!"*

"Good. Good," said a high-pitched voice. *"But, what happens if he isn't hungry?"*

"Further on there is a well, known for the purity of its

water. *I will be in the ladle and when he drinks from me, he will die from my poison,"* said a gravelly voice.

"Yes," shouted the voices.

But then a worried voice asked, *"But what if he isn't thirsty, have we then lost our opportunity?"*

"No," said a deep voice. *"When he arrives at the young woman's house, a bag of straw will be put next to his horse. I will be a red hot poker and when he steps on me, he will burst into flames and die!"*

The voices cheered until a syrupy voice asked, *"But what if he is helped down on the other side? Then what?"*

"I have the perfect solution," offered a sweet-sounding voice. *"I will be a poisonous snake and lie under the bridal bed. When the two are asleep, I will bite the young man. He will certainly die."* The voices cheered, congratulating themselves; sure they would succeed and be liberated, no matter what happened.

The old servant listened, horrified. He knew if he told what he had heard no one would believe him. He had to think of a plan to save the young man.

In the morning, he went to the uncle. *"I have cared for your nephew since his birth. This is the last time I will be able to be of service to him; may I not be the one to lead the procession to the home of his betrothed?"* Moved by the old man's devotion, the uncle gave his permission and the old servant took his place, at the front, leading the way.

As they approached the strawberry fields the young man cried out, *"Stop! I am hungry. I want to eat some strawberries."* The old servant pretended not to hear and walked more quickly. The young man was puzzled but said nothing. Soon they came to the well and the young man yelled, *"Stop! I am thirsty. I want to drink a cup of water."* The old servant walked even faster.

The young man was annoyed and complained to his uncle. "Do not worry," he said. "We are almost there. I will take care of his insubordination when we arrive."

The old servant heard the uncle's words but all he could think about was the bag of straw with the hot poker waiting inside. As the young man prepared to dismount, the old man smacked the horse and it ran a few feet before throwing his rider into the dust, unharmed.

The old servant ran to the young man, helped him to his feet, and dusted off his clothes. The young man was so upset at looking foolish he could not speak. Grateful there was only one more danger to be faced, the old servant listened to the uncle's angry words, all the time wondering how he would kill the snake.

After the wedding festivities, the bride and groom retired to their bedchamber, unaware of the danger that lurked beneath their bed. The old servant quietly crept into the room, sword in hand, and waited until they were asleep. Then, he threw back the rug and with one blow, cut off the head of the snake.

The couple screamed. The uncle and in-laws and servants rushed into the room. "You shall be whipped within an inch of your life," yelled the uncle.

"Please sir," said the old servant, before you punish me, may I explain why I have behaved so strangely?" Knowing how much the old man loved his nephew, the uncle nodded. After the old servant told how he had heard the angry voices in the bag in the young man's room and how they plotted to kill him, he showed them the burned edges of the wheat in the bag and the remains of the poisonous snake. "If all else failed, they were sure the snake would kill your nephew."

"But why?" asked the young man. "I have never harmed them."

"Not intentionally, that is true. But, every time you refused to tell a story, one more story spirit was imprisoned in the bag for all time. This was their last chance to free themselves."

"Oh, no. What can I do?"

"Tell stories to anyone who asks for one."

And he did

About the Author

Imagine a little girl, hiding behind a sofa, snuggled under her covers, or sitting on a rock in the woods. Her eyes are closed. Now imagine yourself inside the little girl's head. She's turned on the theatre in her mind's eye and sees the images of the stories she tells herself.

Years later, Nancy King, the little girl now a grown woman, is still telling stories, traveling the world, helping people in schools, universities, mental hospitals, prisons, recreational centers, battered women shelters, and various kinds of staff development programs to rediscover their creativity and imagination, by finding and sharing their stories in storymaking workshops.

Nancy King holds a Ph.D. from the Union Institute and University in Symbolic Learning and has spent many years intertwined with stories and storytelling. The author of plays, books, and articles, Nancy resides in Santa Fe, New Mexico where she continues to write, weave, study, and teach.

Please visit her website: nancykingstories.com

SELECTED BIBLIOGRAPHY

The Arts and Storytelling:

Applebee, Arthur. (1978). *The Child's Concept of Story.* Chicago, IL: U. of Chicago Press.

Baker, Augusta and Ellin Greene. (1977). *Storytelling: Art and Technique.* NY: R.R. Bowker.

Ball, Chris. (1995). *Taking Time to Act.* Portsmouth, NH: Heinemann.

Barton, B., and D. Booth. (1990). *Stories in the Classroom.* Portsmouth NH: Heinemann.

Bettleheim, Bruno. (1977). *The Uses of Enchantment: The Meaning and Importance of Fairy Tales.* NY: Vintage.

Bruner, Jerome. (1986). *Actual Minds, Possible Worlds.* Cambridge, MA: Harvard University Press.

Cooper, Pamela, and Rives Collins. (1992). *Look What Happened to Frog: Storytelling in Education.* Scottsdale, AZ: Gorsuch Scarisbrick.

Davis, Shari, and Benny Ferdman. (1993). *Nourishing the Heart: A Guide to Intergenerational Arts Projects in the Schools.* NY: City Lore Inc.

Eisner, Elliot. (1973). *The Educational Imagination*. NY: Macmillan.

Eisner, Elliot. (1972). *Educating Artistic Vision*. NY: Macmillan.

Fowler, Charles, ed. (1988). *Can We Rescue the Arts for America's Children: Coming to our Senses--Ten Years Later*. NY: American Council for the Arts.

Fromm, Erich. (1951). *The Forgotten Language: An Introduction to the Understanding of Dreams, Fairy Tales, and Myths*. NY: Grove Press.

Gallas, Karen. (1994). *The Languages of Learning: How Children Talk, Write Dance, Draw, and Sing their Understanding of the World*. NY: Teachers' College Press.

Gardner, Howard. (1985). *Frames of Mind: The Theory of Multiple Intelligences*. NY: Harper Collins.

Gersie, Alida and Nancy King. (1990). *Storymaking in Education and Therapy*. London: Jessica Kingsley Publishers.

Gillard, Marni. (1996). *Storyteller Storyteacher*. York, ME: Stenhouse Press.

Goleman, Daniel. (1995). *Emotional Intelligence*. NY: Bantam.

Heinig, Ruth. (1992). *Improvising with Favorite Fairy Tales: Integrating Drama into the Reading/Writing Classroom.* Portsmouth, NH: Heinemann.

Jones, Bessie. (1972). *Step it Down: Afro American Games and Songs.* Athena, GA: University of Georgia Press.

Jones, Richard. (1970). *Fantasy and Feeling in Education.* NY: Harper & Row.

King, Nancy. (1995). *Playing Their Part: Language and Learning in the Classroom.* Portsmouth, NH: Heinemann.

King, Nancy. (1993). *Storymaking and Drama.* Portsmouth, NH: Heinemann.

King, Nancy. (1975). *Giving Form to Feeling.* NY: Drama Book Specialists.

Koste, Virginia. (1978). *Dramatic Play in Childhood: Rehearsal for Life.* New Orleans, LA: Anchorage Press.

Luthi, Max. (1987). *The Fairytale as Art Form and Portrait of Man.* Bloomington, IN: Indiana University Press.

Maguire, Jack. (1985). *Creative Storytelling: Choosing, Inventing, and Sharing Tales for Children.* NY: McGraw Hill.

Mearns, Hugh. (1959). *Creative Power.* NY: Doubleday.

Moody, William J. (Ed). (1990). *Artistic Intelligences: Implications for Education.* NY: Teachers College Press.

Murdock, Maureen. (1987). *Spinning Inwards: Using Guided Imagery with Children for Learning, Creativity, and Relaxation.* Boston, MA: Shambhala.

Paley, Vivian Gussin. (1981). *Wally's Stories.* Cambridge, MA: Harvard University Press.

Pirrto, Jane. (1992). *Understanding Those Who Create.* Dayton, OH: Ohio Psychology Press.

Remer, Jane. (1990). *Changing Schools Through the Arts: How to Build in the Power of an Idea.* NY: American Council for the Arts.

Saldana, Johnny. (Ed). (1995). *Drama of Color.* Portsmouth, NH: Heinemann.

Sales, Roger. (1978). *Fairytales and After: From Snow White to E.B. White.* Cambridge, MA: Harvard University Press.

Sawyer, Ruth. (1970). *The Way of the Storyteller.* NY: Penguin.

Sternberg, Robert J. (1988). *The Triarchic Mind.* NY: Viking.

Sutton Smith, Brian. (1981). *The Folkstories of Children.* Philadelphia, PA:University of Philadelphia Press.

Vygotsky, Lev. (1986). *Thought and Language.* MA: MIT Press.

Walker, Pam. (1993). *Bring in the Arts: Lessons in Dramatics, Art, and Story Writing for Elementary and Middle School Classrooms.* Portsmouth, NH: Heinemann.

Witkin, Robert. (1974). *The Intelligence of Feeling.* London: Heinemann.

Zipes, Jack. (1983). *Fairytales and the Art of Subversion.* NY: Routledge.

Zipes, Jack. (1995). *Creative Storytelling: Building Community, Changing Lives.* NY: Routledge.

Mythology:

Ausband, Stephen. (1983). *Myth and Meaning, Myth and Order.* Macon, GA: Mercer University Press.

Bachofen, J.J. (1967). *Myth, Religion, and Mother Right.* Princeton, NJ:Bollingen/Princeton University Press.

Beane, Wendell and William Doty, (Eds). (1967). *Mircea Eliade Reader. Myths, Rites, Symbols. Vols. 1 & 2.* NY: Harper Colophon.

Campbell, Joseph. (1968). *The Hero With a Thousand Faces.* Princeton, NJ: Princeton University Press.

Campbell, Joseph. (1978). Myths to Live By. NY: Bantam.

Cook, Roger. (1974.) *The Tree of Life*. London: Thames & Hudson.

Coxhead, David, and Susan Hiller. (1975*). Dreams: Visions of the Night*. *NY:* Avon Books.

Doty, William G. (1986). *Mythography*. Birmingham, AL: University of Alabama Press.

Dunne, John S. (1975.) *Time and Myth*. Notre Dame and London: University of Notre Dame Press.

Eliade Mircea. (1974). *Gods, Goddesses, and Myths of Creation*. NY: Harper & Row.

Eliade, Mircea. (1974). Man and the Sacred. NY: Harper & Row.

Eliade, Mircea. (1975). *Myths, Dreams, and Mysteries*. NY: Harper Colophon.

Eliade, Mircea. (1971). *The Myth of the Eternal Return*. Princeton, NJ: Bollingen/Princeton University Press.

Fromm, Erich. (1951). *The Forgotten Language*. NY: Grove Press.

Goldenberg, Naomi R. (1979). *Changing of the Gods*. Boston, MA: Beacon Press.

Huxley, Francis. (1979). *The Dragon*. London: Thames &

Hudson.

Kirk, G.S. (1970). *Myth: Its Meaning and Functions in Ancient and Other Cultures.* Berkeley and Los Angeles, CA: University of California Press.

Jung, C.G., and C. Kerenyi. (1979). *Essays on a Science of Mythology.* Princeton, NJ: Bollingen/Princeton University Press.

Jung. C.G. (1979). *Man and His Symbols.* NY: Doubleday.

Jung, C.G. (1958). *Psyche and Symbol.* NY: Doubleday Anchor.

Luke, Helen. (1982). The Inner Story: Myth and Symbol in the Bible and Literature. NY: Crossroad Pub.

Luckert, Karl. (1978). *A Navajo Bringing Home Ceremony.* Flagstaff, AZ: Museum of Northern Arizona Press.

Maclagan, David. (1977). *Creation Myths.* London: Thames & Hudson.

Monaghan, Patricia. (1994). *O Mother Sun: A New View of the Cosmic Feminine.* Freedom, CA: The Crossing Press.

Murdock, Maureen. (1990). *The Heroine's Journey.* Boston, MA: Shamhbala Press.

Murray, Henry. (Ed). (1968). *Myth and Mythmaking.* Boston:

Beacon Press.

Olson, Alan M. (Ed). (1980). *Myth, Symbol, and Reality.* Notre Dame: University of Notre Dame Press.

Purce, Jill. (1974). *The Mystic Spiral: Journey of the Soul.* NY: Avon Books.

Robertson, Seonaid. (1963). *Rose Garden and Labyrinth.* London: Routledge and Kegan Paul.

Stewart, Kilton. (1954). *Pygmies and Dream Giants.* NY: Harper Colophon Books.

Van der Post, Laurens. (1979). *Patterns of Renewal.* Pendle Hill, PA: Pendle Hill Press, Pamphlet #121.

von Franz, Marie-Louise. (1978). *Creation Myths.* London: Thames & Hudson.

Young, Jonathan. (Ed). (1996). *Saga: Best New Writings on Mythology.* Ashland, OR: White Cloud Press.

Zolla, Elemire. (1981) *Archetypes.* London: George Allen & Unwin.

Myths and Tales:

Abrahams, Roger. (1983). *African Folktales.* NY: Pantheon.

Albert, Mary. (1983). *How The Birds Got their Colors: An*

Aboriginal Story. Sydney: Ashton Scholastic Pub.

Asbjornsen, Peter Christen and Jorgen Moe. (1960). *Norwegian Folktales.* NY: Pantheon.

Aung, Maung Htin and Helen G. Trager. (1968). *A Kingdom Lost for a Drop of Honey and Other Burmese Folktales.* NY: Parents Magazine Press.

Ausubel, Nathan. (1952). *A Treasury of Jewish Folklore.* NY: Crown Publishers.

Benardete, Seth. (Ed). (1965). *Larousse Greek and Roman Mythology.* NY: McGraw-Hill Book Company.

Biebuyck, Daniel and Kahombo C. Mateene. (Ed. and Trans). (1971). *The Mwindo Epic.* Berkeley and Los Angeles, CA: University of California Press.

Bierhorst, John. (1983). *The Sacred Path: Spells, Prayers, and Power Songs of the American Indians.* NY: William Morrow and Company.

Black Elk. (1953). *The Sacred Pipe.* Joseph Epes Brown. (Ed). Baltimore, MD: Penguin.

Booss, Claire. (Ed). (1984). *Scandinavian Folk and Fairy Tales: Tales from Norway, Sweden, Finland, Iceland.* NY: Avenel Books, Crown Publishers.

Buber, Martin. (1947). *Tales of the Hasidim: The Early*

Masters. NY: Schocken Books.

Buber, Martin. (1948). *Tales of the Hasidim: Later Masters.* NY: Schocken Books.

Calvino, Italo. (1956). *Italian Folktales.* NY: Pantheon Books.

Campbell, Joseph. (1976). *The Masks of God: Creative Mythology.* NY: Penguin Books.

Campbell, Joseph. (1976). *The Masks of God: Occidental Mythology.* NY: Penguin Books.

Campbell, Joseph. (1976). *The Masks of God: Oriental Mythology.* NY: Penguin Books.

Campbell, Joseph. (1976). *The Masks of God: Primitive Mythology.* NY: Penguin Books.

Campbell, Joseph. (1974). *The Mythic Image.* Princeton, NJ: Princeton University Press.

Campbell, Joseph. (1988). *The Power of Myth.* NY: Doubleday.

Carey, George. (1971). *Maryland Folk Legends and Folk Songs.* Cambridge, MD: Tidewater Publishers.

Cavendish, Richard. (Ed). (1980). *Mythology: An Illustrated*

Encyclopedia. London: Orbis Publishing Ltd.

Chalk, Gary. (1984). *Tales of Ancient China*. London: Frederick Muller.

Chandler, Robert. (1979). *The Magic Ring and other Russian Folktales*. London: Faber&Faber.

Chase, Richard. (1969). *Quest for the Myth*. NY: Greenwood Press.

Christie, Anthony. (1968). *Chinese Mythology*. NY: Paul Hamlyn.

Cole, Joanna. (Ed). (1983). *Best Loved Folktales of the World*. Garden City, NY: Anchor Press/Doubleday.

Courlander, Harold and George Herzog. (1947). *The Cow-Tail Switch and Other West African Stories*. NY: Henry Holt & Co.

Crossley-Holland, Kevin. (1980). *The Norse Myths*. NY: Penguin Books.

Cook, Elizabeth. (1976). *The Ordinary and the Fabulous*. London and NY: Cambridge University Press.

Craighead, Meinrod. (1979). *The Sign of the Tree*. London: Artists House, Mitchell Beazley Marketing Ltd.

Davidson, H.R. Ellis. (1969). *Scandinavian Mythology*.

London: Hamlyn.

Davies, Chaz, Ruhl Hamid, and Chris Searle. (1980). *Tales of Mozambique.* London: Young World Books.

Degh, Linda, (Ed). (1965). *Folktales of Hungary.* Chicago: University of Chicago Press.

DePaola, Tomie. (1983). The Legend of the Bluebonnet. NY: G.P. Putnam's Sons.

de Valera, Sinead. (1973). *Irish Fairy Tales.* London: Picolo.

de Valera. (1979). *More Irish Fairy Tales.* London: Picolo.

Dorson, Richard M. (Ed). (1975). *Folktales Told Around the World.* Chicago and London: University of Chicago Press.

Downing, Charles. (1956). Russian Tales and Legends. London: Oxford University Press.

Downing, Christine. (1981). *The Goddess: Mythological Images of the Feminine.* NY: Crossroad.

Drake-Brockman, H. (Ed). (1953). *Australian Legendary Tales.* Sydney: Angus and Robertson.

Feldmann, Susan. (Ed). (1963). *African Myths and Tales.* NY: Dell Publishing Co.

Fisher, Sally. (1980). *The Shining Princess.* NY: A Studio

Book, The Viking Press.

Frazer, James. (Ed). (1965). *The New Golden Bough*. NY: Mentor Books.

Gantz, Jeffrey. 1981. *Early Irish Myths and Sagas*. NY: Dorset Press.

Garfield, Leon & Edward Blishen. (1970). *The God Beneath the Sea*. London: Kestrel Books.

Garfield, Leon & Edward Bishen(1974). *The Golden Shadow*. London: Carousel.

Garner, Alan. (1975). *The Guizer: A Book of Fools*. London: Hamish Hamilton.

Goodrich, Norma Lorre. (1960). *Ancient Myths*. NY: Mentor Books.

Goodrich, Norma Lorre. (1977). *Medieval Myths*. NY: Mentor Books.

Graves, Robert. (1959). *The New Larousse Encyclopedia of Mythology*. NY: Hamlyn Publishing Group.

Graves, Robert and Raphael Patai. (1983). *Hebrew Myths: The Book of Genesis*. NY: Greenwich House.

Gray, John. (1969). *Near Eastern Mythology*. London: Hamlyn.

Green, Roger Lancelyn. (1967). *Tales of Ancient Egypt.* London: Bodley Head.

Grundtvig, Svend. (1928). *The Emerald Fairy Book.* London: John F. Shaw & Co. Ltd.

Haile, Bernard, O.F.M. (1979). *Waterway.* Flagstaff, AZ: The Museum of Northern Arizona Press.

Hamilton, Edith. (1969). *Mythology.* NY: Mentor Books/New American Library.

Haviland, Virginia. (1973). *Told In India.* Toronto: Little, Brown & Co.

Hillerman, Tony. (1972). *The Boy Who Made Dragonfly.* NY: Harper & Row.

Hooke, S.H. (1963). *Middle Eastern Mythology.* London: Pelican.

Hyde-Chambers, Frederick and Audrey. (1981). *Tibetan Folk Tales.* Boulder, CO and London: Shambhala.

In-Sob, Zong. (Ed. and Trans). (1979). *Folk Tales from Korea.* NY: Grove Press.
Isaacs, Jennifer. (Ed). (1980). *Australian Dreaming: 40,4000 Years of Aboriginal History.* Sydney: Lansdowne Press.

Jewett, Eleanore. (1953). *Which was Witch? Tales of Ghosts and Magic from Korea.* NY: Viking Press.

Jones, Gwyn. (1955). *Welsh Legends and Folktales*. London: Puffin.

Jordan, A.C. (1973*)*. *Tales from Southern Africa*. Berkely and Los Angeles: University of California Press.

Kendall, Carol and Yao-wen Li. (1978). *Sweet and Sour: Tales from China*. London: The Bodley Head.

Killip, Kathleen. (1980). *Twisting the Rope and Other Folktales from the Isle of Man*. London: Hodder and Stoughton.

Knappert, Jan. (1980). *Malay Myths and Legends*. Hong Kong: Heinemann Educational Books, (Asia) Ltd.

Knappert, Jan. (1977). *Myths and Legends of Indonesia*. Hong Kong: Heinemann Educational Books, (Asia) Ltd.

Kramer, Samuel Noah. (Ed). (1961). *Mythologies of the Ancient World*. Garden City, NY: Anchor Books, Doubleday & Co.

Lee, F.H. (1932). *Folktales of all Nations*. NY: Coward-McCann, Inc.

Levin, Meyer. (1932). *Classic Hasidic Tales*. NY: Dorset Press.

Lopez, Barry Holstun. (1977). *Giving Birth to Thunder, Sleeping With his Daughter*. NY: Avon Books

Mackenzie, Donald. *(1985)*. *German* Myths and Legends. NY: Avenel Books, Crown Publishers.

Macmillan, Cyrus. (1974). *Canadian Wonder Tales.* London: The Bodley Head.

Manning-Sanders, Ruth. (1976.) *Scottish Folktales.* London: Methuen.

Marriott, Alice and Carol K. Rachlin. (1968). *American Indian Mythology.* NY: Mentor Books.

Marriott, Alice and Carol K. Rachlin. (1975). *Plains Indian Mythology.* NY: Mentor Books.

Marshall, Alan. (1952). *People of the Dreamtime.* Melbourne: Hyland house.

Massola, Aldo. (1968). *Bunjil's Cave.* Melbourne: Lansdowne Press.

McAlpine, Helen and William. (1958). *Japanese Tales and Legends.* London: Oxford University Press.
Megas, Georgios. (Ed). (1970). *Folktales of Greece.* Chicago: University of Chicago Press.

Mercatante, Anthony S. (1978*). Good and Evil: Mythology and Folklore.* NY: Harper & Row.

Mercer, John. (1982). *The Stories of Vanishing Peoples.* London: Allison & Busby.

Miller, Olive Beaupre. (Ed). (1926). *Tales Told in Holland*. Chicago: The Book House for Children.

Monaghan, Patricia. (1981). *The Book of Goddesses and Heroines*. NY: E.P.Dutton.

Mullett, G.M. (1980). *Spider Woman Stories*. Tucson, AZ: The University of Arizona Press.

Kirin, Narayan. (1977). *Mondays on the Dark Side of the Moon*. NY: Oxford University Press.

Neihardt, J. (Ed). (1961). *Black Elk Speaks*. Lincoln, NB: University of Nebraska Press.

Nicholson, Irene. (1967). *Mexican and Central American Mythology*. NY: Paul Hamlyn.

Opie, Iona and Peter. (1974). *The Classic Fairy Tales*. London: Oxford University Press.

Pascheles, Wolff. (No date). *Jewish Legends of the Middle Ages*. London: Shapiro Vallentine & Co.

Petrovitch, Woislav. (1927). *Hero Tales and Legends of the Serbians*. London: George G. Harrap & Company.

Pino-Saavedra, Yolando. (1968). *Folktales of Chile*. London: Routledge & Kegan Paul.

Polsky, Howard W., and Yaella Wozner. (1989). *Everyday Miracles: The Healing Wisdom of Hasidic Stories.* London: Jason Aronson.

Power, Rhoda. (1969). *Stories from Everywhere.* London:. Dennis Dobson.

Qoyawayma, Elizabeth. (1928). *The Sun Girl.* Flagstaff, AZ: The Museum of Northern Arizona Press.

Radin, Paul. (1972). *The Trickster.* NY: Shocken Books.

Randolph, Vance. (1976). *Pissing in the Snow and Other Ozark Folktales.* NY: A Bard Book, Avon Books.

Ransome, Arthur. (1916). *Old Peter's Russian Tales.* London: Nelson.

Riordan, James. (1985). *The Woman in the Moon.* NY: Dial Press.

Roberts, Moss. (1979). *Chinese Fairy Tales and Fantasies.* NY: Pantheon.

Robinson, Gail. (1981). *Raven the Trickster.* London: Chatto & Windus.

Robinson, Gail, and Douglas Hill. (1975). *Coyote the Trickster.* London: Piccolo.

Salkey, Andrew. (Ed). (1980). *Caribbean Folk Tales and Legends.* London: Bogle-L'Ouverture Publications.

Schwartz, Howard. (1983). *Elijah's Violin and Other Jewish Fairy Tales.* NY: Harper & Row.

Shah, Idries. (Ed). (1979). *World Tales.* NY: Harcourt Brace Jovanovich.

Sherlock, Philip. (1966). *West Indian Folktales.* Oxford: Oxford University Press.

Simpson, Jacqueline. (1972). *Icelandic Folktales and Legends.* Berkeley, Los Angeles: University of California Press.

Sleigh, Barbara. (1979). *Winged Magic.* London: Hodder and Stoughton.

Spence, Lewis. (1920). *The Myths of Mexico and Peru.* London: George G. Harrap & Co. Ltd.

Sproul, Barbara C. (1979). *Primal Myths.* London: Rider.
Stephens, James. (1920). *Irish Fairy Tales.* NY: Macmillan Co.

Storm, Hyemeyohsts. (1972). *Seven Arrows.* NY: Ballantine Books.

Stuchl, Vladimir. (Ed). (1979). *American Fairy Tales.* London: Octopus Books Ltd.

Sun, Ruth Q. (1967). *Land of Seagull and Fox: Folktales of Vietnam.* Rutland, VT: Charles E. Tuttle.

Tedlock, Dennis. (Trans). (1985). *Popul Vuh.* NY: Simon & Schuster.

Toor, Frances. (1985). *A Treasury of Mexican Folkways.* NY: Bonanza Books.

Turner, Frederic. (Ed). (1977). *The Portable North American Indian Reader.* NY: Penguin Books.

Uchida Yoshiko. (1955). *The Magic Listening Cap: More Folktales from Japan.* NY: Harcourt, Brace & World, Inc.

Underhill, Ruth M., Donald M. Bahr, Baptisto Lopez, Jose Pancho, David Lopez. (1979). *Rainhouse and Ocean: Speeches for the Papago Year.* Flagstaff, AZ: The Museum of Northern Arizona Press.

Von Franz, Marie-Louise. (1972). *Creation Myths.* Zurich: Spring Publications.
Van Over, Raymond. (Ed). (1980). *Sun Songs.* NY: Mentor Books.

Vyas, Chiman. (1972). *Folktales of Zambia.* Lusaka, Zambia: Neczam.

Waley, Arthur. (1973). Dear Monkey. Indianapolis/New York: Bobbs-Merrill Co. Inc.

Walker, Barbara. (Ed). (1983). *The Woman's Encyclopedia of Myths and Secrets* NY: Harper & Row.

Warner, Rex. (1975). *The Encyclopedia of World Mythology.* NY: Galahad Books.

Waters, Frank. (1969). *Book of the Hopi.* NY: Ballantine Books.

Wenig, Adolf. (1923). *Beyond the Giant Mountains: Tales from Bohemia.* Boston: Houghton Mifflin Co.

Williams-Ellis, Amabel. (1981). *The Story Spirits: Tales from the Far East Africa, and the Caribbean.* London: Picolo.

Wister, A.L. (1907). *Enchanted and Enchanting.* Boston: J.B. Lippincott.

Wolkstein, Diane and Samuel N. Kramer. (1983). *Inanna.* NY: Harper Colophon Books.

Yagawa Sumiko. (1979). *The Crane Wife.* NY: Mulberry Books.

Yolen, Jane. (Ed). (1986). *Favorite Folktales from Around the World.* NY: Pantheon.

Zimmerman, J.E. (1974). *A Dictionary of Classical Mythology.* NY: Bantam Books.

To learn more about other Champion Press, Ltd. titles, sign up for free newsletters, or read excerpts, please visit

www.championpress.com